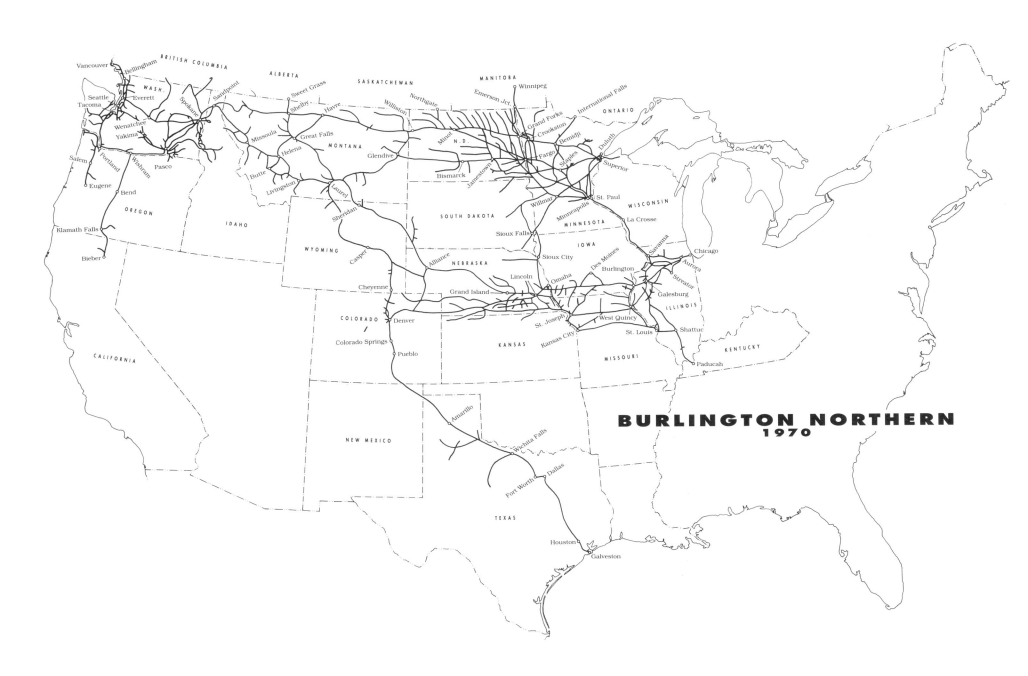

BURLINGTON NORTHERN
1970

BURLINGTON NORTHERN
and Its Heritage

STEVE GLISCHINSKI

For Lori and Robin

This edition published in 1996 by Motorbooks International, Publishers & Wholesalers, 729 Prospect Avenue, PO Box 1, Osceola, WI 54020, USA.

© Andover Junction Publications, 1996

Previously published by Andover Junction Publications, Andover, NJ 07821

Library of Congress Cataloging-in-Publication Data Available.
ISBN 0-7603-0236-7

Printed in Hong Kong

DUSTJACKET PHOTOS: GP38X 2187 stands vigil at Essex, Mont., in February 1988.—MIKE SCHAFER; CB&Q E5A&B Nos. 9912A&B pilot the northbound *Morning Zephyr* at Oregon, Ill., 1964.—JIM BOYD; in 1962, F7A 308-A illustrates GN's classic paint scheme.—BUD BULGRIN; a BN coal train harmonizes with the Wyoming environment in 1991.—ERIK COLEMAN.

TITLE PAGE: Since Burlington Northern was created in 1970, one of the largest revenue producers for the company has been low-sulphur coal, mined in Wyoming and Montana from the "Fort Union Formation" of the Powder River Basin. BN delivers the coal to utilities across its system (as well as off-line) using unit trains, many pulled by 100 wide nose SD60M's delivered to the railroad in 1990-91. SD60M's 9298-9292 are in the siding at Abbott, Neb., waiting for an eastbound merchandise train to pass on Nov. 30, 1991. In 1990, seven of the new 3,800-h.p. units were named to honor former company executives: 9243 for John M. Budd (BN's first chairman), 9244 for Louis W. Menk (the company's first president), 9245 for Robert W. Downing, 9246 for Norman M. Lorentzen, 9247 for Thomas J. Lamphier, 9248 for Richard J. Grayson and 9249 for Walter A. Drexel.—STEVE GLISCHINSKI

FACING PAGE: A westbound cruises above the waters of Lake Pend Oreille near Sandpoint, Idaho.—BLAIR KOOISTRA, COLLECTION OF FRED W. HYDE

INTRODUCTION

On March 2, 1970, a new railroad was created that would become one of the most successful railroad enterprises in the U.S. The company was Burlington Northern, uniting Chicago, Burlington & Quincy, Great Northern, Northern Pacific, Pacific Coast and Spokane, Portland & Seattle railways. The new company was headquartered in St. Paul, my home town. I was only 13 years old at the time, but already had a deep interest in railroading. While it was sad to see the predecessors disappear, it was exciting to be trackside as the first green units appeared, signs were changed and track rearranged. BN quickly became a favorite.

In view of the success of the BN merger, and the impact it had on railroading west of the Mississippi, it is surprising that no single book tracing BN's development, growth and ancestry has been written. BN has largely been ignored, with the exception of the excellent motive-power annuals by Hol Wagner and Robert Del Grosso. This book fills the void by tracing BN through its first 21 years of existence and providing an overview of its five major predecessors.

I have tried to be as complete as possible in covering the huge BN system, but admittedly it would take several volumes to cover every facet of the road's history and operations. I have highlighted what I felt were the most important aspects of the predecessors and BN's history in these pages, but will leave it to future authors to write an in-depth corporate history of the company. Not included is an extensive review of BN's motive power, since this aspect of the company has already been well documented, and more BN motive-power books are in the works from other publishers as this volume goes to press.

Literally thousands of photos were examined for possible use in this book by the book's editor, Mike Schafer, and myself. Choosing the final photos that made it into this volume turned out to be an incredibly difficult task. Many photographers work that we wanted to include had to be left out due to space limitations, and to those contributors we do apologize. We tried to choose photos that best tell BN's story over the last two decades, as well as finding unusual images, going above and beyond the typically sunlit "three-quarter" views of trains that dominate so many other books.

The last portion of the book is organized into chapters covering BN's eight operating divisions as they existed in 1992. Line sales, acquisitions and abandonments are listed for the states that most logically go with that division, even though some of the lines may be outside the 1992 boundaries of that division. For simplicity, I've rounded off the mileages of the lines listed to the nearest mile (3.2 miles is rounded to 3 miles, for example). Only lines abandoned, sold or acquired since BN was formed in 1970 have been included. Maps of each division as they exist in 1992 are also included.

No project of this magnitude could be completed by just one individual. Dozens of railroaders, photographers and former members of BN's management team have assisted me in research, manuscript review and proofreading. They deserve special thanks here: Rik Anderson, Robert C. Anderson, Mike Bartels, Jim Boyd, Peter A. Briggs, Bud Bulgrin, Tom Carlson, Mike Cleary, Mike Del Vecchio, David Duncan, John Gaertner, Gerald A. Hook, Fred W. Hyde, David M. Johnston, Bruce Kelly, Tom Kline, Rick Knutson, Blair Kooistra, Thomas J. Lamphier, John Leopard, Pat Malone, Louis A. Marre, Andy McBride, Dan Munson, Scott Muskopf, Steve Patterson, Dan Poitras, Jeff Lemke, Karl Rasmussen, T. O. Repp, Al Rung, Mike Schafer, Tim Schandel, Jeffrey C. Schmid, Paul D. Schneider, Lorenz P. Schrenk, Dick Schultz, David M. See, Greg Sieren, Greg Smith, Dr. John F. Strauss Jr. and Lori Van Oosbree all assisted me in one way or another.

Another citizen of St. Paul, James J. Hill, could be considered the "Father of Burlington Northern," since he was the first to push for consolidating the predecessor roads in the 19th Century. Now, as the 20th Century draws near its end, Hill's vision has become reality. In the pages that follow, you can see for yourself both the railroads he helped build and the culmination of his dream. This is BURLINGTON NORTHERN—AND ITS HERITAGE.

Steve Glischinski
Shoreview, Minn.
August 1992

JAMES J HILL
EMPIRE BUILDER

FOREWORD

W hen asked to write a forward to this splendid account of what culminated in the formation of the Burlington Northern, I thought who better than I, having served as president of the St. Louis-San Francisco, Chicago, Burlington & Quincy, Northern Pacific and the subsidiaries Colorado & Southern and Fort Worth & Denver, as well as the first president of Burlington Northern.

BURLINGTON NORTHERN AND ITS HERITAGE serves to recall the exciting days and years of putting together the then-largest railway merger in history.

The effort of those involved was inspiring and I am pleased to see this excellently written book record those efforts, as well as detailing the history of each of the constituent lines.

Railfans and historians alike will benefit from the reading of BURLINGTON NORTHERN AND ITS HERITAGE. I commend it to them, and to you.

Louis W. Menk
Carefree, Arizona
August 1992

ABOVE: Bust of James J. Hill, "Father of Burlington Northern", Superior, Wis.—OTTO P. DOBNICK RIGHT: An Alco Century idles away under the stars at Wishram, Wash., in June 1977.—PAUL D. SCHNEIDER

PART I

BEFORE BURLINGTON NORTHERN

Sparkling on a summer morning in 1958, CB&Q's *Morning Zephyr* awaits dispatch from St. Paul Union Depot. On its left flank stands train 32, the *Empire Builder*, just in from the West Coast. Already, Northern Pacific's Chicago-bound *North Coast Limited* has arrived and departed SPUD; the *Builder* will depart next, following a locomotive swap for Burlington motive power, and the *Zephyr* will trail the two flagships down the 427 miles to the Windy City.—BOB CAFLISCH

The creation of Burlington Northern on March 2, 1970, brought to an end the colorful histories of four major railroads that helped settle regions of the United States west of the Great Lakes: Chicago, Burlington & Quincy, Great Northern, Northern Pacific and Spokane, Portland & Seattle. GN also operated the Pacific Coast Railroad, a 32-mile line at Seattle, which it had controlled since Nov. 1, 1951, and was also merged into BN. In a similar vein, Colorado & Southern and Fort Worth & Denver fell under the umbrella of CB&Q.

Each of the four principal merger partners had its own personality and method of operation, but all ensured the survival of the regions they helped establish by providing vital transportation. As much as the four were different, they were also intertwined. As stepchildren of corporate owners GN and NP, both Burlington and SP&S assisted the parent roads in forwarding premiere passenger trains—the Burlington providing access to Chicago and the SP&S to Portland. The same held true for freight, with the two subsidiaries feeding traffic to and from the parent roads.

Although GN and NP were rivals in their own time, they also cooperated in several areas, using each other's tracks (e.g., the line between Seattle and Portland) and terminals, and working together on locomotive orders. The presidents of the parent roads also served in that capacity on the SP&S, as well as sitting on the board of directors of CB&Q.

All four roads were at one time or another under the influence of James J. Hill, the builder of the Great Northern. Collectively, they became known as the "Hill Lines," and since they served a common territory and had similar interests, it was only a matter of time before the issue of consolidation would become a priority, paving the way for the creation of Burlington Northern.

CHAPTER 1

CHICAGO, BURLINGTON & QUINCY

O f all Burlington Northern predecessor lines, Chicago, Burlington & Quincy was largest. In fact, the "Q" was unusual in that it was bigger than both its parent roads (8,430 route-miles at merger, versus 8,263 for GN and 6,682 for NP; CB&Q was 11,000 miles if subsidiaries Colorado & Southern and Fort Worth & Denver are included). Arguably, Burlington was more independent than was SP&S in that it wasn't quite 100 percent owned by the parent companies—GN and NP each owned 48.59 percent. Headquartered in Chicago, CB&Q retained its own offices and executives throughout its existence.

Throughout its history, Burlington went its own way, but nearly always in a manner that was the most direct and profitable. As a Midwestern carrier that depended a great deal on agricultural traffic, CB&Q was the envy of fellow granger roads like Chicago & North Western, Milwaukee Road and Rock Island. It wasn't easy to be a railroad in the Midwest—there were too many miles of track that depended on crops doing well, which often they didn't. CB&Q's competing roads always seemed to be in peril, moving into and out of bankruptcy, while Burlington stood strong, with a fine physical plant and reputation for excellent customer service— freight and passenger.

CB&Q traces its heritage to Feb. 12, 1849, when a group of millers in Aurora, Ill., obtained a charter to build a 12-mile railroad connecting Aurora with the Galena & Chicago Union Railroad, a C&NW predecessor. The Aurora Branch Railroad ran its first train on Sept. 2, 1850, between Turner Junction (now West Chicago), on the G&CU, and Batavia, Ill. Later, the new line obtained trackage rights over the G&CU to operate directly into Chicago.

In 1852, the Aurora Branch changed its name to the Chicago & Aurora, and in 1855 the C&A was authorized to change its name again, this time to the Chicago, Burlington & Quincy Rail Road. Several consolidations with small railroads followed, with the railroad that became a part of BN actually coming into existence in 1864, as the Chicago, Burlington & Quincy Railroad—the same year the road was extended into Chicago.

In the 1860's, Burlington built lines west to Iowa, Missouri and Nebraska, with the all-important line to St. Paul that connected to NP and GN predecessors entering service on Aug. 23, 1886. Interestingly, the name of the railroad that CB&Q established to build the line to St. Paul had a familiar ring to it: Chicago, Burlington & Northern. Another important line opened nine years later when Burlington's extension to the NP at Huntley, Mont., opened. This line would prove to be a boon to BN because of its proximity to low-sulphur coal mines.

By the end of the 19th Century, James J. Hill had developed a keen interest in acquiring a line to Chicago for his Great Northern. Hill also held NP stock and bonds, so a link to Chicago would benefit that road as well. It was logical for Hill to pursue the Burlington, as it would afford him entrance into traffic centers such as Chicago, Kansas City and St. Louis and help keep competitor E. H. Harriman's Union Pacific at bay. Indeed, Harriman turned out to be Hill's most-vigorous competitor for control of the Burlington. Eventually Hill overcame his opposition, partly because CB&Q realized that an end-to-end alliance with Hill would be more politically acceptable than selling to parallel UP, which would reduce competition and give UP more power in the Midwest. Burlington was also a better "fit" with the Hill lines, since it was already handling traffic for them. Thus, on May 21, 1901, CB&Q was sold to NP and GN.

Hill had also formulated plans for his railroads to reach the Gulf of Mexico, and found the link he needed in the lines of Colorado & Southern. C&S extended from a connection with CB&Q at Orin Junction, north of Wendover, Wyo., south along the Front Range of the Rockies, through Denver, Colorado Springs and Pueblo. C&S then plunged even farther south, cutting across the far northeast corner of New Mexico and into Texas. At appropriately named Texline, on the Texas/New Mexico border, began the trackage of the Fort Worth & Denver City, which had been owned by C&S since Dec. 19, 1898. FW&DC cut across the Texas panhandle, through Amarillo to Dallas and Fort Worth, and finally south to Houston and the Gulf of Mexico at Galveston. On

Burlington's steam excursion from Chicago to Galesburg, Ill., on Sept. 6, 1959, was one of its most famous. Featuring O-5b 4-8-4 5632 and M-4a 2-10-4 6315, the double-header operated smoothly until a photo stop at Zearing, where it was discovered that an eccentric rod on the 6315 had bent. It was disconnected and wired out of the way, but a few miles later, at Galva it became disconnected, causing the eccentric on the other side to bend. The powerful 5632 then both pushed the disabled locomotive and pulled the 18-car passenger special into Galesburg. Before the problems, the special pauses by the coal chute at Mendota as a pristine set of Burlington F-units passes with westbound tonnage. Burlington's steam excursion program was a splendid public-relations tool and one of the most aggressive of any railroad of the time. Diesel-powered excursions for schools and other groups, the steam program and a generous amount of passenger and freight advertising gave CB&Q an unusually high public profile.—BUD BULGRIN

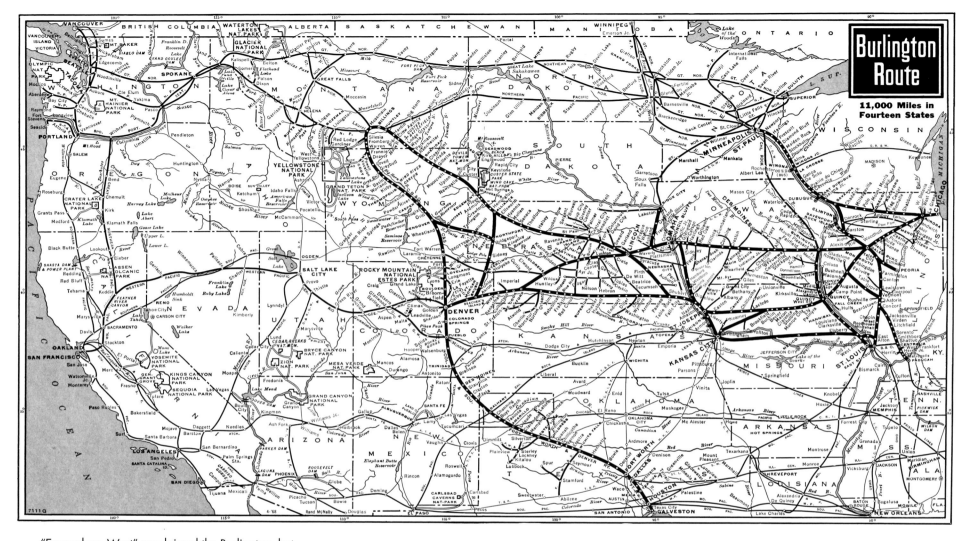

Burlington Route

11,000 Miles in Fourteen States

"Everywhere West" proclaimed the Burlington, but "Everywhere West to the Front Range of the Rockies" perhaps would have been a more-accurate assessment of CB&Q's position in North American geography, as evidenced by this (distorted) map from a 1968 passenger timetable. Nonetheless, with a line extending from Montana to the Gulf of Mexico (through subsidiaries C&S and FW&D), Burlington was well positioned to connect with several roads that did indeed reach the West Coast—and, of course, the Pacific Northwest.

Dec. 19, 1908, CB&Q became owner of C&S, along with subsidiaries FW&DC and other smaller roads in Texas. C&S and FW&DC (the latter became the Fort Worth & Denver in 1951) were henceforth operated as Burlington subsidiaries, with the president of CB&Q also serving as president of the subsidiary lines. Both roads had their own vice presidents, general managers, directors and equipment, which was still lettered for the respective railroads—even after the BN merger when the two became Burlington Northern subsidiaries. C&S was integrated into the BN in December 1981; FW&D followed in December 1982.

Books can and have been written about C&S's other lines in Colorado, which extended west out of Denver deep into the Rockies on tracks of three-foot gauge, including the famed Georgetown Loop route between Georgetown and Silver Plume, Colo. The last of C&S's narrow-gauge trackage west of Denver was abandoned in 1941, and narrow-gauge operations came to a complete end in August 1943 when the 14-mile branch between Leadville and Climax was standard-gauged. The Leadville-Climax branch was not connected to the rest of the C&S after narrow-gauge abandonments, but did have a rail connection with the Rio Grande at Leadville. The line was sold by BN to a tourist railroad after the mine that was its main source of traffic closed.

THE BURLINGTON IN RECENT TIMES combined flashy, innovative services with conservative traits of a well-managed company. Part of this interesting mix can be credited to Ralph Budd, who left Great Northern in 1931 to become Burlington's 17th president. Under Budd's management, the railroad went through its most colorful times, even as the country was gripped by the Great Depression. In 1933 the road ordered a new lightweight, streamlined train from the E. G. Budd Manufacturing Company of Philadelphia (no relation to Ralph Budd). At the time the order was placed, no decision had yet been made as to its power supply. Ralph Budd was approached by H. L. Hamilton, president of Electro-Motive Corporation, to see if he would be interested in placing a newly developed two-cycle, eight-cylinder diesel engine in the new train. Budd embraced the concept, and the diesel revolution that would sweep steam from the railroads of America was born.

According to Richard C. Overton's BURLINGTON

ROUTE: A HISTORY OF THE BURLINGTON LINES, Ralph Budd also was instrumental in naming the new train. One of Budd's officers had suggested that the name of the train begin with the last word in the dictionary because it would be the "last word" in transportation. When Budd looked up the last words in his dictionary, none were appropriate as a train name, but then he remembered some lines from Chaucer's CANTERBURY TALES which spoke of Zephyrus, God of the West Wind, who typified renaissance. Budd suggested the name Zephyr which, although not the last word in the dictionary, did at least begin with the last letter. Little did he know that the name would become a hallmark of the new-era Burlington.

The new Burlington Zephyr, No. 9900, whose superstructure was built entirely of stainless steel using Budd Company's new patented "shotwelding" process, rolled out of Budd Manufacturing on April 7, 1934. It was turned over to the Burlington on April 17. The three-car Zephyr was 196 feet long, carried 70 passengers and could reach speeds up to 120 mph. It cost close to $200,000 and would change passenger railroading forever. The train was first sent on a tour of the eastern part of the country and later several cities in Burlington territory. On May 26, 1934, the train electrified the nation with a nonstop run from Denver to the Century of Progress Exhibition in Chicago in just 14 hours.

The new Zephyr entered regular service on Nov. 11, 1934, making a daily round trip from Lincoln through Omaha to Kansas City; the following year it received the name Pioneer Zephyr. Zephyr 9900 was an immediate success and became the first of an entire fleet of Zephyrs to ride Burlington rails. For example, in April 1935 new Twin Zephyrs began service on the highly competitive Chicago-Twin Cities route on a schedule that was among the fastest in the country. And in 1949, what is perhaps the most-well-known Zephyr was born, the California Zephyr linking Chicago with Denver, Salt Lake City and San Francisco through a cooperative arrangement with Rio Grande and Western Pacific. Today, Amtrak still

The *Pioneer Zephyr* spawned a whole fleet of *Zephyr* trains, descendants of which still operate. In this serene Midwestern scene from August 1959, the *Nebraska Zephyr* calls at Mount Pleasant, Iowa, during its Lincoln-Chicago journey. The articulated trainset serving on No. 12 was originally built as one of the second-edition *Twin Zephyrs* in 1936 and was bumped to *NZ* duties when the Vista-Dome *Twin Zephyrs* arrived from the Budd Company in 1947.—F. L. BECHT

operates a version of the *California Zephyr*, with most of its journey to and from the West Coast on Burlington Northern rails.

ALTHOUGH CB&Q WAS BUSY offering its diesel *Zephyrs* as the "last word" in transportation, it still stuck with steam power for the majority of its freight service in the 1930's and 1940's. Elderly 2-8-2 Mikado types still patrolled branch lines, and new steam power came in the form of magnificent 4-8-4's of the O-5 type (Nos. 5600-5635). The first eight O-5's were built by Baldwin in 1930, but 28 more were constructed by CB&Q's West Burlington (Iowa) Shops in the years 1936-40. One of the 1940-built machines, No. 5632, went on to great fame pulling steam excursions until 1964.

Freight diesel power also came to the Burlington under Ralph Budd's tenure. Like many railroads, Burlington first tested diesel switchers, then leaped headlong into the diesel era with purchases of FT's in 1943 and 1944. More F-units followed throughout the 1940's and into the 1950's. Burlington dieselization was essentially complete by 1958, but between September 1958 and January 1959, four 2-8-2's and a pair of 2-10-4's were pressed into coal service in Illinois. Subsidiary C&S holds the historical distinction of operating the last standard-gauge Class I steam locomotive, keeping 2-8-0 No. 641 in service on the Leadville-Climax branch until Oct. 11, 1962, when it was relegated to permanent display.

Burlington continued to innovate in passenger service with the construction of the first Vista-Dome car in June 1945. While enjoying a cab ride on the Rio Grande through Colorado's Glenwood Canyon, Cyrus Osborn, a vice president of General Motors, was struck by the idea of adding a dome to passenger cars so that riders could enjoy the same see-all view engine crews had. CB&Q President Ralph Budd was intrigued by Osborn's idea—which he turned into reality by having Aurora Shops fit a stainless-steel coach, *Silver Alchemy*, with a dome. Renamed *Silver Dome*, this "pattern dome" put passengers' views above the roof line. It went into test service, was highly successful and (in typical Burlington fashion) started yet another revolution. Soon the Budd Company was building domes for the Q. The innovation spread to other car manufacturers and railroads throughout the U.S. and Canada. In 1947, new Budd-built domes cars entered service on third-edition *Twin Zephyr*s, the first regularly scheduled trains in the world to feature dome cars as regularly assigned equipment.

That CB&Q, GN, NP and SP&S were closely affiliated long before the 1970 BN merger was nowhere more evident than in through Chicago-Pacific Northwest passenger services—trains such as the *Oriental Limited* and *Empire Builder*—jointly operated by the four lines. In the late 1940's, Burlington participated with its parent roads in re-equipping the *North Coast Limited* and *Empire Builder* with streamlined equipment. Five *EB* and *NCL* trainsets were built, and since CB&Q operated approximately one-fifth of the Chicago-Seattle mileage, it owned one of the five sets of each train. The new *Builder* was put in service in 1947, and the *North Coast Limited* began receiving new cars in 1947-48. In 1951, GN again re-equipped the *Builder*, with CB&Q purchasing cars; the railroad also participated in dome-car purchases initiated by NP and GN in 1954 and 1955 respectively.

IN 1949, RALPH BUDD RETIRED from Burlington service and was succeeded by Vice-President-Operations Harry C. Murphy, well-remembered as the man who brought CB&Q through dieselization, yet retained steam for excursions. When other roads were getting out of the passenger business, CB&Q under Murphy in 1956 completely re-equipped the Chicago-Denver-

Back-to-back Burlington E-units splice the frigid Illinois air at Earlville on a January afternoon in 1970 with westbound train 17, the *California Zephyr*. Launched in March 1949, the *CZ* was the most widely known of the *Zephyr* fleet. Burlington, Rio Grande and Western Pacific cooperated in the operation of the nationally famous train between Chicago, Denver, Salt Lake City and Oakland/San Francisco. The *CZ*'s concept—i.e., a train scheduled expressly for sightseeing—centered around the Vista-Dome car, which was (and is) in essence an invention of Cyrus Osborn, a vice president of General Motors in the 1940's, and CB&Q. Despite the train's tri-parte ownership and operation, its design was strictly from the Burlington *Zephyr* fleet mold, with Budd-built stainless-steel cars and Art Deco theming. There were six *CZ* trainsets; two were owned by WP, one by Rio Grande and three by Burlington, not including four spare cars that also worked in the *Ak-Sar-Ben Zephyr* pool. Burlington operated most *CZ* mileage—an irony considering CB&Q's segment, Chicago-Denver, was considered the least scenic.—MIKE SCHAFER

LEFT: Clad in Q's black-and-gray scheme, a pair of NW2's pause on the Rock River bridge at Sterling, Ill., in February 1966. The local was waiting for Chicago & North Western traffic to clear on the CB&Q-C&NW crossing at the end of the bridge.—MIKE MCBRIDE ABOVE: In 1959, Burlington introduced its Chinese red and harbor mist gray livery for freight diesels, principally applied to road locomotives. NW2 605 at Wichita Falls, Texas, in 1967 was the only known switcher to receive the red paint.—TOM HOFFMAN FACING PAGE: The red brought high visibility to Q freights, such as hotshot 97 approaching Oregon, Ill., westbound on July 3, 1964. Three-year-old GP20 931 leads a GP30 and two SD24's.—JIM BOYD

Colorado Springs *Denver Zephyr*—the last all-new passenger train built until after Amtrak.

Score another first for Burlington in the realm of revolutionizing commuter service on a national scale. Working with the Budd Company, CB&Q in the late 1940's developed the high-capacity bilevel gallery-car, the first of which entered service on the road's Chicago-Aurora commuter district in 1950. Today, gallery cars are standard equipment on many North American commuter-rail operations.

In 1960, the *Pioneer Zephyr* was retired from service. President Murphy presented the train to the Museum of Science & Industry in Chicago, after it had logged 3,222,898 miles and carried over one million passengers. Ralph Budd had begun dieselization of the Burlington through this little train, and Harry Murphy had completed it. Now his administration began the task of retiring the fleet of first-generation F-units which had displaced steam. In 1959, Burlington received 16 EMD (Electro-Motive Division, General Motors) SD24's, the first units to wear Q's new Chinese red scheme. In the early 1960's, Burlington placed its first orders for new "second-

generation" power from EMD: Thirty-six GP20's arrived in 1961, followed by 38 GP30's in 1962-63, 22 GP35's in 1963-64 and 40 3,000-h.p. GP40's in 1966-68.

Late in 1964, Burlington broke its tradition of EMD motive power for road-freight service by ordering six U25B road-switchers from General Electric. Other GE orders followed: 12 U25C's in 1965, 16 U28C's in 1966 and 20 U28B's in 1966-67 (ten of which were later upgraded to U30B's). In 1968-69, second-generation-diesel deliveries made further inroads into the ranks of Burlington's older diesels as five more U30B's and 15 SD45's arrived, all delivered in a precursor BN scheme of green with a wide white stripe. Also delivered in experimental BN colors in 1969 were nine U23C's numbered 460-468. Burlington had orders in with GE for four U33C's and with EMD for six SD45's at the time the merger took place, so those units were delivered to BN instead.

Innovation on the CB&Q wasn't restricted to passenger service; the road held a sterling reputation in freight operations as well. Burlington was a pioneer

in jointly operated run-through freights. In the early to mid-1960's, when "foreign" road power was an uncommon sight on most railroads, Union Pacific locomotives made regular appearances on the Q. They were usually mixed with Burlington power on the joint UP-CB&Q symbol freight CGI (for Chicago-Grand Island). The hottest freight on the Chicago-Twin Cities line, Chicago-Seattle No. 97, regularly carried Great Northern power to expedite passage through the Twin Cities, where a change in motive power between the two roads normally occurred.

President Murphy retired from the Burlington in 1965, and was replaced on Oct. 1 by Louis W. Menk, who formerly headed up the Frisco. Although his tenure at CB&Q was short, it was memorable. Many enthusiasts decry the Menk administration for killing the road's steam excursion program, and Menk was thought by some to be anti-passenger. Menk's main task was to increase Burlington's sagging earnings—in 1965 the road only netted $16.6 million on revenues of $270 million. During Menk's short time at Burlington's helm, however, the road renewed passenger-train advertising, issued new

flashy timetables and even reversed an earlier decision to eliminate food service on some trains. But
Menk made no bones about the fact that trains
which ran empty were a drain on his road's treasury,
and that if people really wanted money-losing passenger trains, then they ought to pay for them.

Menk left the Burlington in September 1966 to
become president of the Northern Pacific; he was
replaced by William J. Quinn, formerly of the Milwaukee Road. Passenger deficits continued, but the
railroad continued to operate the *Denver* and *California Zephyr*s in fine style, even as other services were

discontinued or combined with other trains. Not
until after CB&Q disappeared was the question of
what to do about the "passenger train problem"
finally answered.

One hundred twenty-one years after the Aurora
Branch was chartered, Burlington Route slipped into
Burlington Northern—and into history, leaving
behind a legacy of silver streamliners, fast freight
trains and customer service second to none.

ABOVE: Subsidiaries Fort Worth & Denver and Colorado & Southern extended the reach of Burlington
Route from Colorado and Wyoming to the Gulf of Mexico. With grinding insistence, a gang of Colorado &
Southern SD's wearing both the old and new schemes
wind their way south near Walsenburg, Colo., with
train 75. Interestingly, it was a C&S SD9 (No. 828) that
first wore the red scheme, following wreck rebuilding in
March 1959. The date of this scene is Feb. 25, 1968,
and the C&S main line is now freight-only, Denver-Dallas passenger trains 7 and 2 having been discontinued
less than a half year earlier.—STEVE PATTERSON

RIGHT: Flagship passenger run of C&S-FW&D was the *Texas Zephyr*, a Denver-Dallas train inaugurated in 1940; connecting service between Dallas/Fort Worth and Houston was handled by the *Sam Houston Zephyr* and the joint FW&D-Rock Island *Twin Star Rocket*. In this view at Vernon, Texas—the first town of significant size west of the crew change point of Wichita Falls—on Aug. 5, 1967, the southbound *TZ* No. 7 slides into town behind a double-A pair of FW&D E5's. Only months earlier, the *TZ*'s nameless companion train on the Denver-Dallas/Fort Worth route had been discontinued, resulting in a rescheduled *TZ* bolstered with additional head-end traffic. Little more than a month after this scene was recorded, the train would become one of the first major members of the *Zephyr* fleet to get the axe. FW&D also had a pair E8's that could show up on the *Zephyr*, so seeing the steely E5's was in no way assured.—TOM HOFFMAN

LEFT: Hazy sun veils a trio of F's easing over the Aurora-Galesburg main line—and their own train holding on the westbound track—at Zearing, Ill., to pull interchange with the New York Central. It's a winter morning in 1966, but for Q's F-unit fleet, it's twilight time.—JIM BOYD ABOVE: E-units—five of them—obscure the fact that this is in reality a freight move. It's November 1969, and the photographer is at the Broken Bow, Neb., passing siding on the Lincoln-Billings line to record the rare passage of a Montana stock train, probably destined for the Kansas City stock yards. Behind the E's is a drover coach for cattlemen accompanying their livestock.—RAN VARNEY

Covered wagons and hood units rumble into Montgomery, Ill., on a lazy June evening in 1965 with a mixed manifest headed for Chicago. The train-order signal at Montgomery Tower has been shorn of its semaphore blades—a certain indication that the facility has been recently closed. Montgomery, located just west of downtown Aurora, was the junction of Burlington's 57-mile Streator Branch with the Aurora-Galesburg main line. In 1964, the interlocking here gained tragic notoriety when Q's westbound combined *Ak-Sar-Ben/American Royal Zephyr* collided head on with Rock Island's eastbound combined *Corn Belt Rocket/Golden State*, detouring over the Burlington between Ottawa, Ill., and Chicago.—RON LUNDSTROM

LEFT: Burlington's role as a forwarder of traffic off the lines of owners Great Northern and Northern Pacific was nowhere more evident than in the realm of passenger operations. With just shy of 100 miles left in their transcontinental journeys, the east-bound *Empire Builder* and *North Coast Limited*—combined east of the Twin Cities to Chicago—head out of Oregon, Ill., and across the Rock River on a late summer day in the mid-1960's. BELOW LEFT: CB&Q actively pursued run-through arrangements with other lines at a time when U.S. railroads were still isolationists. This scene at Cicero Yard, Chicago, in the mid-1960's illustrates the practice, with train CD-CGI (Chicago-Denver combined with Chicago-Grand Island) at left and a New York Central-CB&Q run-through from Elkhart, Ind., at right. BELOW: Pure Rio Grande GP30's westbound at Naperville Curve with the CD in summer 1965 demonstrate a power-pool operation with Colorado's best-known rail-road.—THREE PHOTOS, JIM BOYD

BELOW: Looking virtually brand new, caboose 13977 belies its steam-era heritage. About the only clue to the late date of this view—1969—is the brightness of the fresh coat of red paint (darker shades were the norm for Q hacks in earlier years). Some of these wooden classics even made it into Burlington Northern.—MIKE SCHAFER

Postwar CB&Q was a curious, delightful mixture of the antiquated and the modern. The road was a leader in rail passenger transportation, was nearly always first in line to employ the latest diesel technology and kept its physical plant up-to-date; e.g., following World War II, Q replaced elderly depots with attractive modern structures at a number of strategic cities. Yet, inexplicably (except perhaps in the name of frugality), Burlington harbored pockets of history well into its last decade—the 1960's. ABOVE: A staged scene at a museum? No, motorcar 9735 was into 1967 the motive power for a local freight based at Bushnell, Ill.

RIGHT: At Oregon, Ill., in 1964, where *Zephyrs* had flashed by only hours earlier, the Oregon mixed readies for its seven-mile trip up the Mount Morris branch. The prestigious *Morning Zephyr* was listed in timetables as a connection to the mixed, which had originated at Eola Yard east of Aurora, Ill., and dodged those same *Zephyrs* while working its way west to Oregon.—BOTH PHOTOS, JIM BOYD

Shimmering in the night lights of Galesburg roundhouse in October 1963 stands a mighty trooper of yore: power car 9908-*Silver Charger*. Electro-Motive built the shovelnose locomotive (with baggage section) in 1939 for the *General Pershing Zephyr*, which ran between St. Louis and Kansas City. Following the *Pershing's* discontinuance in 1949, *Silver Charger* could be found in various other passenger duties, but, like its motorcar ancestor on the previous page, it spent its final days in miscellaneous—mostly non-passenger—assignments. One of *Silver Charger's* more-interesting duties during this period was the handling of U.S. and company (CB&Q) mail and paychecks to West Burlington (Iowa) Shops, as well as U.S. Army guard cars to the Iowa Munitions Plant at Dayman, three miles west of West Burlington. These cars (disguised as baggage cars) were brought to Galesburg on Nos. 11-35—the combined *Nebraska Zephyr/Kansas City Zephyr,* cut from the trains while they were being separated and then transferred to the 9908. The 9908 followed No. 11 to West Burlington and Dayman as a caboose hop. In 1966, shortly after it was retired, *Silver Charger* was donated to the St. Louis Museum of Transport.—BOB BULLERMAN

Burlington passenger service ranged from the sublime to the minimal. Most of the passenger trains the road operated on any given day (or at least on any given weekday) weren't high-speed *Zephyr*s, but suburban runs between Chicago Union Station and Aurora. RIGHT: A two-car "dinky" —as commuter trains are known on the Burlington—on track 1 approaches the Naperville stop as the westbound *California Zephyr* on track 3 overtakes its more-mundane brethren. Interestingly, both of these services were conveyed to government agencies following the BN merger. Burlington suburban services became a ward of Chicago's West Suburban Mass Transit District and the Regional Transportation Authority/Metra while Amtrak carried forth the *California Zephyr* tradition.—JIM BOYD BELOW: Omaha-Billings, Mont., trains 41 and 42 were less fortunate. They were abruptly discontinued in the middle of their runs on Aug. 14, 1969, much to the consternation of passengers. . . and a congressman who happened to be aboard. Here, train 42 makes its evening stop at Newcastle, Wyo., on Aug. 28, 1967.—GEORGE BERRISO

FACING PAGE: The famous and not-so-famous share the confines of the Clyde roundhouse at Chicago just two days before Christmas 1963. Principal star of Burlington's warmly remembered steam excursion program was Northern 5632, here awaiting her last season as an operating celebrity. The 4-8-4 was unceremoniously scrapped in the 1970's.—JIM BOYD ABOVE: Surrounded by smiling Mother Nature, triple GE's churned over the Sinsinawa River bridges with ore Extra 145 East along the Mississippi River north of Portage, Ill. At this point, CB&Q trains were operating on Illinois Central trackage rights from East Dubuque to Portage, Ill. The date is June 22, 1967, and the train's 10,060 tons of Minnesota iron ore are destined for the steel mills of Granite City, near St. Louis.—MIKE NELSON

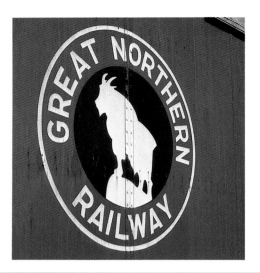

CHAPTER 2

GREAT NORTHERN

Railroads, it seems, more than other industries, are companies which reflect the personality of the individual who sits in the president's chair. This being so, it can be argued that Great Northern was shaped by the personality of its founder, James Jerome Hill. Born in the small town of Rockwood, Ont., in 1838, he came to the U.S. at the age of 18. He arrived in St. Paul on July 21, 1856, by steamboat after taking a train from Chicago to Dunleith (now East Dubuque), Ill., on the Mississippi River. When Hill stepped off the boat onto the levee at St. Paul, he probably little realized he would be responsible for changing the face of the city—and the Northwest—forever.

A hard worker with a shrewd head for business, Hill in short order became a forwarding agent for the steamboat companies and, ten years after his arrival, served as an agent for the First Division of the St. Paul & Pacific Railroad. Hill began a successful steamboat business on the Red River of the North, which helped establish his fortune.

In 1878 he entered the railroad business, purchasing with other partners the struggling StP&P, which had reached St. Cloud in 1867. It built west from Minneapolis through Breckenridge and into the Dakotas in 1871. The StP&P was also the first railroad to operate a train in Minnesota, connecting St.

Paul with St. Anthony (later Minneapolis) on June 28, 1862. Hill pushed the StP&P to completion, reaching a connection with a Canadian Pacific branch from Winnipeg at St. Vincent, Minn., in 1879. Since CP's transcontinental route was not yet complete, traffic to and from Winnipeg had to move over Hill's line, immediately making it profitable. By completing the line on time, a land grant was also awarded, of over two million acres. Hill was off and running on his journey to become the "Empire Builder."

Hill established the St. Paul, Minneapolis, & Manitoba to take over the StP&P in May 1879 and pushed further into North Dakota. But, unlike some rail builders, Hill proceeded cautiously. He actively promoted the colonization of the sparsely settled territory his railroad served, to ensure continued traffic for his company. With his background in water transportation, Hill established a steamboat company which carried wheat on the Great Lakes, received from his trains at the twin ports of Duluth, Minn., and Superior, Wis. Always concerned that his line be well-constructed, he established Great Northern's tradition of engineering excellence, paying close attention to grade and curvature, which BN benefits from even today on its northern transcontinental route. Hill was also concerned with financial stabili-

ty: Unlike NP and several other Western roads, GN never suffered through bankruptcy.

The "Manitoba" pushed west to Minot, N.D., in 1886 and into Montana in 1887. The goal was to connect with the Montana Central Railroad, which would build from Great Falls to the Montana capital of Helena. The connection with MC was reached in October 1887 after very rapid construction. In 1889, Hill established the Great Northern Railway Company, which leased the Manitoba, eventually purchasing it outright along with several other subsidiary railroads.

To the west lay the Pacific coast, which would become a gateway for even more markets, this time overseas. In 1890 the go-ahead was given for GN to build to Puget Sound—no easy task, since the railroad had to cross the formidable Rocky Mountains. Concerned that heavy grades would mean extra costs, Hill employed engineer John F. Stevens to find a pass through the mountains. Stevens located a hidden pass near the Marias River in today's Glacier National Park which required only a 1 percent grade

ABOVE: Rocky, possibly one of the most-recognized symbols in American railroading, adorned GN equipment, timetables and advertising for nearly a half century.—MARV NEILSEN, COLLECTION OF OTTO P. DOBNICK

Nights could be long and cold in Great Northern country. GN E7 509 and an F-unit mate are about to brave a chilly, 504-mile trip north from St. Paul into the prairies of Minnesota and Manitoba with the *Winnipeg Limited*. The *Limited* of the 1960's carried coaches, Pullmans and a sleeper-buffet-lounge, traveling the GN route through Fergus Falls, Grand Forks and Crookston to the Canadian border at Noyes. Trains crossed the border one mile to Emerson Junction, where CN crews took over for the final 66-mile lap into the Manitoba capital. The Winnipeg train was a regular hangout for GN E7's—units that originally had been built for *Builder* service. In 1969, sleepers and the St. Paul-Grand Forks leg were eliminated in favor of an across-the-platform connection at Grand Forks with the *Western Star*. Two years later the train disappeared with the advent of Amtrak.—JIM HEUER

This map of the Great Northern from a 1939 passenger timetable clearly illustrates the empire built by James J. Hill in his quest to link America's bread belt to the Pacific Northwest with steel rails. It also emphasizes the importance of anchor roads SP&S and CB&Q; in fact, one has to examine the map closely to see that SP&S is a separate entity at all, so thoroughly has the map artist weaved it into the fabric of GN. The full impact of dieselization was still a few years off, thus "oil and electric locomotives" were touted for "the clean, scenic" route. Note also the profile, which points out that only 55 miles of the railroad was above 4,000 feet elevation—the lowest mountain crossing of any of the northern transcontinentals.

westbound and 1.8 percent eastbound. Only one helper district was required, while to the south, NP had to contend with two. GN's location along the south border of what would become Glacier Park would later prove a boon to its passenger department, which promoted direct service to park entrances.

In Washington state, Hill faced another problem: the Cascade Range. Here, Stevens located another pass, which today bears his name, but the grades were not as favorable as the crossing of the Rockies. The railroad had to resort to expensive switchbacks on steep grades and construct huge trestles to conquer the mountains. To protect the line against avalanches, many miles of expensive snowsheds were also built. Although a grueling stretch of rail-

road to operate, the Stevens Pass route nonetheless allowed GN to complete the line to the West Coast in 1893, with the first passenger train reaching Seattle from St. Paul on July 4. In 1900, the switchback line over the Cascades was eliminated with the opening of the 2.5-mile original Cascade Tunnel. However, the tunnel still didn't resolve the problems of steep grades and snowsheds. Partial relief came with the electrification of the tunnel in 1909, one of the shortest stretches of mainline electrification ever in North America.

Hill was responsible for other achievements as well. He was instrumental in establishing the Spokane, Portland & Seattle to give GN and NP direct access to Portland. He also established the

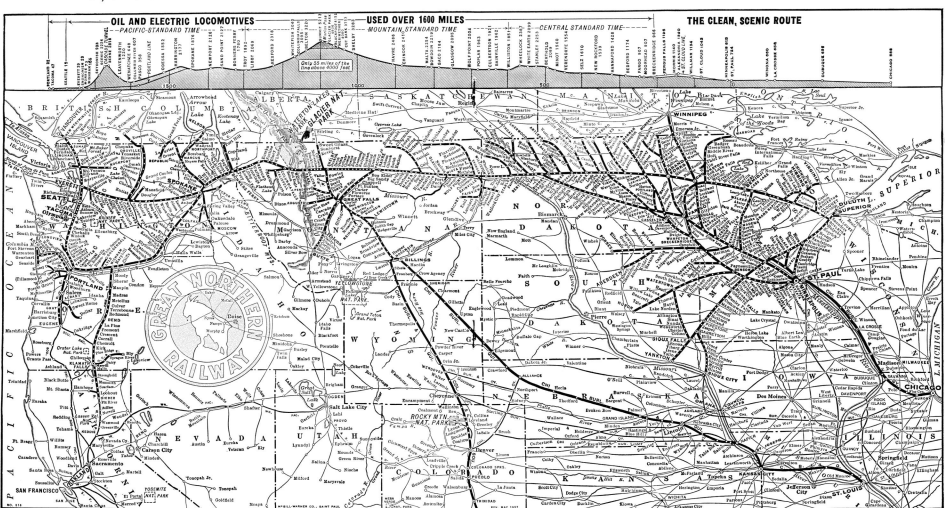

Great Northern Steamship Company, which increased his reach all the way across the Pacific.

In 1907, he turned over the leadership of GN to Louis W. Hill, his son, who moved up to chairman of the board in 1912. Interestingly, Louis Hill was succeeded by Carl R. Gray, a former vice president of the St. Louis-San Francisco Railway, which BN would absorb 68 years later. Still, Hill continued to be active in the affairs of the company he had built, heading to his office in St. Paul each day from his mansion on Summit Avenue. In May 1916, he became ill with an infection from an old hemorrhoid, and despite efforts by doctors, including the famed Mayo brothers, the infection spread. Hill fell into a coma and died in St. Paul on May 29 at the age of 77. At the hour of his funeral, 2 p.m. on May 31, every train on the Hill Lines came to a stop for five minutes—a fitting tribute to the builder of the Great Northern empire.

In the period following Hill's death, the company continued to prosper. GN was under Federal control during World War I, returning to private operation in 1920. The mantle of GN presidency was passed to Ralph Budd in October 1919. Like the Hills, the Budd family would have a profound influence on the fortunes of the company. In 1927, Budd, like Hill, attempted to merge the partners that eventually became Burlington Northern, but political and economic climates of the times prevented it. In 1930, the ICC would approve a merger—which was to happen under the name Great Northern Pacific Railway—but only on the condition that GN and NP relinquish control of CB&Q. They refused, and the case was dropped in 1931.

Under Ralph Budd, GN upgraded its steam fleet, purchasing 28 4-8-2's for passenger service and, in 1929-30, 20 magnificent 4-8-4's, referred to as the "Empire Builder" type in GN annual reports. In 1925, huge 2-8-8-2 articulateds arrived from Baldwin; GN later built its own 2-8-8-2's at its Hillyard (Wash.) Shops, which also built three Class 0-8 Mikados in 1931-32, the heaviest "Mikes" ever built. These were followed by 22 more, rebuilt from Class O-7 Mikados in 1944-46, the last of GN's steam designs. The Budd administration also was responsible for the purchase of GN's first diesel, 600-h.p. oil-electric 5100, built by Ingersoll-Rand in 1926 for use in the Minneapolis/St. Paul terminal.

Probably Ralph Budd's biggest achievement, and certainly the highest profile, was the construction of the new Cascade Tunnel and the line relocation that eliminated the tortuous grades and snowsheds on

ABOVE: "Home" for GN passenger trains in the Northwest was King Street Station, Seattle, where on a March morning in 1967 two of GN's lesser-known runs ready for their departures. On the right stands the morning northbound *International,* complete with parlor-lounge-observation car properly equipped with a neon drumhead; to the left is GN's contribution to the joint UP/NP/GN "pool service" trains on the Seattle-Portland route, southbound train 460. SDP40 320 leads the nameless run, which is a mixed bag of heavyweight and lightweight equipment.—RON LUNDSTROM LEFT: Flagship of the GN, of course, was the "Incomparable" *Empire Builder,* and rarely was that claim disputed. The eastbound *Builder* sweeps along Puget Sound near Edmonds, Wash., in 1963.—GIL HULIN

the old line. At 7.79 miles, the new tunnel was the longest in the Western Hemisphere (until CP opened a longer tunnel in 1989) and was completed in only three years and 47 days. Electrification was also extended from Wenatchee to Skykomish, Wash., through the new tunnel, a distance of 72 miles, and new, more-powerful electrics were purchased. The tunnel opened officially Jan. 12, 1929.

Over the years, GN used several types of identifying symbols, but none were more recognizable than Rocky, the Rocky Mountain goat whose likeness adorned Great Northern literature and equipment from 1921 to 1970. William P. Kenney, a GN vice president who later was elevated to the presidency, is credited with the idea of including the goat in the company emblem—prompted by the prevalence of Rocky Mountain goats in Glacier National Park. Over the years, the goat's appearance changed slightly until 1936 when a silhouetted goat appeared, with the words "Great Northern Railway" in a circle. This emblem remained in use until 1967 when GN adopted a modernized symbol, with the goat (featuring a more-trim physique) remaining in silhouette with stylized lettering below the emblem. At the same time, GN introduced the "Big Sky Blue" colors that were its standard until the birth of BN.

In 1929, in addition to being the year Cascade Tunnel was opened, GN introduced its most famous passenger train, the *Empire Builder*. The all-new heavyweight train debuted June 10, becoming the premiere train on the route. The *Oriental Limited*, inaugurated in 1905 and upgraded in 1924, assumed secondary status until it was dropped on March 29, 1931, during the Great Depression. A Seattle-Spokane day train, the *Cascadian*, was also put into service in September via the new Cascade Tunnel route. GN actively promoted its trains, even going so far as renaming smaller mainline stations in Montana so they sounded more romantic. According to the book GREAT NORTHERN RAILWAY, A HISTORY, Louis Hill came up with the idea. For example, Lubec, Mont., became "Rising Wolf" while Kilroy, Mont., became "Spotted Robe."

In the late 1920's and early 1930's, GN expanded its reach into California to compete with Southern Pacific. GN and NP initially were to cooperate in building a line south from Bend, Ore., at the south end of the SP&S-controlled Oregon Trunk Railway,

toward California. NP backed out, concluding that traffic would be too light and that it might offend SP, with which it had traffic arrangements.

GN decided to go it alone. First, after some hard bargaining, it gained trackage rights over SP between Chemult and Klamath Falls in northern Oregon; next, the railroad rebuilt a logging line south from Bend 24 miles and constructed a new line beyond to Chemult; this extension was completed in 1928. GN didn't stop at Klamath Falls. Realizing that a connection with Western Pacific would provide access to

Clad in the classic GN colors of Omaha orange and Pullman green, GN Geeps hustle southbound toward Sioux City, Iowa, with train 419 near the Minnesota/Iowa border in August 1968.—RON LUNDSTROM

markets in California, GN built south 91 miles from Klamath Falls to Bieber, Calif., while WP constructed a line north 112 miles from Keddie, on its Oakland-Salt Lake City main line, to Bieber. This route, completed in 1931, came to be known as the "Inside Gateway" because it provided a shortcut to SP's coastal gateway route. After the BN merger, the Inside Gateway became an important route for the new carrier until WP was merged into Union Pacific in 1982.

In 1931, Ralph Budd moved on to the presidency of CB&Q and was succeeded by William P. Kenney, who eventually set the company on the road to dieselization. In the fall of 1937, GN ordered two 900-h.p. switchers from General Motors subsidiary Electro-Motive Corp. Pleased with the performance, GN's board authorized the purchase of 12 more switchers in September 1938 for delivery the following

ing year. The purchase price was slightly under $1 million for all twelve units. Kenney did not live to see diesels come into general use, dying on Jan. 24, 1939. Frank J. Gavin was elected to replace him as the sixth GN president.

More diesel purchases followed. By the end of 1939, the road owned 29 diesels, but it wasn't until EMC's streamlined FT locomotive No. 103 came to GN rails in 1940 that the road was convinced of the diesel's utility on road hauls. After demonstrating what it could do on passenger, freight and even ore trains on the Mesabi Range, GN ordered several quantities of FTs beginning in 1941, eventually owning 96 units.

During the World War II years, President Gavin was thinking ahead to the period after the war—and was concerned how GN would fare when peace came again. Gavin recognized the efficiency of the diesel and, despite wartime restrictions, fought for the purchase of more diesel power—even though new steam locomotives could be delivered more readily. As early as 1943, Gavin had decided that a new *Empire Builder* should be put in service as soon as possible when the war ended. GN got a jump on Twin Cities-Northwest competitors NP and Milwaukee Road by being the first to order new streamlined equipment to re-equip the *Builder*. Pullman-Standard would be GN's builder of choice, and received an order for five *Empire Builder* sets, consisting of 12 cars each (CB&Q would own one set). The *Builder*'s older, heavyweight equipment was transferred to a revived *Oriental Limited*. The new *Builder* debuted Feb. 23, 1947, pulled by two-unit sets of EMD E7's, which were delivered in 1945.

One of the more spectacular aspects of the new streamliner was its paint scheme—Omaha orange and Pullman green with gold striping. The first large-scale application of those famous colors had been on the FTs delivered in 1941, and the scheme—considered by many to be one of the finest railroad paint schemes ever—can be largely credited to the Electro-Motive design team in their locomotive styling section in Detroit. Eventually the scheme spread to all road freight diesels, switchers, electrics and even motorcar "doodlebugs." GN's very first diesel switchers had been garbed in a sombre black scheme with a large herald on the center of the long hood, so the orange-and-green scheme was a welcome change.

The new *Empire Builder* brought significant revenue to GN, earning over $5 million in its first year of operation. So successful was the streamlining that in 1949 Gavin announced the purchase of 115 more streamlined cars at a cost of $14.8 million. Delivered in 1950-51, the order included two five-car sets for the *Internationals* between Seattle and Vancouver, B.C., and another five cars for the *Red River* between St. Paul and Fargo. The bulk of the equipment was used to once again re-equip the *Empire Builder*. Dubbed the "Mid-Century *Empire Builder*," the new train entered service June 31, 1951. The 1947 cars were placed on a new secondary train on the transcontinental route, the *Western Star*, and the *Oriental Limited* name then retired. (The *Star* had a slower schedule, so an additional *Western Star* trainset was built, since six sets were required to protect the schedules.) Thus, GN had in five short years put two all-new streamliners on its transcontinental route, a feat that NP and Milwaukee would be hard pressed to match. Unfortunately, the growth of the publicly funded Interstate highway system and air travel in the 1950's would soon render GN's new equipment decisions academic, even with the 1955 addition of sixteen dome coaches and six full-length Great Domes to *Empire Builder* consists.

A month before the second streamlined *Empire Builder* entered service, Frank Gavin became chairman of the board while Vice President-Operations John Budd—son of former GN and Burlington president Ralph Budd—was elected GN's seventh, and last, president. For the next 19 years, Budd's steady hand would guide GN fortunes. It would be John Budd's administration which would complete dieselization, promote new marketing strategies, purchase "second-generation" diesels and, finally, guide the road into Burlington Northern.

LIKE MANY RAILROADS, GN dieselized with EMD's ubiquitous F-units: FTs and F3's in the 1940's, F7's in the 1950's. But GN also was one of the first owners of GP7's, EMD's "general purpose" freight locomo-

Though they were not GN's first diesels per se, the FT's were its first road diesels and thus the first to have major impact on steam operations. (Likewise, FT's were the first major road freight diesel purchases for NP and CB&Q.) Aglow in the moonlight of a spring evening in 1959, an A-B FT set commingles with later-model "covered wagons" at the fueling station at Minneapolis Junction. GN had a fleet of 96 FT's, purchased between 1941 and 1945; all were retired or traded in on new power before the BN merger.—BOB CAFLISCH

ABOVE: Brand-new GP30's prepare to leave Hillyard, near Spokane, Wash., in June 1963. The GP30's held at least three "firsts" on GN—as the first true "second generation" diesels on the railroad; the first to wear the simplified orange-and-green scheme; and the first units to run short hood forward. Previous GN diesel practice was to operate long hood forward for collision protection. Some of the GP30's survived—rebuilt as GP39's—into the 1990's. The Hillyard facilities didn't fare as well, being dismantled in the mid-1980's, with only a station sign remaining where GN once built its own steam power.—JACK WHEELIHAN

ABOVE: Far more obscure than EMD's relatively popular GP30 model was the NW5, of which GN owned ten. The 186 is shown with the northbound Fargo-Portland Junction (N.D.) mixed train at Erie, N.D., on a summer evening in 1959. Erie is 34 miles from Fargo on a branch that left the Surrey Cutoff at Erie Junction and ran north 33 miles to Portland Junction, where it connected with the line from Vance to Larimore and Hannah.—RUSS PORTER

tive, buying 23 of the units in 1950, 30 in 1951 and three in 1953. GN also owned two unique locomotive designs that were GP7 predecessors: seven NW3's (a GN-only model) and ten NW5 road-switchers, all of which featured steam boilers for passenger service.

The last regular-service steam plied GN rails in 1957. During July and August, six 2-8-2's and two 0-8-0's working out of Minneapolis, Willmar and Breckenridge in Minnesota made steam's last stand on the Great Northern. One steam locomotive saved by GN, 4-6-2 1355, is being restored in Sioux City, Iowa, for operation, as is a 4-8-2 sold to SP&S for display. In addition to wiping out steam, GN diesels forced the end of electric operations. After blower fans were installed in Cascade Tunnel to force out diesel exhaust, electric operations were terminated in 1956.

PRELIMINARY DISCUSSIONS toward merger began between GN and NP in 1955. In the meantime, GN continued to improve its physical plant, opening the $6.5 million Gavin electronic classification yard in Minot, N.D., named for the former GN president. Continuing Hill's practice of improving the physical plant, GN in 1957 built 1½ miles of new line where the main runs along Puget Sound between Seattle and Everett, Wash. The soil in the bluffs was unstable, and during rainy weather frequent slides blocked the tracks. A new line, dubbed the "million dollar mile," was constructed an average of 100 feet offshore and placed in service Nov. 27, 1957. GN was also an early user of welded rail and Centralized Traffic Control, and expanded the use of both during the 1950's and 1960's.

The biggest change to come to a GN line was caused by the construction of Libby Dam in western Montana. The new dam on the Kootenai River, built by the U.S. Army Corps of Engineers between 1966 and 1971, resulted in a reservoir 90 miles long (part of it in Canada) that inundated a portion of GN's original main line. Sixty miles of new line were constructed between Jennings and Stryker including the seven-mile long Flathead Tunnel under remote Elk Mountain, at the time second only to Cascade as the longest tunnel in the Western Hemisphere. Drilling on the tunnel commenced Oct. 3, 1966. The new line, fifteen miles shorter than the old, was opened after the merger on Nov. 7, 1970.

Like Burlington, GN began replacing its F-unit fleet in the the 1960's. Seventeen GP30's were delivered in 1963, followed by an order for twenty-four GP35's in 1964 and 1965. The GP30's introduced a simplified version of the orange-and-green scheme, doing away with the gold striping and making more-extensive use of green paint. The last vestige of the 1947 *Empire Builder* paint scheme on its original passenger locomotives ended when E7 511 arrived in St. Paul from Duluth, Minn., on the *Badger* on Sept. 19, 1965. Shortly thereafter, the 511 was repainted in the simplified scheme.

Great Northern also turned to General Electric for new power in the 1960's. Twenty-four U25Bs arrived in 1964-65, followed by six four-axle U28Bs in 1966. GN acquired historic power in 1966, purchasing the first production SD45. Numbered 400, the 3,600-h.p. unit was named *Hustle Muscle* and retained that moniker while in service for BN. The unit has been preserved in Duluth and is still operational. *Hustle Muscle* was the first of eight SD45's delivered in 1966; nineteen more followed in 1967-68. For passenger service, the road purchased six steam-generator-equipped 3,000-h.p. SDP40's in 1966 (among the last units delivered in orange and green) and eight SDP45's in 1967. Fifteen U33C's delivered in 1968-69 wore the new Big Sky Blue colors.

Among the more-interesting latter-day GN diesels were the F45's, essentially SD45's with full width "cowl" bodies. The fully enclosed engine compartment made servicing easier for crews during freezing

weather encountered across much of the system. Although rearward visibility was restricted, GN embraced the units and began buying them in quantity right up to the merger, with the intention of having enough F45's to pilot most of its transcontinental freights. Fourteen units, Nos. 427-440, arrived in 1969 at a cost of more than $4.2 million, with units 441-452 scheduled for delivery in 1970. The merger intervened, and the locomotives became BN 6614-6625. BN continued the practice of buying

Under the big blue skies of eastern Washington, a westbound freight treads its way through Spokane near Fort Wright Junction on a July afternoon in 1963. A pair of veteran F-units lead two EMD newcomers, GP20's—builder EMD's first turbo-charged Geeps—in a scene that reflects the waning years of the "boxcar era," a time when TOFC (trailer-on-flat-car) was in its infancy and terms like "double-stack" were unheard of. The tracks in this area were removed a decade later as part of BN's massive line relocation project in Spokane.—Jack Wheelihan

BELOW: Great Northern updated its diesel fleet in the 1960's with second-generation motive power. Though EMD had been the favored builder for most units since dieselization, General Electric became a contender with 24 U25B's delivered to GN in 1964-65. Two "U-boats" teamed with a GP30 stand ready at Minneapolis Junction for their next assignment in October 1965; power delivered by EMD and GE during this period wore a simplified orange-and-green scheme.—RON LUNDSTROM RIGHT: Old colors meet new near the Twin Ports as a pristine A-B-B-A set of F-units clad in Big Sky Blue lead an ore train into a meet.—JIM BOYD

F45's, purchasing twenty more in 1971, and throughout most of the 1970's the units could be found leading BN's priority trains.

When merger finally came, it was a testament to GN that most of its superbly engineered transcontinental route became BN's. Former GN men dominated the executive office's of the new company in its first decade, including John Budd, BN's first chairman, Robert Downing, who became vice chairman and chief operating officer, and Thomas Lamphier, who served as BN president from 1976 to 1979.

GN remains well-remembered. Orange-and-green streamliners, "Rocky" the Great Northern goat and handsome 4-8-4's are all fondly recalled. Unlike Northern Pacific, which introduced the 4-8-4 "Northern" type but failed to save even a single example of its "super steam" locomotives, GN preserved one of its classic machines. Class S-2 4-8-4 No. 2584 was placed on display adjacent to the depot in Havre, Mont., on May 15, 1964. With all the steam locomotive revivals that have taken place in the 1970's and 1980's, there is hope that 2584 may steam once again, reviving the spirit of the Great Northern.

LEFT: Swiss Alps, U.S. style—A pair of GN "U-boats" arrive at the yard in Whitefish, Mont., in late 1969. In the background is the Swiss-styled Whitefish depot, which also provided office space for the division superintendent. Note wood reefers at left, still being used at this late date.—STEVE PATTERSON BELOW: West of Whitefish, a pair of SDP40's cant into a curve with train 28, the east-bound *Western Star*, in 1968. In the early 1960's, the *Star*—which originally was to have been called the *Evergreen*—was combined with the old *Fast Mail*, which greatly increased the head-end mail and express business handled by the train. All 6,000 horsepower generated by the two units will be needed to pull the heavy *Star* over Marias Pass, 50 miles to the east.—HAROLD A. EDMONSON

Between Seattle and Portland, GN exercised trackage rights on NP. The station agent at Vancouver, Wash., just across the state line from Portland, hoops orders to a southbound freight headed by an Alco FA in 1964.—GIL HULIN

LEFT: Great Northern's large fleet of covered wagons was put to good use on the Iron Range of Minnesota. FT's and F7's wiped out steam on the ore runs in the 1950's, and even neighboring Missabe Road leased F-units from the GN during a 1958 traffic upsurge. A set of orange and green F's splits the semaphores near Carlton, Minn. with an eastbound ore drag for the Allouez, Wis. ore docks. GN maintained double track between Brookston, Minn. and Superior to handle the ore traffic.—RON LUNDSTROM

LEFT AND BELOW: We're in grain country, the heart of GN operations, as GP20 2032 and two fellow Geeps hustle their way northward through the Minnesota countryside in the mellow light of the evening of July 3, 1968, with train 420 en route to Willmar, Minn. The train originated at Garretson, S.D., junction of the Sioux City (Iowa) and Yankton (S.D.) branches.—BOTH PHOTOS, RON LUNDSTROM

Daily service between the Twin Cities and Minot, N.D., was provided by the *Dakotan*, which supplemented the Twin Cities-Fargo *Red River* streamliner. In May 1966, GN No. 3, the westbound *Dakotan*, is shown commencing its 529-mile run from St. Paul Union Depot with an short consist: RPO-baggage, cafe-coach and an ex-Katy day coach. Number 3 will make its last trip in 1969.—JIM ASPLUND

ABOVE: Following its 154-mile run down from the Twin Ports (Duluth, Minn./Superior, Wis.), the *Gopher* cools its paws at Minneapolis Great Northern Station on a late spring evening in 1965. Hallmark cars of the *Gopher* and its companion St. Paul-Duluth train, the *Badger*, were two modernized heavyweight parlor-buffet observation cars, the *Twin Cities* and the *Twin Ports*. Since both were used for both trains, both featured dual drumheads.—Ron Lundstrom RIGHT: Also at Minneapolis, but in climes about 40 degrees cooler, SDP45 331 and an F-unit cohort await their next assignment at Minneapolis Junction engine terminal in 1969.—Jim Heuer

FACING PAGE: Probably one of GN's better-known branch operations was the "Hutch" job, in the 1960's based out of Lyndale Junction in Minneapolis. Each weekday, the Hutch headed west out of Lyndale 12 miles to Wayzata, junction with the 44-mile line to Hutchinson. The branch was a regular haunt for one of GN's oddball NW5 locomotives—usually the 186, here buzzing along the Minnesota prairies (and past one of the state's more than 10,000 lakes) on a fine autumn day in 1967. The Hutch also featured an incredibly long caboose converted from a boxcar that was used for mail and express. The elderly (built in 1946) NW5 light roadswitchers would live to see BN green paint; some even ran until 1981.—Jim Boyd

CHAPTER 3

NORTHERN PACIFIC

MAIN STREET OF THE NORTHWEST

Northern Pacific, like rival Great Northern, had its share of dominant and colorful personalities over its history, no less among them Abraham Lincoln. The nation's 16th president, signed the federal charter authorizing NP's construction on July 2, 1864. The area NP would traverse was largely inhabited by Indians and had only recently been explored by captains Meriwether Lewis and William Clark on their Northwest expedition of 1804-06. By the mid-19th Century, momentum was building for the construction of a transcontinental railroad across the Western United States.

Although consideration was given to a northern route along what finally would become the NP, a more southerly route was chosen that headed west from Council Bluffs, Iowa, to California. However, supporters of a northern route, notably Josiah Perham, an Eastern rail promoter, continued to lobby for its construction. Perham made powerful friends in Congress and was able to persuade them to submit a bill that asked the government only for land grants, and to rely upon private financing of the actual construction. The bill passed on May 31, 1864, and was signed into law by President Lincoln. The land grants would, in time, become very valuable and would serve as the nucleus of Burlington Northern's land resources.

Securement of financing proved difficult. Eventu-ally Perham became disillusioned and sold the charter, which was amended in Congress to allow mortgaging of the railroad and the land grant. Construction bonds were then sold to purchase supplies and begin the work of building a railroad. Financier Jay Cooke, well experienced in bond sales, entered the picture and became NP's chief backer. Cooke shrewdly figured that the land grants would be of great value once the railroad was completed. Construction began in July 1870 at Thompsons Junction (near the present-day town of Carlton, Minn.), juncture with the Lake Superior & Mississippi Railroad, which ran from St. Paul to Duluth and would one day become the NP main line between those two cities. Construction also began on the western part of the line just north of Portland, Ore., at the town of Kalama, Wash., in December 1870.

Overly rapid construction of the NP led to the collapse of Jay Cooke and his company in 1873 and triggered a financial panic that gripped the nation; construction ceased. The western section of the line had been completed to Tacoma, Wash., while the eastern section had reached Bismarck, N.D. With the panic and little traffic, NP fell into receivership. Delays in construction continued until, under the leadership of Charles B. Wright, confidence in the company was renewed and additional money was raised. NP then continued its march across North

Dakota, and in Washington construction proceeded on a third front, near Ainsworth, heading toward Spokane.

The Oregon Railway & Navigation Company was building rail lines in the same area, and one of the men who controlled the company, Henry Villard, saw NP as a threat to his plans for a transportation monopoly along the Columbia River. Convinced that NP was headed for OR&N territory, Villard secretly raised money and purchased enough NP stock to gain control, becoming the company's president.

Villard pushed the NP to completion—although at such a rapid pace that construction was sometimes shoddy. The main line was completed at Independence Gulch, Mont., on Aug. 22, 1883, but a huge ceremony was put together at nearby Gold Creek on Sept. 8 to officially mark NP's opening; access to NP lines from Portland to Tacoma and Seattle from the Spokane area was provided by OR&N. In 1884, Villard left the NP as his financial empire collapsed, and in 1887 the OR&N fell under the control of Union Pacific.

To gain independent access to its West Coast sec-

ABOVE: NP's celebrated monad logo harkened to the ancient Orient, but the well-remembered symbol could be found on the most-modern of NP equipment, including the Vista-Dome cars of the *North Coast Limited.*—MIKE SCHAFER

It's the noon hour on a July day in 1969 in the high country of eastern Washington state; heat rising from the lava rockbed mingles with the sun's rays, shrouding this sparsely settled region in a veil of oppressive heat. The stillness is soon parted by distant air horns, and six high-horsepower Northern Pacific locomotives representing builders Electro-Motive and General Electric scream past like desert banshees, with eastbound tonnage out of Pasco, Wash. SD45 No. 3603 and companions leave little doubt that this indeed is the "Main Street of the Northwest," stretching from the shores of Lake Superior to the coast of the cool blue Pacific.—MIKE SCHAFER

LEFT: NP's frugal side is aptly illustrated in this view of St. Paul-International Falls train 11 at St. Paul Union Depot on a rainy late evening early in the 1960's. Conveyance for the few adventurous passengers utilizing the train for its 339-mile overnight trip to the Canadian border town was an ancient, but well-maintained heavyweight coach, dating from the pre-World War I years. A steam-generator equipped Geep—NP purchased a pair of GP7's in 1950 just for this service—provided propulsion. The train was later cut back to Little Falls, Minn. and was replaced by a bus in 1968. —JIM BOYD

RIGHT: Jamestown, N.D., was a major rail center on the NP and a hub for its regional branch lines. The region around Jamestown was one in which NP made extensive use of gas-electric "doodlebugs" to serve small, branchline communities. At the Jamestown station in the early 1950's, car B-22 waits for passengers from a mainline train, probably No. 3, the remnant of the *Alaskan.* NP branchline passenger service in North Dakota remained intact through much of the 1950's, thanks to the stubborness of the North Dakota Public Service Commission, which steadfastly refused to allow its elimination. The last doodlebug operated out of Jamestown on June 17, 1961, on a run to Wilton.—ALEXANDER MAXWELL

tion, Northern Pacific built its own railroad over the Cascades, attacking the mountains at Stampede Pass after following the Yakima River west from Pasco, Wash. Like the GN which would come later, NP had to build switchbacks and endure steep grades until the completion of 1.8-mile Stampede Tunnel in May 1888. Still, grades remained: up to 2.2 in both directions. Other significant mountain grades on the NP were in Montana. At Bozeman Pass, just west of Livingston, trains required helpers in both directions on grades up to 1.8 percent westbound and 1.9 percent eastbound. At Mullan Pass near Helena, westbound trains required helpers on grades of 2.2 percent, with eastbounds facing a 1.8 percent grade. These grades would play into Burlington Northern's thinking when it selected the GN route for its principal main line across Montana and Washington.

In 1893, NP's chief engineer, E. H. McHenry, saw a Korean flag at the Chicago World's Fair bearing a monad emblem. Devised in 1017 A.D. by Chinese scholar Chow Lien Ki, the monad, in the Orient, symbolizes eternal life represented by darkness and light. McHenry "imported" the emblem to the NP, and it was soon being used on equipment, stations and company literature. It continued to be NP's most recognizable symbol until the BN merger.

The same year McHenry saw the monad, the railroad went bankrupt (along with many other railroads) due to the silver panic of 1893. Once again, over-expansion played a role, since NP had built too many branch lines before traffic had grown enough to support them. GN's James J. Hill took advantage of NP's precarious position and with help from financier J. P. Morgan purchased much NP stock, eventually becoming a significant voice in operations. Hill's acquisition of the Burlington in 1901 gave NP (and GN) access to Chicago from the Twin Cities, with CB&Q ownership split between the two roads. Hill then combined his railroads into the Northern Securities Company. Had this company remained intact, the history of Burlington Northern would be entirely different, since BN in effect would have come into being in 1901, not 1970. However, the "trust busting" era of President Theodore Roosevelt was in full swing, and the Northern Securities Company—judged by the Supreme Court to be in violation of the Sherman Anti-Trust Act—was dissolved.

Because Hill was part owner, and simply because NP did not have a lot of cash, NP became more conservative and began tending more to business during this period. The company under a succession of

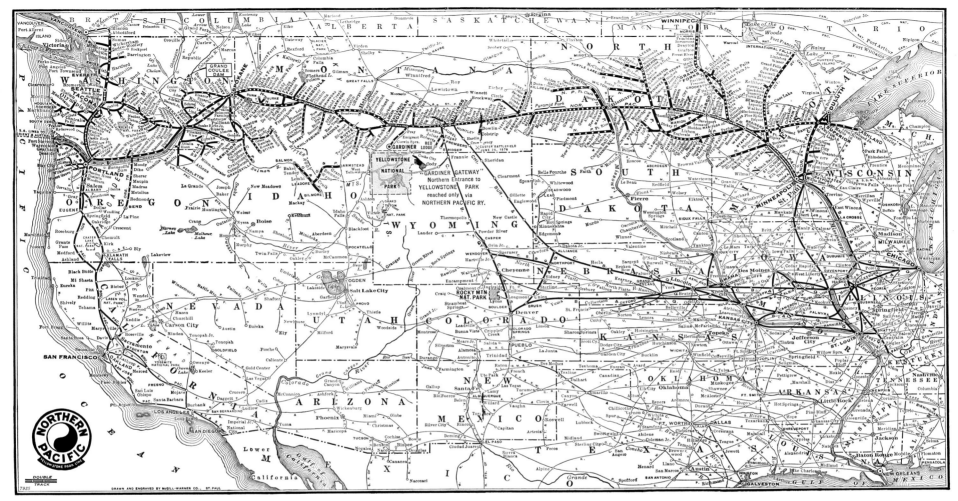

managements concentrated on upgrading its physical plant. In 1924, the company completed automatic block signaling over the entire St. Paul-Seattle main line, as well as the Seattle-Vancouver (Wash.) and St. Paul-Duluth lines, a program which had begun in 1909. The signals were virtually all of the semaphore type, which became a trademark of NP publicity photos in the ensuing years.

Management also acquired up-to-date rolling stock and locomotives for its premiere train, the *North Coast Limited*. The *NCL* was one of the oldest name trains in the Northwest, inaugurated on April 29, 1900, and also was the first entirely electrically lighted train in the Northwest. Intended as a summer-only train, the *North Coast Limited* proved so popular that year-round operation was instituted in

1902. The train was re-equipped by Pullman in 1909 in anticipation of passengers headed for the Alaska-Yukon-Pacific Exhibition in Seattle that year. Always NP's flagship, the *NCL* operated up to the merger and continued under BN auspices until Amtrak.

Northern Pacific became known—much more than the other pre-merger roads—as a user of large steam power. NP was first to use the 4-8-4 locomotive type, which was named "Northern" after the railroad. NP received the first of its Class A Northerns from American Locomotive Company in 1926 as part of an order for 12 locomotives. It continued to develop and refine its 4-8-4 designs, purchasing 36 more from Baldwin between 1934 and 1943. NP 4-8-4's were famous for pulling the *North Coast Limited* between St. Paul and Livingston, Mont., without

Northern Pacific went to a lot of places that rival Great Northern did (Minneapolis/St. Paul, Duluth, Grand Forks, Spokane, Seattle)—and a lot that it didn't (Ashland, Wis., Bismarck, N.D., Bozeman and Missoula, Mont.). NP's more-southerly route across the northern tier between the Twin Cities and Spokane was arguably more scenic overall. (The grandness of GN's route through Glacier Park had its price—the endless flat prairies of North Dakota and eastern Montana; NP followed scenic river valleys in the southern portions of those states.) Like GN, NP served a major national park, Yellowstone, which prompted an earlier NP slogan, "Yellowstone Park Line," visible under the emblem on the map from a 1939 passenger timetable.

LEFT: As with Burlington and Great Northern, NP's first road diesels were Electro-Motive FT's, 44 of which were delivered in 1944-45. They remained in active service longer than those of CB&Q and GN (or, for that matter, probably longer than any other Class I carrier); here, two sets of A-B FT's sandwich two later models on a freight at Yardley, Wash., in March 1967.—RON LUNDSTROM BELOW: Dressed in the black/yellow ochre scheme, two of NP's 176 GP9's work at Silver Bow, Mont., in 1965. Catenary supports for the adjacent Milwaukee Road main line serve as a reminder as to how close NP's principal competitor in the region could be—BUD BULGRIN

"World's Largest Steam Locomotives," the Yellowstones worked mainly between Glendive, Mont., and Mandan, N.D., where the railroad had a "sawtooth" profile. Later, some were transferred west to the Rocky Mountain Division to serve as helpers on NP's stiff grades. The last of the Yellowstones were scrapped in 1957, and the only survivors of this wheel arrangement are three Duluth, Missabe & Iron Range Yellowstones on display in Minnesota.

The Yellowstones weren't the only chapter in NP's large-locomotive development. In 1936, it received the first of what would become a fleet of 47 4-6-6-4 "Challengers." This time Alco remained the primary builder, erecting all of NP's Challengers between 1936 and 1944. The 4-6-6-4's were intended for service over mountainous terrain west of Livingston with the exception of Stampede Tunnel—the locomotives were too big for its narrow confines. The last NP Challenger operated in 1957.

LIKE GREAT NORTHERN, NP was committed to offering the highest-quality mainline passenger service. Consequently, a year after GN debuted the *Empire Builder*, NP unveiled an upgraded *North Coast Limited* using heavyweight cars purchased between 1925-30. The new train entered service on May 14, 1930, and featured such amenities as radios, showers and a barber shop. NP passenger trains served Yellowstone National Park via the Park Branch from Livingston to Gardiner, Mont., at Yellowstone's northern border. The railroad took full promotional advantage of its proximity to the park, even adopting the slogan "Yellowstone Park Line" for a time. It's dining cars were also noted for fine food; one of its most famous menu items was the "NP Big Baked Potato" grown in the on-line state of Washington.

In 1947, the *North Coast Limited* began receiving new streamlined equipment from Pullman-Standard. Unlike the *Empire Builder*, the *NCL* was streamlined gradually, as cars were received from the builder. Modified heavyweight cars continued to be used in *NCL* consists until more cars were purchased in the early 1950's. Initially, NP streamlined cars wore dark green with a lighter green window band edged in yellow. One of highlights of the train was the observation-buffet-lounge sleeping cars, of which six were built (one was owned by CB&Q). The *North Coast Limited* name, complete with monad emblem, was carried on an illuminated tailsign on the rear of the car. All these cars survived into the 1990's.

On Nov. 16, 1952, new, faster schedules were implemented so that the *North Coast Limited* could

change, a distance of over 1,000 miles—one of the longest single locomotive assignments in the U.S. In 1933 NP purchased Timken Roller Bearing 4-8-4 No. 1111, the first steam locomotive to be equipped with roller bearings. Renumbered 2626 by NP, the famous machine served the railroad well until 1957 when it pulled a special excursion train on its final run. The following year, despite the pleas of preservationists, the engine was unceremoniously scrapped.

Although large, the 4-8-4's were far from being NP's biggest steam locomotives. Another locomotive developed by the road was the 2-8-8-4, or "Yellowstone" type, named for the river paralleled by NP in Montana and the name of the division to which the locomotives were initially assigned. The first, built by Alco in 1928, was 125 feet long, 16 feet 4 inches high and weighed 559 tons; eleven more followed in 1930, built by Baldwin. For years hailed as the

better compete with Milwaukee Road and GN streamliners. Westbound the schedule was cut by 12 hours, while a nine-hour saving was achieved eastbound. On the same date a new train, the *Mainstreeter*, was inaugurated, running on approximately the *Limited*'s old schedule and handling many of the stops that had been dropped by the speeded-up *NCL*. As the *NCL* received more new cars, older equipment was reassigned to the *Mainstreeter*. Beginning in 1953, locomotives and cars of the *North Coast Limited* began wearing a new two-tone green paint scheme conceived by noted industrial designer Raymond Loewy, who also designed interiors for new passenger equipment to arrive in 1954.

Seven dome coaches and a like number of dome sleepers arrived that year with Loewy-designed interiors. A year later, "Lewis and Clark Travelers' Rest" buffet-lounges, also designed by Loewy with interiors finished by NP's Como Car Shops in St. Paul, were added to *NCL* consists. At the same time, stewardess-nurses began staffing the train. After the arrival of domes, the train was always referred to in promotional material as the "Vista-Dome *North Coast Limited*." Still, the railroad wasn't finished: It added new "Holiday Lounge" cars to the *Mainstreeter* in 1956, and six new Budd-built diners to the *NCL* in 1958—the last conventional single level diners built prior to Amtrak. In 1959, Slumbercoaches (economy sleepers) were added to the train.

After World War II, NP adopted the celebrated slogan it carried until merger day: "Main Street of the Northwest." The diction was appropriate, for although GN had the better route profile, NP served more of the population centers of North Dakota, Montana and Washington. In the 1950's traffic flourished along the "Main Street" under the guiding hand of President Robert S. Macfarlane. Like John Budd at GN, he rose to the presidency in 1951 and would be at the helm during the critical years leading to the merger. Under his administration, NP dieselized and continued to rebuild its physical plant, even as merger talks progressed. In 1955, NP opened a huge new classification yard at Pasco, Wash., at a cost of $5.5 million—a yard still used by BN.

About 35 percent of NP's gross ton-miles were

handled by diesels by 1950. Already, NP had subscribed to Electro-Motive's pioneering FT locomotives after test runs by demonstrator FT 103 over the railroad. Forty-four units were delivered in 1944 and 1945 in 10 A-B-B-A sets. Before the FT's arrived, NP had purchased only diesel switchers, but once they had proved their worth, NP entered the road of

NP maintained pride in its star streamliner, the *North Coast Limited*, right to the end. The *NCL* gets a dousing at Livingston, Mont.—BOB SCHMIDT

dieselization, a process well-documented in the book NORTHERN PACIFIC DIESEL ERA, 1945-1970 by Lorenz P. Schrenk and Robert L. Frey.

For *North Coast Limited* power, NP used three-unit sets of dynamic-brake-equipped EMD F3's, delivered in 1946-47. F7's were added in 1949, and F9's followed beginning in 1954. The road acquired

both freight and passenger F-units en masse until the last F9's were added to the roster in 1956. Counting the FT's, NP owned close to 200 F-units, with the newer members surviving well after the BN merger— some right into 1981. NP also purchased 20 GP7's and was a booster of the GP9, buying 176 of them between 1954 and 1958. Also added to the roster were Baldwin and Alco switchers, as well as 18 Alco RS11 road-switchers in 1958 and 1960. With the invasion of all this diesel power, NP steam was wiped out. Class W-3 Mikado 1713 made the last trip, a Duluth-Superior transfer run, on Jan. 17, 1958, ending NP's steam era. However, in 1992 two preserved 1907-built engines were back in action: Class S-10 4-6-0 No. 328 in Minnesota and L-9-class 0-6-0 1070 in Washington state.

In 1960, NP bought nine GP18's from EMD, then plunged into the high-horsepower diesel era in 1964-65 with the purchase of thirty 2,500-h.p. U25C's from General Electric (three of the units were rated for 2,750 h.p); twelve U28C's came in 1966 and ten U33C's in 1969. NP also went for the EMD SD45 in a big way, adding thirty of the 3,600-h.p. units between 1966-68. NP had twenty additional SD45's on order at merger time that instead wound up on BN.

Robert Macfarlane left the president's chair in 1966, moving up to chairman, and Louis W. Menk moved over from CB&Q to replace him. Menk would be at the helm on merger day, but that day may not have occurred had not Macfarlane and GN's John Budd collaborated in the 1950's to explore the possibility of merger. Menk became BN's first president, and guided the company through its formative early years.

When Menk came to NP in October 1966, the handwriting was already on death notices for the passenger train. Even pro-passenger Macfarlane had been forced to cut away at losing local passenger services, even though the company had made a last-ditch effort to upgrade them by purchasing six Rail Diesel Cars in the 1950's and 1960's. On Jan. 5, 1967, NP eliminated service between St. Paul and Duluth, and later that year, local service between St. Paul and Jamestown, N.D. In 1968 service to International Falls, Minn., was cut and replaced by a bus, and in 1969, Twin Ports-Staples, Minn., and

LEFT: Stepsister to the famed *North Coast Limited* was the *Mainstreeter*, whose main job was to serve the multitude of stops on the Chicago-Seattle route skipped by the *North Coast Limited*. Following its cross-country trek, No. 1 gingerly approaches the platforms of Seattle's King Street Station early one March morning in 1967.—RON LUNDSTROM

Fargo-Winnipeg trains left the timetable. By merger time only the *North Coast Limited*, *Mainstreeter* and a Portland-Seattle round trip remained.

Initially the National Railroad Passenger Corporation—Amtrak—was not kind to routes formerly served by NP passenger trains. On April 30, 1971, the final *North Coast Limited*s and *Mainstreeter*s departed Chicago, Seattle and St. Paul. Amtrak retained Seattle-Portland service, but the route between Pasco and Seattle initially was the only other principal ex-NP line to host passenger trains after Amtrak, when the *Empire Builder* was rerouted to this line (between Spokane and Pasco, trains alternated between the NP and SP&S routes). However, only weeks after Amtrak was born, strong pressure from Montana Senator Mike Mansfield resulted in the reinstatement of passenger service over the NP route between Minneapolis and Spokane, a run that became the *North Coast Hiawatha*.

Northern Pacific lines under BN control fared worse than the former routes of the other merger partners. Many Minnesota and Washington NP branch lines were abandoned, and most of the branches in North Dakota were sold to regional Red River Valley & Western in 1987. Even the main line wasn't safe: The route over Stampede Pass was taken out of service in 1983 and the Pasco-Cle Elum (Wash.) portion sold to Washington Central in 1986. The Huntley-Sandpoint, Idaho, portion of the main line was deleted from BN's map in November 1987 when it was leased to Montana Rail Link.

Parts of the NP are still vital to BN: the Seattle-Portland main and Sandpoint-Spokane-Pasco routes remain busy, as is the line through eastern Montana and the Dakotas to Minnesota, where coal trains operate on streetcar-like headways. Between St. Paul and Casselton, N.D., the NP route is also also the main route for BN's fleet of transcontinental intermodal trains. Out here at least, the slogan "Main Street of the Northwest" still means something.

RIGHT: NP's cadre of Budd-built Rail Diesel Cars saw a variety of services. One of NP's more-obscure RDC wanderings was Spokane-Lewiston (Idaho) trains 311 and 314, operating as a day turn out of Spokane; this run saw the first use of NP RDC's, in 1955. Schedules coincided at Spokane with the *Mainstreeter* so as to permit-Seattle-Lewiston travel. Here, southbound 311 stops at the college town (Washington State University) of Pullman early in the 1960's. Passenger service on the Palouse & Lewiston branch ended in 1966.—GIL HULIN

ABOVE: Following a spectacular descent from Homestake Pass, the westbound *North Coast Limited* pauses at Butte in February 1965. Union Pacific's *Butte Special* idles nearby during its all-day layover at its namesake; it will depart in about three hours for the overnight run to Salt Lake City.—GIL HULIN LEFT: It was the NP main line that linked the Northwest's two most-prominent cities, Seattle and Portland, but passenger service over the route was provided through a cooperative arrangement between NP, GN and UP, with each road providing one daily Seattle-Portland round trip. Collectively, they were known as the "Pool Trains," and they formed the basis for later Amtrak service on the line. NP's northbound Pool No. 407 is at Vancouver, Wash., in 1969.—GEORGE BERISSO

ABOVE AND RIGHT: Northern Pacific entered its high-horsepower diesel era with 30 imposing U25C's from General Electric in 1964-65, followed by a group of U28C's in 1966. With their boxy design, wide, flat noses, Cyclopian single-piece front windshields and silver trucks, the locomotives of these series were among the most formidable and impressive diesels NP ever owned. Here, 15,300 horsepower worth of U25C's and a U28C strongarm a freight out of Northtown Yard in Minneapolis in summer 1966. Leading the pack is new "class" U28C No. 2800.—BOTH PHOTOS, JIM BOYD

ABOVE AND RIGHT: Chasing the setting sun, the westbound Vista-Dome *North Coast Limited* strikes out of Missoula, Mont., in 1969. The glowing sunset provides a fitting finale for passengers who have enjoyed a splendid day of sightseeing along the rivers, valleys and peaks of Big Sky country. The *North Coast*'s trip through Montana stretched nearly 800 miles in the space of about 18 hours.—BOTH PHOTOS, MIKE SCHAFER

RIGHT: At Pasco, Wash., the *North Coast Limited*'s Portland cars were separated from the Seattle section and combined with Spokane, Portland & Seattle train 1 and 31, the latter comprising the *Empire Builder*'s Portland cars, which SP&S No. 1 handled from Spokane along with its own equipment. This scene at Pasco in August 1963 shows the vice versa: NP Baldwin DRS6-6-15 No. 525 is nudging onto the three *North Coast* cars from Portland that have arrived on SP&S train 2-32 (SP&S's Portland-Spokane local and the *Empire Builder*). It will pull the cars from 2-32 and tack them onto the *North Coast* Seattle section, which will arrive shortly. The unique Baldwin (NP had but one of this model; it was re-engined with an EMD prime mover in 1959) will then switch the *North Coast* to properly position the three add-ons within the main-stem train.—GIL HULIN

The *North Coast Limited* was one of the oldest name trains in operation when it departed Seattle and Chicago for the final time on April 30, 1971, just one day after its 71st birthday. Though it outlived its parent railroad by some 14 months, the *North Coast* fell to history when Amtrak arrived and was survived by its long-time but younger (by 29 years) competitor, the *Empire Builder.* LEFT: The two rivals share Great Northern station in Minneapolis following a fresh siege of snow on a February evening in 1969; both trains had traveled as one over the Burlington from Chicago to St. Paul where they were separated, commingling briefly again at Minneapolis before resuming their respective runs to Seattle.—MIKE SCHAFER/LIGHTING BY JIM BOYD ABOVE: Buffet-observation-lounge cars were a fitting conclusion to NP's best, glistening at St. Paul in March 1967.—RON LUNDSTROM RIGHT: The lighted gate sign at Minneapolis beckoned passengers boarding one of America's all-time great streamliners.—JIM HEUER

CHAPTER 4

SPOKANE, PORTLAND & SEATTLE

THE NORTHWEST'S OWN RAILWAY

The Spokane, Portland & Seattle Railway was the youngest of the four large carriers that became Burlington Northern in 1970—and would be the last to formally disappear. The SP&S, whose slogan was "The Northwest's Own Railway," got its start in 1908, and its purpose was clear: to give NP and GN a direct route from eastern Washington to Portland, Ore. Before the SP&S line was built along the north bank of the Columbia River, GN and NP sent their Portland traffic via a circuitous route over the NP by way of Seattle and Tacoma, or via rival Oregon Railway & Navigation Company (OR&N). Construction of a line from Spokane directly to Portland would give the two roads a straight shot from that area to the Oregon city.

During the 1890's, James J. Hill had particular concern about the OR&N. The railroad ran for 212 miles along the Columbia's south bank from Portland to Wallula, Wash., where it connected with NP. OR&N also connected with Union Pacific-controlled Oregon Short Line and had branches in several areas, as well as steamship service on the Snake, Willamette and Columbia rivers. OR&N provided NP—and GN—with the most-direct access to Portland. E. H. Harriman, a keen rival of Hill's, managed to gain control of the OR&N when his UP leased the line in 1887 and then purchased the majority of its stock two years later. Anxious for their own direct

line to Portland, GN and NP incorporated the Portland & Seattle Railway Company on Aug. 22, 1905. The new railroad would be owned 50 percent by each company; neither would have a controlling interest.

In August 1905, the construction firm of Siems & Shields was retained to build the line from Vancouver, Wash. (near Portland) to Kennewick, near Pasco, Wash. Construction began in January 1906 after the fledgling P&S had fought off the OR&N both in the courts and along the right-of-way, as the Harriman Lines tried to stop the progress of the P&S near Portland. In September 1906, Hill decided the P&S should be extended into Spokane to connect with the GN, and once again Siems & Shields were given the job.

Because the Portland & Seattle was built relatively late, more-modern construction techniques were used, with the result that the railroad was and is superbly engineered. Construction proceeded on several fronts at once, and steam shovels were used to speed efforts. On Feb. 1, 1908, the name of the company was changed to Spokane, Portland & Seattle Railway. In March 1908, the Vancouver-Kennewick line was completed (SP&S used NP tracks from Kennewick into Pasco). Thanks to the Columbia River, the railroad was able to maintain an 0.2 percent eastbound ruling grade despite being

surrounded by cliffs and mountains. The line east of Pasco toward Spokane didn't open until May 1909; it was spectacular, with no less than five large viaducts and six tunnels.

Another notably scenic railroad was the Oregon Trunk, connecting with the SP&S at Wishram, Wash., and running south 151 miles to Bend, Ore. Hill had determined that central Oregon would be a worthy objective, as he would soon have direct access to Portland. Engineer John F. Stevens, who had located Great Northern's line through the Cascades and Rockies, once again helped Hill survey the railroad. Stevens determined that the best route south would be through the rugged Deschutes River Canyon.

A railway was already in the works along the Deschutes. The Oregon Trunk Line had been incorporated by a group of Seattle bankers and a railroad contractor in 1906. The group had already surveyed the Deschutes route, as had another company—the Deschutes Railroad, a Harriman concern. Stevens met with the Trunk's owners in 1909 and was able to procure the option to buy their stock, which he did on Sept. 6, 1909. The Oregon Trunk Line was renamed the Oregon Trunk Railway Company, and it became a subsidiary of the SP&S.

ABOVE: SP&S office car drumhead, 1969.—MIKE SCHAFER

An eastbound Spokane, Portland & Seattle freight with a four-unit set of Alco FA's and FB's crosses Great Northern's Fort Wright trestle over the Spokane River at West Spokane in June 1963. At the west end of the bridge was Fort Wright Junction, where SP&S trains curved onto the GN main for the trip to GN's Hillyard Yard. All four units are clad in the SP&S' original diesel paint scheme. Everything in this photo is now gone: the bridge, the diesels, even the SP&S itself.—JACK WHEELIHAN

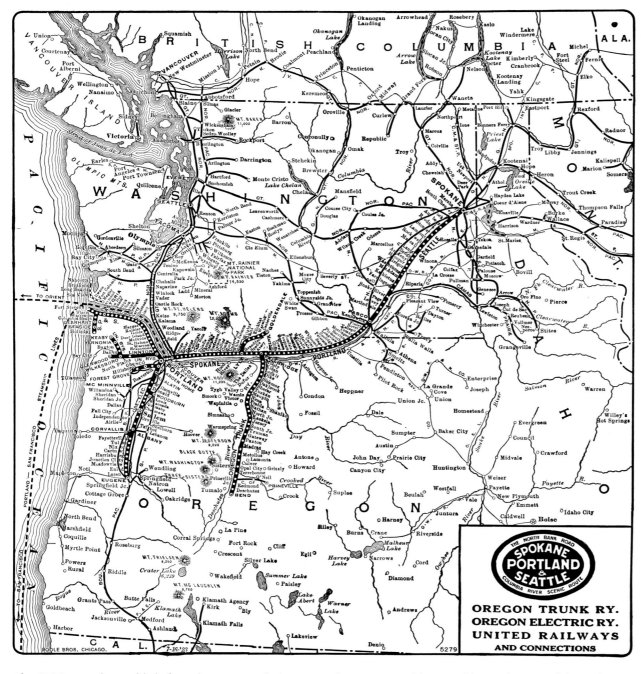

The SP&S map changed little from this version which appeared in a 1925 public timetable. By the time of the Burlington Northern merger 45 years later, only a few short branches had vanished, and in fact some growth had occurred. SP&S subsidiary Oregon Electric gained trackage rights over Southern Pacific from Albany to Lebanon, Ore., and built from Lebanon to Sweet Home, Ore., in 1931. It also built the Holley Branch from Sweet Home through Holley to Dollar. The lines opened for traffic April 1, 1932.

Construction progressed south, with the OT on the west bank of the canyon and the Deschutes Railroad on the east. But at milepost 75, OT crossed over to the east bank to avoid an Indian reservation, running afoul of Deschutes Railroad workers who were also grading and laying track. The situation became tense, with workers on both sides harassing the others. In 1910, a compromise was worked out with the OT building to Bend, but with the Deschutes having trackage rights; joint terminals were also built. James J. Hill drove OT's golden spike at Bend on Oct. 5, 1911. In 1935, Deschutes successor Union Pacific was granted trackage rights from Ainsworth, Ore., across the Columbia from Wishram, to Davidson, and the east bank line was abandoned. The OT became more important with the GN extension to Klamath Falls and Bieber, Calif., in 1928-31 and a connection with the Western Pacific.

SP&S also controlled two other rail lines: the United Railways and the Oregon Electric. The OE, an electric interurban line, was acquired in February 1910. It had been incorporated in 1906 to build south from Portland to Roseburg, Ore., and had reached Salem in November 1907; SP&S extended the road south to Eugene in 1912. Electric operation continued until 1945, when diesels took over.

The United Railways Company was established in 1906 and built from Portland to Wilkesboro, Ore. Hill acquired the line as a feeder for the SP&S in 1910, and in 1924, URC assumed control of the Portland, Astoria & Pacific, which had built from Wilkesboro to County Line.

SP&S operated as a separate company until Jan. 1, 1933, when complete control was exerted by GN and NP. Previous to that, SP&S had its own executive department and officers. Under the new arrangement, the president of one of the parent companies would also serve as SP&S president on an alternating-year basis; the parent road executive not serving as president would become SP&S vice president. Work previously done by SP&S departments at its Portland offices were turned over to the parent roads as much as possible. Almost 500 people lost their jobs under cuts made in 1933. Between 1933 and 1940, the company was operated as a division of its parents, under a Portland-based superintendent, who reported to GN and NP general managers in Seattle. However, in 1940 the parent roads appointed a vice president and general manager based at Portland. He ran the day-to-day operation, reporting directly to the chief executives of GN and NP.

SP&S is probably best known as the forwarder of

GN and NP passenger trains. The "North Bank Road" (as it was sometimes called because of its location along the Columbia), took GN trains from Spokane to Portland and NP trains from Spokane or Pasco to Portland. Shortly after the road opened for service, SP&S implemented a day train (Nos. 1 and 2) and a night train (3 and 4). For a brief time, 1 and 2 carried a through sleeper for NP's *North Coast Limited.*

In 1924, when GN's *Oriental Limited* was upgraded, SP&S 1 and 2 were given the *Oriental* name since it connected with the GN train at Spokane; meanwhile, Nos. 3 and 4 received the *North Coast Limited* name. In 1929, the connecting point for the *North Coast Limited* was moved from Spokane to Pasco.

UNTIL THE 1930's, SP&S relied primarily on used steam power such as 2-8-0's, 2-6-2's and 2-8-2's from the parent roads. The only new power were a handful of 0-6-0's and 4-6-0's, plus ten 4-4-2's, all built prior to 1912. In 1927-28 and 1930, six 4-6-0's built in 1910 were upgraded to 4-6-2's, but it was evident that the motive-power fleet was aging. SP&S was able to tag onto NP orders from American Locomotive Works for six 4-6-6-4's and three 4-8-4's from Baldwin, all identical to NP designs except that the SP&S engines burned oil. The 4-6-6-4's were the first new power in 24 years when they arrived in 1937. The three Northern's were delivered in 1938 and entered passenger service. During World War II, SP&S received two more "Challenger" articulateds, which once again had been tacked to an NP order. Delivered in 1944, the pair would be the last steam power received by the road, except for two Challengers that had gone to GN which were sold back to SP&S in 1946 and 1950.

After the war, when GN and NP upgraded and streamlined their passenger services, so did SP&S. The road ordered 13 streamlined passenger cars in 1946 that were delivered over the next four years to serve in *North Coast Limited, Empire Builder* and regular SP&S consists. The upgraded trains operated on faster schedules, so some schedule swapping took place to preserve the level of service that existed before the streamliners came. Local service along the main line continued to be provided by a pair of trains on a daylight schedule.

GN's *Empire Builder* streamliner arrived first in 1947, with SP&S handling one through sleeper and coach to and from Portland. In 1952, when the *North Coast Limited* was speeded up, SP&S trains 1 and 2 (the *Empire Builder* connection) began receiving the *Limited*'s cars in Pasco. At the same time, the sec-

ABOVE: SP&S's principal passenger runs were unnamed Nos. 1 and 2 between Portland and Spokane (SP&S people called it the "Streamliner"). They were combined with the Portland sections of two of the most-famous name trains in North America— the *North Coast Limited* and *Empire Builder.* Number 1 left Spokane late in the evening, providing overnight service to Portland; eastbound No. 2 left the Rose City in late afternoon. Number 2 has just arrived Pasco, Wash., in August 1963. As the nose of F3A 801 gets a dousing, the *NCL* cars will be pulled from the consist; the *Empire Builder* cars will be relayed to the *Builder* at Spokane.—GIL HULIN

ABOVE: Perhaps SP&S's most-unusual "passenger" train (such as it was) was the Oregon Trunk mixed between Wishram, Wash., and Bend, Ore. A popular run with sportsmen, the mixed snaked its way along the canyons of the Deschutes River into areas accessible to the public only by way of the train's classic steel combine. Southbound 102 is shown early in the morning at Redmond, Ore., in 1967. The trains lasted as mixeds on Burlington Northern as well, until Amtrak arrived on May 1, 1971; they were the only mixeds operated by BN.—GIL HULIN

LEFT: SP&S was synonymous with Alco. The 34-unit FA/FB fleet was the road's hallmark, and the flatnose covered wagons could be found on just about all parts of the system. Three FA's and two Great Northern Geeps head the joint SP&S-GN Inside Gateway freight at Bend, Ore., during the small hours of a July day in 1969. BELOW: Alco built 2,370 examples of its venerable RS3 model, and SP&S owned 29 of them (two having been purchased used from GN). A pair of RS3's bask in the hot sun of a July day in 1969 at Wishram, the first division point out of Portland and junction with the Oregon Trunk line to Bend.—BOTH PHOTOS, JIM BOYD

ondary *Mainstreeter* began operation, and SP&S trains 3 and 4 provided the new train with a Portland connection. In 1954-55, when GN and NP dome cars arrived, SP&S received two cars as its contribution to the NP train and one for the *Empire Builder*.

The "Northwest's Own Railway" became popular with students of railroading because of its use of American Locomotive Company (Alco) diesel power— SP&S was the only heavy user of Alcos in the Northwest. Like its parent railroads, SP&S's first diesels were switchers. In 1940 four diesels arrived for switching service at Portland: two 1,000-h.p. Alco S2's and two Baldwin VO1000's. Baldwin, in Eddystone, Pa., had submitted a bid at the same price as Alco, and since the horsepower was the same, SP&S split the order between the two builders. Two 660-h.p. Alco S1's switchers were delivered in 1941.

With the traffic increases caused by World War II, more switchers were ordered: a single Baldwin in 1942, six Alco S2's in 1943 and another pair of Baldwins in 1945. Over time, SP&S found the mechanical reliability of the Alcos to be far superior to the Baldwins, so no more Eddystone products were

ordered. Alco RS1's and RS2's arrived in the years 1945-50.

The first true road diesel power came in the form of two F3's ordered from Electro-Motive for SP&S's new streamlined train; they were delivered in 1947. Three other EMD's—1000-h.p. NW2's—came the following year. Although the road preferred Alco switchers, EMD could deliver the NW2's faster, so it got the order. Road freight dieselization got underway in 1948 with the arrival of six of Alco's streamlined FA1 cab units. SP&S eventually would own 34 Alco FA and FB units, including eight purchased from parent Great Northern.

Since the *North Coast Limited* still had not been speeded up and SP&S's streamliner was serving only as the *Empire Builder* connection in the late 1940's, the two F3's were more than ample for the shorter train. Thus, a 2,000-h.p. E7, No. 750 (the only E-unit ever owned by SP&S), was purchased from EMD in 1948 for use on the *Builder* connection, which allowed the two F3's to be used on other, heavier trains; a third F3A joined the roster at this time.

In the 1950's, SP&S's march toward dieselization continued. Four F7A's came in 1953 to fully dieselize passenger service, and 18 Alco RS3's came in 1950-55 to finish off the steam. Parental intervention influenced future diesel orders, with GN suggesting EMD power and NP, Alco—probably due to financial considerations. A compromise was reached: the next SP&S order would be split between both builders: Six EMD GP9's (four equipped with steam boilers for passenger service) were ordered in August 1955 along with nine additional RS3's.

The last SP&S steam run began on June 22, 1956, when 4-6-6-4 No. 910 handled the "Scribner Turn" out of Spokane, swapping power with eastbound diesels at Scribner (which took the turn back

to Spokane) and continuing west to Wishram. On June 23, the 910 headed out of Wishram to Vancouver and steam was finished. Two locomotives were preserved: 2-8-2 No. 539 (ex-NP 1762), displayed at Vancouver, and 4-8-4 No. 700, donated to the City of Portland and placed in Oakes Park in 1958. Another steam locomotive, 4-8-2 No. 2507, was purchased

No inferiority complex here: An SP&S billboard advises Portland motorists that "Our wheels are just as big!" Move over UP, NP and SP.—GEORGE BERISSO

from GN and relettered for display at Maryhill, Wash.

In 1990, the 700 was returned to service by the Pacific Railroad Preservation Association. Its first test run operated from Portland to Longview, Wash., on June 13, after which the 700 returned to home rails on a Portland-Wishram round trip on June 28, 1990. The trip recreated the May 20, 1956, excursion which closed out steam passenger service on the SP&S. Restoration efforts are also underway on the 2507, which has been returned to its GN livery.

In 1959, local trains 5 and 6 were discontinued, but SP&S's other passenger business remained stable into the 1960's. Trains 1 and 2 continued as the connecting train for the premiere GN and NP stream-

liners, while 3 and 4 provided connections for the secondary *Mainstreeter* and *Western Star*. SP&S even bought a brand new RPO car in 1961 and picked up several used passenger cars from the Missouri-Kansas-Texas Railroad in the 1960's to bolster its passenger car fleet. Service continued under Burlington Northern until the advent of Amtrak, when the direct connection to Portland was eliminated.

SP&S's most-unique passenger operation was the Wishram-Bend mixed train on the Oregon Trunk. Elderly heavyweight combines trailing strings of freight cars cruised through the isolated Deschutes River Canyon, stopping to drop off or pick up passengers—mostly sportsmen—and freight just about anywhere. The combines featured bay windows for the conductor and portable flood lights for night unloading. The unusual service continued right up to Amtrak.

In the 1960's, SP&S faced the prospect of replacing diesels nearing the end of their life expectancy and once again turned to its old, economical friend Alco. The first "second-generation" Alco power to arrive were seven Century 424's in 1964. The 2,400-h.p. locomotives carried a new paint scheme: a broad yellow ochre stripe surrounded by Pullman green, which became the new standard for the railroad (it was supposedly the yellow of NP and the green of GN). In 1965-66, sixteen 2,500-h.p. C425's came onto the roster, with several FA's traded in to Alco on the purchase. This was followed by an order for six big 3,600-h.p. C636's, delivered in early 1968 with more FA trade-ins. Late in the year, four more C636's arrived, along with two unusual C415 1,500-h.p. center-cab switchers. They would be the last Alco's received by SP&S. In 1969, with Alco soon to close its doors, SP&S ordered six 2,000-h.p. GP38's from EMD. The units weren't to be delivered until February 1970, and with the Supreme Court approving

the merger that month, the units were given BN colors and numbers.

Following the merger, the ex-SP&S lines remained a source of fascination. In mid-1970, BN shifted 18 ex-NP Alco RS11's plus some RS3's from the Midwest to the SP&S to consolidate all Alco power in one location. Throughout the 1970's, the Alcos, together with F-units from the predecessors lines, roamed for-mer SP&S lines, making the Northwest a haven for rare motive power. Run-through power off the Western Pacific from the ex-GN connection at Bieber made consists even more colorful (GN/SP&S power pooling to Bieber had begun in 1958). The last FA cab units continued in service until 1972, and the remaining Alcos were finally retired in 1980.

On Oct. 26, 1981, Amtrak reinstated direct

FACING PAGE: SP&S took enough of a fancy to Alco products that it acquired 35 of the manufacturer's second-generation "Century"-series locomotives. Two Centurys descend into the Spokane River valley with a transfer from GN's Hillyard complex at Spokane on a stifling hot afternoon in July 1969. ABOVE: Eastbound No. 2-26-32 slides into Vancouver, Wash., in July 1969.—BOTH PHOTOS, MIKE SCHAFER

Spokane-Portland service over BN's former SP&S main line west of Pasco when the passenger railroad added a Portland section to its Chicago-Seattle *Empire Builder*. Between Spokane and Pasco, Amtrak trains had used the ex-NP westbound and the ex-SP&S eastbound, with shifts at BN's option—a practice which continued until October 1984 when the *Builder* began using the NP in both directions.

BN shifted mainline traffic off SP&S's scenic "High Line" between Spokane and Pasco to the parallel NP line in 1987 and abandoned the High Line two years later. Nonetheless, the Pasco-Portland ex-SP&S main remains a vital part of the BN system, and most other SP&S lines, including the remote Oregon Trunk, remain intact. For tax reasons, the Spokane, Portland & Seattle was leased by BN at merger and continued to exist, at least on paper, until Nov. 1, 1979, when it was liquidated. Not until then was the "Northwest's Own Railway" truly gone for good.

ABOVE: In the pre-merger days of separate yard facilities, transfer runs often interlinked the predecessor railroads. Their payload having been delivered to the NP, two FA's pick their way out of Yardley at Spokane, Wash., in March 1967; meanwhile, an NP Baldwin switcher tends to its mundane chores.—RON LUNDSTROM LEFT: SP&S was a favorite among the country's medium-haul lines that included the likes of Monon, Western Pacific and Delaware & Hudson, thanks to an interesting blend of motive power. A combination of old and new Alcos hustles west from Wishram along the wide Columbia River in 1969.—MIKE SCHAFER

PART II

A NEW RAILROAD COMES OF AGE

An eastbound coal train, bound for Houston Power & Light in Smithers Lake, Texas, pounds through Osage, Wyo., on Aug. 31, 1979. The new Orin coal line had not yet opened, and this route, which led east over Nebraska's Crawford Hill, was being stretched to the limit of its capacity. Today, most coal trains destined for Denver and Texas points exit the Powder River Basin southward via the Orin Line, through Guernsey, Wyo., and Sterling, Colo.—STEVE PATTERSON

On March 2, 1970, Burlington Northern, Inc. became America's newest railroad. The merger that took place that Monday climaxed more than 15 years of discussion, planning and legal effort toward unification. Thanks to earlier false starts, the railroads were ready for the events of M-Day. Once again, timetables were printed, the locomotive renumbering system prepared and plans laid for connecting the best lines of the five major partners. Still, complete unification would take time: The elimination of duplicate facilities and the construction of a new yard in the Twin Cities and connections at Sandpoint and Spokane would take years to complete.

Unlike the acrimonious New York Central-Pennsylvania merger of 1968, the merger partners enjoyed good relationships. NP and GN had been striving toward a common merger goal for decades, and by virtue of their joint control of CB&Q and SP&S, the executives of the parent roads had already worked together to run a railroad. There was no "red team vs. green team" rivalry that helped derail Penn Central.

The success of the BN merger can also be attributed to geography. Most BN territory was immersed in growth and prosperity throughout the 1970's. BN lines passed close to incredibly huge deposits of low-sulphur coal, which would replace grain as the largest single commodity carried by the railroad before the end of the 1970's. Tapping these deposits would require an astronomical outlay of capital, but the constant flow of coal would help insulate the railroad from periodic economic recessions that affected other railroads.

By the end of the decade the railroad could no longer be termed "new." It had come of age, offering improved, single-line service to 17 states and two Canadian provinces, as merger planners had promised. The company was strong enough to add another railroad to its ranks: the St. Louis-San Francisco (Frisco) which would place BN in more growing markets. This addition would prove advantageous, as BN's second decade would bring new challenges from other railroads, motor carriers and a deregulated marketplace.

CHAPTER 5

THE FIRST DECADE OF BN

1970-1980: UNIFICATION, GROWTH AND THE COAL BOOM

If you stand at the James J. Hill mansion on Summit Avenue and gaze down at the view of downtown St. Paul, you cannot help but notice the large microwave tower atop the former Burlington Northern Building, now known as the First Trust Center. The building was for decades the home of two Burlington Northern predecessors: Great Northern and Northern Pacific. The building was divided in half, with each railroad occupying 50 percent of it. A wall divided the two halves, but on the 10th floor, which housed the executive offices of the two companies, there was a single unmarked door connecting the two. In the 1950's, GN President John Budd and NP President Robert S. Macfarlane determined they would attempt to remove the wall that divided the building. . . by pursuing a merger of their companies, as well as the other railroads they controlled.

Budd and Macfarlane began their discussions riding back to St. Paul after a Burlington board meeting in Chicago. The men conceived a new system that would be huge: over 23,000 miles at merger, not including subsidiary railroads. With the subsidiaries, the new railroad could extend south from Colorado to the Gulf Coast, thanks to Burlington's Colorado & Southern and Fort Worth & Denver railroads. The merger would also include GN-owned Pacific Coast Railroad Company.

The move toward merger in the 1950's was not the first effort to unite the railroads. James J. Hill had attempted to do so through the Northern Securities Company at the turn of the century. Ralph Budd, John Budd's father, had tried again in the 1920's when he was head of GN. After preliminary discussions, GN, NP and Burlington directors agreed in 1925 to proceed with a merger. The new company would be called the Great Northern Pacific Railway Company, with Burlington controlled under stock ownership and the SP&S under lease. On July 28, 1927, a formal merger application was filed with the Interstate Commerce Commission.

A major concern of all parties involved in the proposed consolidation was competition. GN and NP officers felt the two systems complemented, rather than competed, with one another. Merger opponents saw things differently. States, cities, farmers and businessmen were opposed for fear the new company would monopolize rail transportation in its service area. Other railroads objected bitterly, particularly Milwaukee Road—and with good reason: If it included CB&Q, the new company would boast nearly 2½ times as much track and would have income many times larger than parallel Milwaukee.

In February 1930 the ICC approved the merger with four conditions. Three were minor, but the

fourth called for GN and NP to sell their interest in CB&Q in a thinly-veiled attempt to protect the Milwaukee. Losing the Burlington and thus access to Chicago was an unacceptable price for GN and NP. This, combined with mounting political, public and labor opposition to any type of merger, resulted in a decision by the railroads to withdraw their merger application on Jan. 31, 1931. The battle was lost, but not the war.

In the 1950's, Budd and Macfarlane could see that the benefits of a merger would be far-reaching. In many cities, the duplicate yards, depots and support facilities of NP and GN could be eliminated. Although the two roads roughly paralleled one another from St. Paul to Seattle, NP's route was saddled with several tortuous grades. Great Northern clearly had superior routes, with only two difficult passes to cross, at Montana's Marias and Stevens Pass in Washington. If these lines could be brought under one banner, traffic could be re-routed to the best routes, with enormous cost savings.

In 1955, the two roads set up a special committee to study consolidation. Legal, corporate and engineering aspects were all explored. GN had the better

---

ABOVE: SD9 6138 has traded its CB&Q Chinese red and gray for BN green, black and white.—PAUL D. SCHNEIDER

Ex-Great Northern F45 6601, on an eastbound train destined for the former CB&Q "River Line," passes a westbound trailing an ex-Q caboose at Hoffman Avenue interlocking in St. Paul, Minn., on May 16, 1971. Behind the train is massive Daytons Bluff, for decades a St. Paul landmark and site of ancient Indian burial mounds. The F45 still wears the "Big Sky Blue" scheme GN adopted in 1967; it took BN until 1977 to paint its last unit in its huge motive-power fleet Cascade green.—E. L. KANAK

physical plant and earnings history, while NP had a few superior rail routes but many attractive non-railroad assets. The consolidation committee employed the consulting firm of Wyer Dick & Co. to study the economics and implementation of the merger. The companies faced the problem of how stock would be exchanged from the old roads to the new carrier. The two presidents agreed that old shares would be exchanged for new on a one-to-one basis, with GN shareholders receiving an extra half share of preferred stock. In 1960, the railroads' boards approved the committee plans for merger. On Jan. 12, 1961, the Great Northern Pacific & Burlington Lines, Inc. was incorporated as the entity to be used in merger filings, and on Feb. 17, 1961, a formal merger application was presented to the ICC.

Hearings were held across the area served by the railroads in question. Proponents argued that consolidation would bring faster and better service for customers, while opposing railroads argued that their revenues would be severely eroded by the strong new company. Union leaders, fearful of losing jobs, argued against the proposal. Worse, the U.S. Department of Justice opposed the merger plan, stating that loss of competition would create a monopoly, violating antitrust laws. Nonetheless, in 1964 ICC Examiner Robert Murphy recommended to the ICC that the roads be allowed to consolidate. As part of his approval, he suggested that C&NW and Milwaukee Road be given access to several areas not previously served, along with other concessions.

In 1966 the ICC rejected the proposed merger. The commissioners did not find substantive reasons why the railroads should be allowed to merge, citing concerns about loss of competition and jobs and that the carriers already appeared to be financially well off.

The "Northern Lines," as the four railroads were called, refused to give up. In mid-1966 they asked the ICC to reconsider its decision. The railroads had worked with C&NW and Milwaukee Road on concessions which greatly reduced their opposition. New agreements with organized labor, including lifetime job-protection agreements, softened union opposi-

tion as well. Macfarlane, NP president since 1951, was elected chairman of the board effective Oct. 1, 1966, with Louis W. Menk moving over from CB&Q to take the reins as president. Menk worked vigorously on the merger, and when it finally came to pass, he would serve as BN's first president.

EARLY IN 1967, the ICC agreed to reconsider the case, and late in the year the commissioners reversed their

Portent of the impending merger was CB&Q GP40 No. 629, the first unit to wear what would become Burlington Northern colors; it received the scheme in August 1968 with "BURLINGTON" stenciled on its cab sides, with room for the "NORTHERN" to be added later. The Q received 29 new locomotives from GE and EMD in 1968-69 in the proposed BN scheme.—JIM BOYD

earlier decision, approving the consolidation. Still, opposition remained from several quarters, and the ICC delayed merger implementation to allow appeals. At last, the Commission gave final approval.

The name and emblem of the new company came from the New York industrial design firm of Lippincott & Margulies. It was generally agreed that the GNP&B name was too long and unwieldy, so Lippincott developed a new name, made public in March 1968: "Burlington" from the CB&Q was combined with "Northern" from GN and NP. Lippincott & Margulies also designed the BN logo.

Inventing a color scheme proved to be a little more difficult. Lippincott originally proposed retaining the "Big Sky Blue" paint scheme, which it had developed

for GN in 1967, but NP management was less than pleased with this idea. Green was then proposed, but of a hue completely different than any used by NP and GN. The new "Cascade green" represented the rich forest country BN would serve in the Northwest, as well as the timber industry, one of railroad's major customers. Managements approved, and Cascade green became BN's official color.

New forms and letterhead were printed with the logos, as well as employee timetables, set to take effect on "M-Day," May 10, 1968. But again, the dream was delayed. On May 9, the Department of Justice once more expressed its opposition to the marriage, this time requesting that Chief Justice of the Supreme Court Earl Warren temporarily stay the order allowing merger. Warren did, and the employee timetables immediately became collectors' items. Arguments were heard by a three-judge court who eventually ruled in favor of merger. Again appeals were filed, this time to the entire Supreme Court. It was now late 1968, and the Court would not hear the case until the fall of 1969. When the case finally came up, the Department of Justice remained steadfast in its view that the merger would eliminate competition and not be in the public interest.

On Feb. 2, 1970, Northern Lines finally achieved victory when the Supreme Court approved the consolidation, affirming the decision of the ICC and lower courts that merger benefits would outweigh any negatives and that it was, indeed, in the public interest. Merger Day was now set for March 2, 1970. The new company born that day was Burlington Northern, Inc. Burlington Northern Railroad Company, the name presently used, would not come into existence corporately until May 14, 1981. Interestingly, the first BN employee timetables did not go into effect until Tuesday, March 3, 1970.

John Budd became chairman, and Louis Menk was appointed president. William Quinn of the Burlington originally was to become vice chairman, but he instead chose to return to the presidency of Milwaukee Road, after which the BN position of vice chairman was eliminated. Former NP President

Robert Macfarlane became BN's chairman emeritus.

Upon completion of merger "paperwork," the real job began of melding four large railroad systems into one. BN kicked off the operation in high style. The first Burlington Northern freight, Chicago-Seattle No. 97, departed Chicago in foggy weather on Monday March 2, 1970, powered by newly delivered BN GP38's. The GP38's weren't the only locomotives in the spotlight on M-Day. Ex-CB&Q E8's 9942 and 9943 also shared the glory, leading the combined *Afternoon Zephyr/Empire Builder/North Coast Limited* from Chicago to St. Paul.

One of the first jobs the new company faced was the monumental task of renumbering locomotives, which at merger totaled nearly 2,000. A special committee of transportation and mechanical department employees of the component roads was formed to develop a program. A new numbering system had been prepared for the abortive merger in 1968, so in essence it was ready to go in 1970. By late that year, most units were renumbered.

Another huge job for the new company was the repainting its locomotive fleet. The first unit to wear Cascade green had been Burlington GP40 629, painted in an experimental scheme in August 1968. In final revisions of this scheme, the white flanking stripe was eliminated (except on passenger units) while four wide 45-degree white stripes replaced the narrow V-stripes on the noses. BN freight units carried either this scheme or a slightly altered version of it (depending upon the dimensions of the locomotive) into the 1980's, when the railroad began studying ways to make its fleet more visible for safety reasons.

Before they were cycled through the paint shops,

BN's locomotive fleet took on a "rainbow" appearance, with predecessor-road locomotives often straying far from their old haunts. Units from all four roads were mixed, creating lash-ups that were a riot of color. It took until Sept. 9, 1977, when ex-SP&S RS3 4064 was outshopped at Spokane, for BN to become an all-Cascade green railroad. Of course, many units never saw the new scheme, having been retired from service before seeing a BN paint brush.

New trains came into being, thanks to the ability of the company to take advantage of new routings (see Close-Up on pages 64-65). Prime among the new services was No. 3, a new mail train introduced between Chicago and Seattle on April 24, 1971. The end of BN intercity passenger service on April 30, 1971, would mean the end of regular schedules to carry U.S. mail. Thus, No. 3 took over where the passenger trains left off, with mail carried in trailers on flatcars (TOFC), in passenger express box/baggage cars or Flexi-Vans. A top speed of 65 mph was established for the new service, with a total elapsed Chicago-Seattle running time of 50 hours for the 2,181-mile trip—an average speed of 44 mph. However, the train frequently made the trip in 45 hours or less (at that time, 45 hours was the scheduled running time of the *Empire Builder*). Other than quick crew changes, the train only made five intermediate stops to set out or pick up. At Yardley, the ex-NP yard in Spokane, Portland cars were transferred to train 197 for delivery to that city. Initially, the train was dubbed *Pacific Zip*, after the postal "zip" code. It continues in operation today as No. 3, one of the few trains to carry the same number during its entire BN

LEFT: Aptly illustrating BN's rainbow years is this scene of a BN freight at Northtown Yard in Minneapolis three months after merger on June 2, 1970. A former-CB&Q GP30 has teammates in the form of a GN U25B, CB&Q GP20, NP U25C and, wearing GN's three-year-old Big Sky Blue, a GP9.—E. L. KANAK BELOW: Shorn of its monad emblem, NP F9 804 leads a freshly painted GP30 and a Southern Pacific unit through Vancouver Junction, Wash., in the summer of 1972. Although BN worked quickly to apply the Cascade green, the sheer number of units involved meant that predecessor paint schemes could be seen well into the mid 1970's.—G. E. STADTER

existence, and it remains one of "hottest" trains on the northern transcontinental route.

Changes in physical plant came too. Line modifications made on the old Q at Plattsmouth, Neb., in 1976 eliminated a 10-mph curve; another four-mile change west of Gillette, Wyo., reduced 12 curves to three. A new by-pass built at West Fargo, N.D. helped speed movements through that terminal. And in Minneapolis, one of BN's largest post-merger projects ushered in improved traffic flow through the Twin Cities: the redesign, expansion and reconstruction of the ex-NP Northtown Yard.

In July 1973, the company was restructured to streamline the management of its two largest components: The Transportation Division was created to handle the railroad and its two subsidiaries—BN Transport, Inc., a trucking company, and Burlington Northern Air Freight, a national air freight forwarder established in 1972. The new Resources Division managed BN's real-estate, timber and mineral holdings.

UPON MERGER, THE NEW COMPANY at first maintained the motive-power policies of its predecessors, receiving their final new diesel orders and placing new orders for EMD F45's, SD45's and GE U33C's. Minority and elderly power, such as Baldwin and Alco switchers, was stricken from the roster by the end of 1973. But one year after merger, BN had found a road locomotive very much to its liking: the 3000-h.p. SD40. The only other SD40's on the roster at merger were 13 units delivered to Colorado & Southern in 1967-68. Great Northern had rostered a slightly different version, the SDP40. Intended for passenger service, these were essentially SD40's that had been elongated to accommodate boilers for generating steam for passenger train heating. With the arrival of Amtrak in 1971, the six ex-GN units were placed in freight service.

In 1971, BN placed its first order for 25 SD40's, Nos. 6300-6324. In the SD40, BN found a unit that was versatile: It was equally at home pulling coal or merchandise trains. In 1972, EMD introduced the SD40-2, with improved electrical components and a slightly longer frame. BN began purchasing them in

large quantities beginning in 1973, and continued to do so throughout the decade. The numbers tell the story: Between 1971 and the end of 1980, BN had acquired 837 new SD40/SD40-2's (eight were inherited from Frisco).

Why so many new locomotives? The answer can

Text continued on page 66

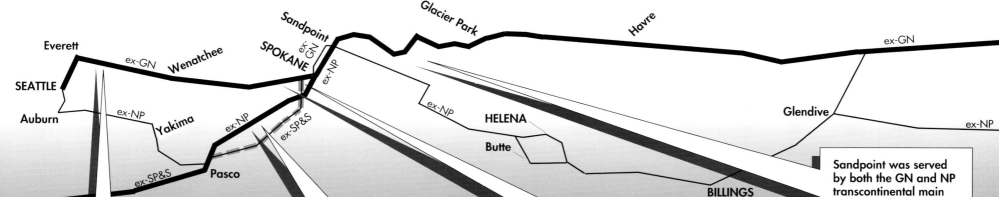

Between Spokane and Seattle, BN chose the ex-GN route over the Cascade Range and along Puget Sound because of the heavy improvements that had been made to it in premerger years. Principal terminal in Seattle is comprised of Balmer Yard and Interbay Engine Terminal; intermodal traffic goes to the ex-NP Stacy Street Yard or South Seattle, a new yard near Boeing Field.

ONE OF THE PRIMARY *benefits of the merger was the elimination of duplicate trackage. BN combined the best parts of its predecessor lines to create the finest possible traffic arteries. A case in point is the main route between Chicago and the Pacific Northwest, host to such transcons as train 3, the former Pacific Zip. The route includes some of the most well-engineered segments of all four pre-Frisco predecessors, as well as some new construction. Here's how the puzzle pieces were fit together...*

BN trains used both the ex-NP and the former SP&S between Spokane and Pasco, Wash., with the NP serving westbound and SP&S eastbound traffic. Eventually, following studies of locomotive performance and fuel consumption, this pattern was reversed—and on June 29, 1987, became academic when BN ceased operations on most of the high-maintenance SP&S line, rife with numerous tunnels and large trestles. For the last lap from Pasco to Portland, traffic is handled over the former SP&S line along the Columbia River. Main terminal in the Portland area is the ex-SP&S yard at Vancouver, Wash.

Spokane was witness to dramatic changes ushered in by BN. For years prior to the merger, the goal had been to link GN, NP and SP&S lines in the city into a single route. Five routes were studied, and by June 1970 the NP route was selected, while Havermale Island on the Spokane River—location of the GN depot—was chosen as the site for the 1974 World's Fair. Ground-breaking commenced on March 2, 1971, and work was completed Dec. 6, 1972. Eliminating GN's route (also used by SP&S) over Havermale and tying it to the NP and SP&S was a complicated proposition. BN mastered the problem by constructing nearly seven miles of new railroad and ten new bridges, including Latah Creek Trestle—4,260 feet long and 212 high. This massive bridge runs west from the NP over Latah Creek on the west side of downtown. The west end of the bridge forms a "wye," the north leg of which leads to the ex-GN route to Seattle, while the south leg connects with the ex-SP&S to Pasco; the ex-NP line to Pasco heads southwest from Sunset Junction, at the east end of the bridge. When most of the ex-SP&S route to Pasco was taken out of service, eight miles of it were retained between Latah Junction and a new connection to the ex-NP—known as Lakeside Junction—was built at Fish Lake, Wash. This gave BN a bidirectional double-track route from that point into Spokane, also used by UP. Generally, Portland-bound trains now use the former SP&S line Spokane-Lakeside because of fewer grades, while eastbounds use ex-NP.

Sandpoint was served by both the GN and NP transcontinental main lines, but the only connection between the two was via the "Humbird Spur," a track hardly suitable for high-speed movements. NP had the superior route to Spokane, where NP facilities were to be utilized, so BN built a new connection between the two lines at Sandpoint just east of the former-NP depot. From this location, known as Sandpoint Junction, traffic from both lines (the NP route now belonging to regional railroad Montana Rail Link) heads along the ex-NP line for 68 miles to Spokane, making this single-track "funnel" among the busiest of BN routes.

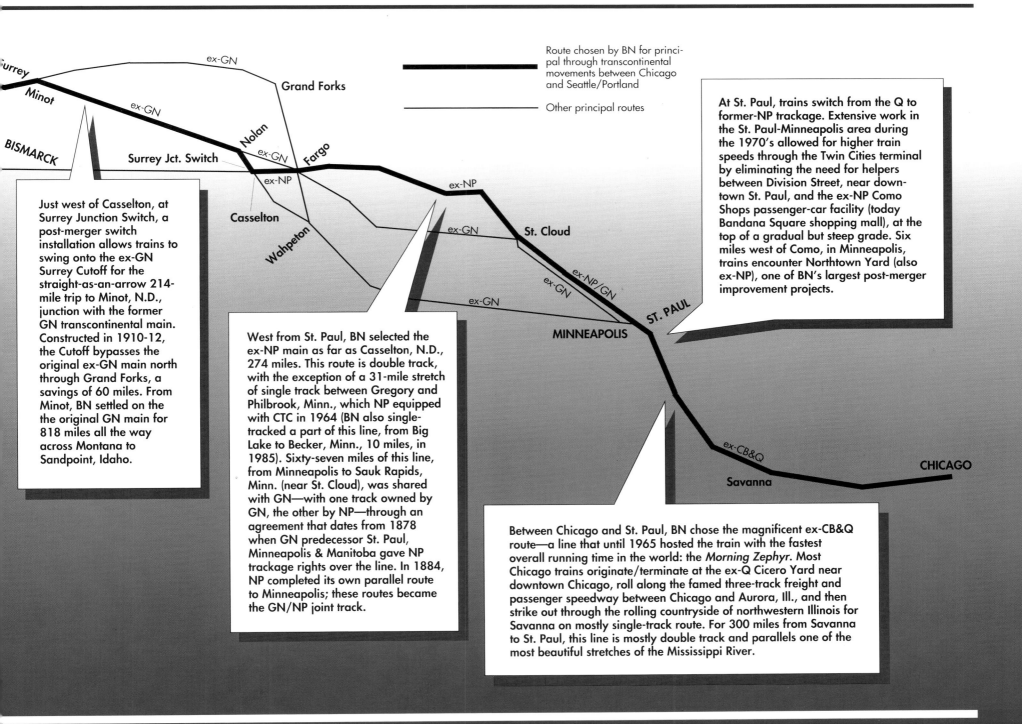

Route chosen by BN for principal through transcontinental movements between Chicago and Seattle/Portland

Other principal routes

ex-GN

Surrey

Minot

BISMARCK

Grand Forks

Nolan

ex-GN

Surrey Jct. Switch

ex-GN

Fargo

Casselton

ex-NP

Wahpeton

ex-NP

ex-GN

St. Cloud

ex-NP/GN

ex-GN

ex-GN

MINNEAPOLIS

ST. PAUL

ex-CB&Q

Savanna

CHICAGO

Just west of Casselton, at Surrey Junction Switch, a post-merger switch installation allows trains to swing onto the ex-GN Surrey Cutoff for the straight-as-an-arrow 214-mile trip to Minot, N.D., junction with the former GN transcontinental main. Constructed in 1910-12, the Cutoff bypasses the original ex-GN main north through Grand Forks, a savings of 60 miles. From Minot, BN settled on the the original GN main for 818 miles all the way across Montana to Sandpoint, Idaho.

West from St. Paul, BN selected the ex-NP main as far as Casselton, N.D., 274 miles. This route is double track, with the exception of a 31-mile stretch of single track between Gregory and Philbrook, Minn., which NP equipped with CTC in 1964 (BN also single-tracked a part of this line, from Big Lake to Becker, Minn., 10 miles, in 1985). Sixty-seven miles of this line, from Minneapolis to Sauk Rapids, Minn. (near St. Cloud), was shared with GN—with one track owned by GN, the other by NP—through an agreement that dates from 1878 when GN predecessor St. Paul, Minneapolis & Manitoba gave NP trackage rights over the line. In 1884, NP completed its own parallel route to Minneapolis; these routes became the GN/NP joint track.

At St. Paul, trains switch from the Q to former-NP trackage. Extensive work in the St. Paul-Minneapolis area during the 1970's allowed for higher train speeds through the Twin Cities terminal by eliminating the need for helpers between Division Street, near downtown St. Paul, and the ex-NP Como Shops passenger-car facility (today Bandana Square shopping mall), at the top of a gradual but steep grade. Six miles west of Como, in Minneapolis, trains encounter Northtown Yard (also ex-NP), one of BN's largest post-merger improvement projects.

Between Chicago and St. Paul, BN chose the magnificent ex-CB&Q route—a line that until 1965 hosted the train with the fastest overall running time in the world: the *Morning Zephyr*. Most Chicago trains originate/terminate at the ex-Q Cicero Yard near downtown Chicago, roll along the famed three-track freight and passenger speedway between Chicago and Aurora, Ill., and then strike out through the rolling countryside of northwestern Illinois for Savanna on mostly single-track route. For 300 miles from Savanna to St. Paul, this line is mostly double track and parallels one of the most beautiful stretches of the Mississippi River.

be found in the Powder River Basin of Campbell County, Wyo., and southern Montana, where huge reserves of low-sulphur coal lie close to the earth's surface. Since merger, BN revenues have steadily increased from the transportation of this coal to markets across the U.S. An example of how important these movements became can be found in the statistics: In 1970 BN carried three million tons of coal and ran an average of one unit coal train weekly. In 1975, volume was up to 40.7 million tons, and the average number of unit trains loaded was 11 daily. Revenues from coal hauling increased to $211 million, up from $143 million in 1974, an increase of 48 per cent—a fourfold increase since 1970. In 1976, coal pulled ahead of grain as the largest producer of revenue for the company. In 1981, 112.1 million tons of coal were carried, more than twice the tonnage of just six years before, and by 1988 this was up to 129 million tons.

Low-sulphur coal came into great demand thanks to the passage of the Clean Air Act of 1970, which required coal-burning companies to reduce sulphur emissions. The easiest way to comply was to use coal that did not have a high sulphur content. BN was in the lucky position of having lines adjacent to coal seams in Montana and Wyoming, where subbituminous coal has a sulphur content that's nearly fourth fifths less than bituminous coal mined in the Eastern U.S. Most mines served by BN are a part of what geologists refer to as the "Fort Union Formation," estimated to contain 600 billion tons of recoverable coal in a seam 300 miles long and 100 miles wide.

NP and CB&Q had both mined coal in the area, mainly for use in their steam locomotives, but by the 1960's there was little interest in the Powder River Basin because power companies could rely on cheap, $3-per-barrel oil. It was also expensive to bring coal all the way from the hinterlands of Wyoming and Montana to generating stations in the East and Midwest, when coal from nearby underground mines was available.

In rapid succession after passage of the Clean Air Act, energy companies began leasing mineral rights and opening mines—and asked BN to move the coal. BN was still unifying the operations of its predecessor roads, but worked out an arrangement whereby the power companies paid for mine spurs, with BN paying them back based on usage; power companies

LEFT: Like several other U.S. railroads, BN honored the nation's 200th birthday by introducing a special Bicentennial scheme, which was applied to three units. On Feb. 5, 1977, Bicentennial SD40-2 No. 1876 wheels past a Milwaukee Road snowplow holed up at Rochelle, Ill., with Milwaukee's local job. Milwaukee Road trains on that road's Janesville (Wis.)-Ladd (Ill.) route had trackage rights on BN from Flagg Center through Rochelle to Steward Junction, Ill.—LLOYD RINEHART BELOW: From the start, BN maintained a high-profile public-relations standing through a number of approaches, including involvement with community activities such as Scouting and school functions. Other endeavors were more modest, but important nonetheless. As a part of a celebration sponsored by the City of Rockford, Ill., for the 1977 sesquicentennial of railroad service to the city, the second-largest in the state, railroads serving Rockford provided equipment for a special display. Glistening-clean BN GP7 1575 stands proudly beside a then-new Amtrak Amfleet coach and Chicago & North Western's Bicentennial Geep at the Illinois Central Gulf/Amtrak Rockford depot.—MIKE SCHAFER/LIGHTING BY RANDY OLSON

also purchased their own hopper cars. In 1973, the Arab oil embargo boosted energy prices and the need for domestic coal became even greater.

Unfortunately, not all BN routes were up carrying such heavy loads. The main coal route to the Basin was the ex-CB&Q line west from Lincoln, Neb., via Grand Island, Neb., and Sheridan, Wyo., hooking up with the ex-NP main line at Huntley, east of Billings. This now-busy line is presently referred to as the "central corridor," but in 1970, although it was in good shape, the line had jointed rail and hosted only a moderate amount of traffic.

Another BN coal route—also made up largely of ex-CB&Q trackage—takes coal from the Basin area to south-central U.S. points and is appropriately referred to as the "southern corridor." Two arms of the route, one striking east from Wendover, Wyo., and one south from Alliance, Neb., join at Northport, Neb., and head south to a junction with the Chicago-Denver main line at Brush, Colo. South of Denver, BN coal trains use the Santa Fe/Rio Grande Joint Line to Pueblo, Colo., then BN (ex-C&S)/Rio Grande joint track to Walsenburg, Colo. Ex-C&S and FW&D trackage heads from there toward Texas.

BN's other primary coal routes are of ex-NP and Milwaukee Road ancestry. The ex-NP line east of Billings has two branches which serve mines near

Huntley. The NP heads east through Glendive and into southern North Dakota (referred to as the "northern corridor") to Superior, Wis., and the Twin Cities. At Moorhead, Minn., some coal trains cut south to the Twin Cities via the ex-GN line through Breckenridge and Willmar, Minn. At Terry, Mont., the former Milwaukee Road transcontinental route heads from a junction with the ex-NP main into the Dakotas. This route was acquired by the State of South Dakota in 1982 and leased to BN.

Some of these lines were better than others in the 1970's, but as the decade progressed, huge sums were expended to upgrade them to handle the tremendous flow of coal and 15,000-ton trains. Since merger, BN and C&NW (which entered the Basin in 1984) have spent an incredible 2.5 billion dollars to build new track, upgrade and signal the old, and purchase new locomotives and cars. Between 1973 and 1977 alone, BN invested $201 million just in coal-related improvements.

By 1972 the railroad had correctly figured that coal business would go nowhere but up and began setting aside the funds to handle it. Construction started on a modest scale that year when BN supervised the building of a spur from Donkey Creek, near Gillette, Wyo., south to the Belle Ayr Mine, 14.8 miles; Amax Minerals, which owned the mine, paid for the spur. In 1973, a 14-mile spur was built from Campbell, just west of Donkey Creek, to Eagle Butte, where up to six mines would be located. Near Sheridan, Wyo., a 22.6-mile spur was constructed north from Dutch to serve mines at Decker, Mont.

The "Achilles heel" of BN's coal lines was Crawford Hill in far northwest Nebraska, west of Alliance. The hill, which was more of a mountain, required trains heading east from Belle Ayr or other mines to take on helpers at Crawford, Neb., where the assault of Pine Ridge began. The railroad negotiated grades of up to 1.55 percent, 10-degree curves at Horseshoe and Breezy Point and Nebraska's only railroad tunnel. To solve the problems, BN first rebuilt the line over the hill in stages, in 1976-82. The tunnel was bypassed, double-track and CTC (Centralized Traffic Control) were installed and a huge track-relocation project was instituted to reduce maximum curvature to 8 percent. Helpers remain, but getting over the hill isn't as difficult as it once was.

The second step was more daring—and expensive: build a new railroad to bypass Crawford and reach southern points in the coal basin more quickly. A new line south could cut as much as 155 miles

Text continued on page 72

LEFT: BN's rainbow era netted a pot of coal, not gold, in the form of the Powder River Basin. By the end of the company's first decade, low-sulphur coal traffic had become a gold mine for the railroad. Amid a blast of exhaust, coal Extra 7101 East exits the east portal of the only railroad tunnel in Nebraska, on Aug. 30, 1979. The 750-foot bore through Pine Ridge was constructed in 1889 at the top of Crawford Hill near Belmont, Nebr., one of the highest points in Nebraska, at an elevation of 4,496 feet; Crawford is 3,678 feet above sea level. It was abandoned following the Crawford Hill rebuilding project.— STEVE PATTERSON

ABOVE: BN retained a number of passenger cars for use on company business trains and excursions. Business trains operated systemwide, giving officers and officials the opportunity to look over the property—and giving observers the rare chance to see an all-BN-painted consist. Rebuilt F-units powered many of the specials, but another kind of F-unit also occasionally got the call: the F45, a "cowled" version of EMD's standard SD45. Fourteen were built for GN in 1969, with BN receiving 12 in 1970 (ordered by GN) and 20 in 1971. Two of the 3,600-h.p. units are about to duck under U.S. Highway 10 at Lincoln, Minn., with a financial analysts' special returning to Northtown from a Western inspection tour on Oct. 8, 1978.—STEVE GLISCHINSKI ABOVE RIGHT: Still wearing his CB&Q attire—including Burlington Route lapel pins— the conductor of the last westbound *Black Hawk/Mainstreeter/Western Star* prepares to highball from Aurora on a stormy April 12, 1970. The loss of this overnight denizen of the Chicago-Twin Cities route left the *Mainstreeter* and *Western Star* without Chicago connections, which further eroded those services.—MIKE SCHAFER

*T*oday, the mention of "Burlington Northern" prompts visions of fast intermodal trains behind GP50's, leviathan SD60's heading long strings of coal-laden hoppers, and mixed-bag merchandise runs in the charge of stout SD40-2's. Few associate BN with being a passenger carrier. Yet, for 14 months, Burlington Northern operated its own network of intercity passenger trains, from "M-Day," March 2, 1970, to Amtrak Day on May 1, 1971. Locomotives and rolling stock sported BN livery, public timetables were published, and the railroad even had its own passenger department.

By the time of the merger, the predecessor roads were facing a dilemma. All four roads had a long tradition of providing superior passenger service, based on a belief that it was a good public relations tool, if not a money-making proposition—which it wasn't. But by 1970, the deficits incurred by CB&Q, GN, NP and SP&S could no longer be offset by positive public relations. In 1969 the passenger services of BN's predecessors lost a staggering $38,320,000, calculated on a solely cost-related basis; during BN's first year, 1970, the figure was over $40 million. Further, even though BN passenger equipment was some of the best in the U.S., it would soon need replacement, a cost which the new railroad could ill afford to spend on a losing service that at the time appeared to have no future. The most effective way to deal with the losses was to eliminate trains.

By 1970, predecessors GN, NP and CB&Q had already pared much of their operations to a "core" system. NP was down to three trains, the North Coast Limited, Mainstreeter and one Seattle-Portland train. Pro-passenger GN's network was somewhat more extensive with the Empire Builder and secondary Western Star; a pair of trains between St. Paul and Superior, Wis.; a single International between Seattle and Vancouver, B.C.; one train as part of the Seattle-Portland "pool;" a Havre-Great Falls (Mont.) Rail Diesel Car; and the Grand Forks (N.D.)-Winnipeg Winnipeg Limited remnant.

SP&S's service at the time of the merger was pretty much the status quo of what had always been: Two trains each way between Portland and Spokane to handle through cars for the Western Star, Mainstreeter, North Coast Limited and Empire Builder. Probably the most unique service to survive the merger was the mixed train between Wishram, Wash., and Bend, Ore.

The last public system timetable issued by the CB&Q on Jan. 18, 1970, was simple, printed on a single long sheet, but it still contained schedules for a number of trains. Queen of the fleet was the Chicago-Oakland California Zephyr, jointly operated with Rio Grande and Western Pacific. The other Burlington flagship was the Denver Zephyr between the Windy City and Denver. Chicago-Twin Cities service included the Empire Builder, North Coast Limited, Morning Zephyr, Afternoon Zephyr, Black Hawk, Western Star and Mainstreeter. These trains were combined in various ways such that there were actually only three trains in each direction daily except Fridays and Sundays, when there were four.

The Q still offered a variety of local passenger services right up to M-Day, although most by then were coach-only accommodations: the Ak-Sar-Ben (formerly the Ak-Sar-Ben Zephyr) between Chicago and Lincoln; the American Royal (also once a Zephyr) between Chicago and Kansas City; unnamed trains 11 and 12 (remnants of the Nebraska Zephyr) between Chicago and Omaha; the "Quincy Local" between Chicago and West Quincy, Mo.; and one Kansas City-Omaha local.

On March 2, 1970, all these trains came under one operator, Burlington Northern. During the short period BN operated intercity passenger service, the

railroad tended to keep the original railroads' cars and locomotives on the their respective routes. The exception were ex-Burlington E8 and E9 units, which began running through to Havre on the Western Star and, for a time, on the Empire Builder.

BN issued its first system timetable effective April 26, 1970, and changes came soon after. The new railroad inherited several petitions to discontinue passenger trains, with the first to face the axe

The sad state of the passenger train just prior to Amtrak is graphically illustrated in this scene of an emaciated BN *Empire Builder/Morning Zephyr*, waiting for westbound freight 97 at Stratford, Ill., in March 1971: Three coaches, a diner, sleeper and lounge-observation (substituting for the Great Dome lounge) were all that was necessary for the modest passenger loads on this day.—MIKE SCHAFER

being one of the most famous, the California Zephyr. Early in 1970, the Interstate Commerce Commission finally agreed to let financially frail WP out of the operation, and the last true CZs departed Chicago and Oakland on March 21, 1970—only 19 days after the BN merger. The CZ was replaced with a BN-Rio Grande pseudo CZ service coordinated with Southern Pacific's City of San Francisco. The operation was deluxe, however, offering dining, sleeping and dome cars, including the CZ's trademark Vista-Dome sleeper-observation-lounge.

The next train to leave the timetables was the overnight Chicago-Twin Cities Black Hawk, which made its last trip on April 12, 1970. In August

1970, the Ak-Sar-Ben made its last trip, and the following month BN pulled one of the two sets of Gopher/Badger trains off the St. Paul-Superior run. Clearly, if some action wasn't taken to relieve the railroad of its huge passenger deficits, it would only be a matter of time before the revered North Coast Limited and Empire Builder faced termination.

A solution came from Washington, D.C., late in 1970 when President Nixon signed into law the Railroad Passenger Service Act of 1970, creating Amtrak. BN became a part of the new system and was relieved of its passenger service (and losses). To obtain this relief, BN paid Amtrak $33.4 million, for which it received stock in the new corporation. Interestingly, BN Chairman Louis W. Menk was elected to serve on Amtrak's Board of Directors.

When Amtrak took over most U.S. passenger service on May 1, 1971, most of BN's service was eliminated, save for the Empire Builder west of Minneapolis, the Denver/California Zephyr; two trains on the Seattle-Portland route and the Seattle-Portland segment of a Seattle-San Diego train. In a strange twist, BN became obligated by the State of Illinois to operate the Quincy Local until May 10, 1971, thanks to a court order obtained by Quincy College.

After Amtrak, BN abandoned coach yards and depots, retired it's ex-GN and CB&Q E7 fleet, sold what remaining equipment it could to Amtrak . . . and closed the final chapters of the very colorful passenger histories of Q, GN, NP and SP&S. BN continues to operate several passenger trains under contract with NRPC, including the Empire Builder (west of the Twin Cities), California Zephyr (Chicago-Denver) and Illinois Zephyr (the Quincy Local reincarnated). Between Seattle and Portland, BN handles the Mount Rainier, Coast Starlight and the Pioneer. In addition, BN retained a selection of rolling stock for special-train service and on occasion has hosted passenger excursions—steam included—for various groups. Further, BN continues to operate, under contract for Chicago's Metra, one of the nation's finest suburban train routes—Chicago-Aurora. So for BN, the passenger train remains a reality that reflects a proud past.

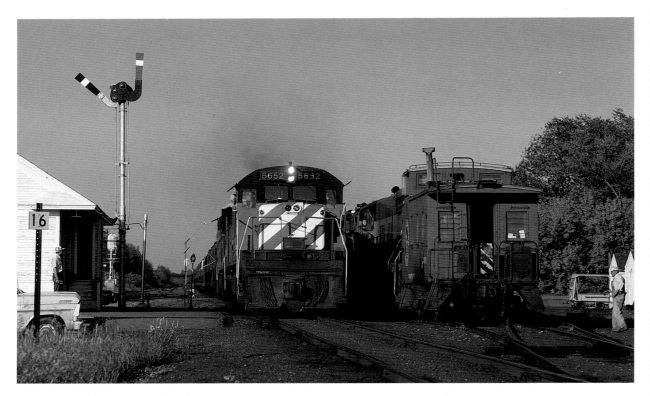

ABOVE: On July 4, 1977, all-rail ore train NT400 with U28C 5652 (ex-Q 564) picks up orders at the GN/DM&IR depot in Calumet, Minn. NT400 traveled from the National Steel Mine near Keewatin, Minn., to Granite City, Ill. The SD9's in the siding are the switch run out of Kelly Lake, which serviced a natural ore mine at Canisteo, Minn.—ROBERT C. ANDERSON

off the distance some unit trains traveled and tap several new mines then already in the development stage. The railroad gave the go-ahead to the new "Orin Line" in late 1972 and made formal application with the ICC for construction. It would extend south 116 miles from the original Belle Ayr mine spur to a point near Orin, Wyo., on the Wendover-Billings line. As BN prepared to build the new line and rebuild Crawford Hill, the coal boom continued.

In 1973 the ICC received another application to build into the Basin from competitor Chicago & North Western. Rather than construct parallel lines, the Commission directed BN and C&NW to build a joint line. The two carriers worked out a joint ownership arrangement, and the ICC approved the start of construction (which BN would supervise) in 1976. That year, six miles of track were built from Belle Ayr to Cordero Mine, followed by another 23 miles in 1977. At that point there came a two-year hiatus caused by environmental concerns, after which construction proceeded. A last-spike ceremony was held

on Nov. 6, 1979. The ceremonial first train, powered by five SD40-2's lead by the 7159, originated at the Kerr-McGee Jacobs Ranch Mine at Reno Junction, Wyo., and was destined for the Public Service Company of Oklahoma. BN paid $113 million for the new line, which includes 26 bridges.

Meanwhile, C&NW was having its troubles. Originally, the railroad wanted to rebuild its own Casper line from Fremont, Neb., to a connection with the new joint BN-C&NW line at Orin, some 640 miles. The track was in terrible condition, and financing was difficult to come by. Delays followed, with BN pushing C&NW to pay for its share of the new line or give up its interest. North Western came up with an alternative: It would become a partner with Union Pacific in the movement of coal from the Basin.

The new plan called for C&NW to build a 56-mile line from Joyce (South Morrill), Neb., on UP's North Platte (Neb.)-South Torrington (Wyo.) grain branch north to a connection on C&NW's Fremont-Casper route. About 45 miles of the old C&NW route would

be totally rebuilt, from Crandall to Shawnee, Wyo. Another six miles of new line would also be constructed from Shawnee to Shawnee Junction on the new BN line, ten miles north of Orin. UP would provide $60 million in financing for the venture. C&NW crews would handle trains from Basin mines to South Morrill, where UP crews would take trains east to the C&NW at Fremont, as well as points on the Union Pacific system.

BN was less than enthusiastic about UP's incursion into coal country, but a series of ICC rulings favored allowing the competitors into the Basin. C&NW paid BN $76 million for its half of the Orin Line in 1983, then built its new connection to the Union Pacific in only 14 months, opening officially on Aug. 16, 1984. Under ICC pressure, BN in 1986 granted half ownership in the line to C&NW all the way to East Caballo Junction (15 miles south of Donkey Creek), giving the North Western access to all the mines on the Orin Line.

To tote all the coal tonnage, BN in the 1970's invested heavily in the aforementioned SD40-2's. But EMD wasn't alone in supplying power: General Electric built 39 U33C's, 184 3,000-h.p. U30C's (including four C&S units built in 1968) and 242 3,000-h.p. C30-7's that were added to the roster between 1971 and 1981 (25 more U33C's came from predecessor roads). The U33C's have since been retired, as have most of the U30C's, replaced by SD60's or SD60M's. To service the coal power and unit trains, construction began in 1977 of a $47 million, state-of-the-art diesel and car shop in Alliance. The 110-acre Alliance complex officially opened in September 1979. Originally, over 600 units were assigned to the shop for maintenance. To keep track of locomotives and rolling stock, BN installed a computerized traffic control system, named COMPASS (Complete Operating Movement Processing and Service System), which locates any locomotive or car at any time.

COAL WASN'T THE ONLY COMMODITY BN transported in its first decade. Farm and forest products continued to be important, accounting for 44 per cent of revenues in 1977. To handle wheat and grain traffic, 3,100 new covered hoppers were purchased by 1977.

In 1977, BN completed a $67.4 million taconite-handling facility at the Allouez ore dock near Superior, Wis., to accommodate burgeoning taconite business. Great Northern had first moved unit trains of taconite in 1967, and business continued to grow into the 1970's. Expansions of the National Steel Company taconite plant near Keewatin, Minn., and the opening of the Hibbing (Minn.) Taconite Plant in 1976 resulted in even heavier tonnages of ore passing through the Allouez docks.

During the Great Lakes shipping season, loaded taconite trains head to a receiving station at Allouez where they are automatically dumped into an underground hopper, two loads at a time, 40 cars per hour. After unloading, the pellets* move over a two-mile conveyor belt to the docks where they are loaded onto boats via 18 shuttle conveyors. The docks can accommodate 1,000-foot vessels. The big boats can be loaded with 52,000 long tons of taconite in four to five hours. With the installation of the conveyor system, BN eliminated the traditional sorting method of locomotives switching ore cars atop the docks. In 1991, BN shipped over 11 million gross tons of pellets from Allouez in 277 vessel cargoes.

Superior also became the site of yet another coal-related project. Detroit Edison Company built a $25 million coal-transloading facility on the south shore of St. Louis Bay, opened in 1976. Coal trains pass through the complex on a large loop track. This facility received nearly 12 million tons of coal from BN trains in 1991. Most of the coal goes to Detroit Edison power plants in Michigan.

IT MAKES FOR INTERESTING SPECULATION to look back on BN's first two decades and observe the condition of the railroads most effected by the merger. Concerned about its deteriorating financial and competitive position, Milwaukee Road in 1973 petitioned the ICC for inclusion in BN. Five years later, the Commission denied the petition, reaffirming that it wanted a competitor in BN territory. Milwaukee appealed, but abandoned the case in 1980, instead requesting access to the Powder River Basin, which it never received. On Dec. 19, 1977, the Milwaukee Road declared bankruptcy, and in 1980 it abandoned its Pacific Coast extension. In 1985, its mileage much reduced, the Milwaukee Road disappeared when it was sold to the Soo Line.

Chicago & North Western, the nation's eighth-largest railroad, still competes with BN, but its Midwest mileage is much reduced. As of the early 1990's, the company was loaded with debt, thanks to a leveraged buyout in 1989 led by Blackstone Capital Partners. Financially, C&NW relies heavily on revenues generated by transporting coal from the

*Taconite is a type of hard rock containing fine particles of iron ore. It is not useful as it comes from the mine, but the fine iron particles in it can be removed after crushing, concentrating and pelletizing. The resulting berry-size pellets are easier to transport than regular iron ore, which in winter tends to freeze in clumps making car unloading difficult at best.

Powder River Basin and serving as a direct feed for UP to Chicago from Fremont, Neb. Another BN competitor, Rock Island, was liquidated in 1980.

It's important to remember the environment BN faced as it was beginning operations. Passenger

Old unit, new look. NW5 990 (ex-GN 190) gets a bath at the new Northtown Yard facilities near Minneapolis in August 1978.—STEVE GLISCHINSKI

trains were on the wane, and thus the public's perception was that the railroad industry as a whole was dying as well. Fueling the fire was the fact that, just three months after the BN merger, on June 21, 1970, Penn Central Railroad declared bankruptcy—at that time the largest U.S. company ever to do so. To its credit, BN mounted an effort to fight the negatives and establish a stronger public identity via television and newspaper ads. One of the biggest successes was the 1973 film "Portrait of A Railroad," which won awards for excellence and was seen by

more than 500,000 people at Expo '74 in Spokane.

Opportunities for expansion were available in the 1970's, and BN took advantage of them, although not all were successful. In October 1974, the railroad made a $3.4 million offer to purchase the 256-mile Green Bay & Western, which interchanged 64 percent of its traffic with BN at East Winona, Wis. BN was anxious to access profitable paper mills served by the "Green Bay Route."

Nonetheless, three railroads with substantial Wisconsin trackage were concerned about BN's proposed penetration into the state's interior. C&NW, Milwaukee Road and Soo Line made a counter offer in 1975 to buy GB&W for $4 million. The Department of Justice opposed the counter proposal. Nonetheless, BN eventually decided to redirect its energies and stopped courting GB&W in late 1977.

BN had better luck acquiring another, far more-strategic railroad. On Feb. 1, 1977, Burlington Northern announced it was conducting a joint study with the 4,674-mile St. Louis-San Francisco (Frisco) Railway on the feasibility of merger. The new combination made sense: BN would get direct routes from Kansas City and St. Louis to Texas; eliminate duplication in those two cities; and tap growing Southeast markets. The Frisco addition would enlarge BN to over 29,000 miles (not including subsidiaries FW&D and C&S), making it close to becoming the nation's first coast-to-coast railroad, stretching from Pensacola, Fla., to Puget Sound.

The chief executives of the two companies signed an agreement of merger and plan of reorganization on Nov. 15, 1977, and filed a formal application with the ICC on Dec. 28. The companies stated that a merger would result in annual savings of $32.8 million within three years of unification. Opposition from other railroads, plus court actions and ICC deliberations, would cause the case to be dragged out into 1980.

Burlington Northern's first decade was strong and vibrant, but it ended on a note of sadness. John Budd—former GN president, one of the architects of the BN merger, and BN's first chairman and CEO—died in St. Paul on Oct. 25, 1979.

BN's first decade as an operating company was nearly over. Four railroads had successfully been blended into one, and a fifth major railroad was about to join the huge system. The next decade would see many changes in the corporation itself, as well as the regulatory environment. By the time it was 20 years old, BN would bear little resemblance to the predecessor roads that came together in 1970.

CHAPTER 6

ENTER THE FRISCO

GATEWAY TO THE OZARKS AND THE SOUTHEAST

The St. Louis-San Francisco Railway that was absorbed into BN in 1980 dates from 1849, when the Missouri Legislature authorized incorporation of the Pacific Railroad. Construction began at St. Louis in 1851 using 66-inch-gauge track. The line ran into funding difficulties, and, in an attempt to garner financing from the legislature, the South-West branch of the Pacific Railroad was incorporated. Construction began from the main line of the PR at Franklin (today Pacific), Mo., on July 19, 1853, heading southwest toward Rolla. This branch, rather than the main line, would be Frisco's ancestor.

Rolla was reached by 1860. At the end of the Civil War, the State of Missouri took over the South-West Branch and sold it to General John C. Fremont, who reorganized it as the Southwest Pacific Railroad, but Fremont defaulted on his installment payments. In 1868 the railroad was again reorganized, this time as the South Pacific Railroad. This line managed to extend the railroad west through Springfield to Pierce City, Mo., by 1870. That year the South Pacific was conveyed to the Atlantic & Pacific Railroad.

The A&P was chartered in 1866 to build from Springfield, Mo., to the Pacific. A&P narrowed the line to standard gauge in 1870-71 and built 73 miles of track from Pierce City into Vinita, in Oklahoma Indian territory. A&P leased the old PR in 1872 and

operated it until 1876, but entered receivership in 1875. Both systems were sold at auction the following year. The A&P within Missouri became the St. Louis & San Francisco Railway, incorporated Sept. 7, 1876, while the line to Oklahoma retained the A&P name. The PR went on to become the Missouri Pacific, which merged into Union Pacific in 1982.

Several SL&SF line extensions into Kansas, Oklahoma and Arkansas followed, and in 1883 a new line east from Franklin to St. Louis was opened. This gave the railroad direct access to St. Louis over its own route; it previously had to use PR/MP trackage.

In the meantime various lines such as MP, Santa Fe and Southern Pacific fought to keep the railroad from building farther westward to the Pacific, which they viewed as their territory. In 1879 Frisco/A&P and Santa Fe signed an agreement wherein the two railroads would jointly build and own an A&P line to the coast. By 1883, A&P was complete through Arizona to an SP connection at Needles, Calif. Santa Fe ended up obtaining total control of SL&SF in 1890, but the relationship was short-lived. In 1893, the same panic that caused the bankruptcy of Northern Pacific claimed Frisco and Santa Fe; both entered receivership. When Frisco emerged in June 1896, it was independent of the Santa Fe, having been reorganized as the St. Louis & San Francisco Railroad

Company. Santa Fe retained A&P lines to the West, and Frisco was denied ever reaching California.

In 1898, line extensions reached Oklahoma City, and in 1901 the Frisco crept again into Texas, eventually reaching Fort Worth and Dallas by trackage rights. One of the biggest extensions of the Frisco empire occured when the Kansas City, Fort Scott & Memphis Railway Company was leased in 1901. This was actually a company organized by SL&SF to acquire the Kansas City, Fort Scott & Memphis Railroad which had lines that stretched from Kansas City to West Memphis, Ark., and from Memphis, Tenn., to Birmingham, Ala. The two segments were joined at Memphis by a car ferry across the Mississippi River, until it was replaced by a bridge in 1892. These newly acquired lines crossed the Oklahoma-Texas route at Springfield, Mo.

The Reid-Moore Syndicate, a group of speculators who acquired a number of railroads early in the 20th Century, gained control of the Rock Island in 1902 and SL&SF in 1903. While under Reid-Moore control, Frisco purchased the Chicago & Eastern Illinois, gaining access to Chicago, and also reached the Gulf Coast cities of Houston, Brownsville and New Orleans by control of the Gulf Coast Lines. Benjamin F. Yoakum had become SL&SF's general manager in 1896 (later becoming president), and in 1909

ABOVE: It's Frisco's final autumn as hot merchandise train No. 33 flies across the Little Piney Creek trestle near Jerome, Mo., on Oct. 20, 1980. The four GP40-2's will need all 12,000 horsepower they can generate to conquer the 1.6 percent grade of Dixon Hill on their race from St. Louis to Springfield and beyond. Frisco acquired a fleet of 25 GP40-2's in 1979, its last full year as an independent company.—JERRY PYFER FACING PAGE: Frisco's "coonskin" emblem adorned the front of steam locomotives, diesels and seemingly just about everything else SLSF owned. This sign was mounted on top of the Yale Yard freight house facing Airways Road in Memphis, Tenn.—MIKE BLASZAK

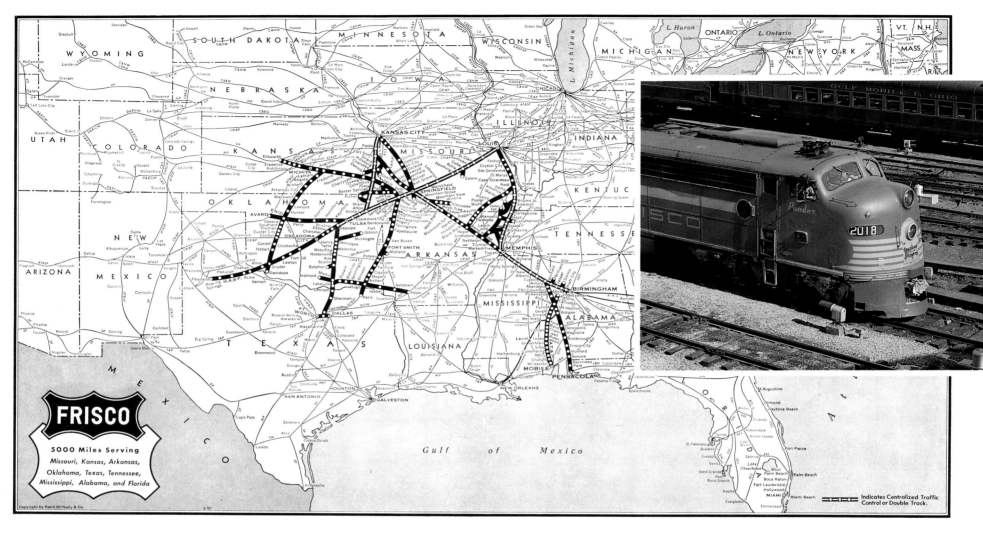

FRISCO

5000 Miles Serving

Missouri, Kansas, Arkansas,
Oklahoma, Texas, Tennessee,
Mississippi, Alabama, and Florida

Copyright by Rand McNally & Co.

Indicates Centralized Traffic
Control or Double Track.

he managed to get the Frisco free of Reid-Moore. The railroad once again fell into bankruptcy in 1913 and was sold, emerging as the St. Louis-San Francisco Railway Company on June 19, 1916—without the C&EI and GCL. There followed a period of physical improvements, such as the installation of automatic semaphore signaling over 900 miles of track.

The passenger train that for decades would be the pride of the Frisco—the *Meteor*—was inaugurated between St. Louis and Tulsa in 1902. It was extended to Texas to compete with Katy's *Texas Special*, inaugurated in December 1915 between St. Louis and San Antonio. During World War I, when U.S. railroads were under government control, the United States Railway Administration (USRA) ordered the

re-routing of the *Texas Special* onto the more-direct Frisco line between St. Louis and Vinita, which saved 78 miles over the all-Katy routing.

In July 1925, SLSF reached the Gulf Coast by purchasing the Muscle Shoals, Birmingham & Pensacola Railroad, which operated 142 miles of track from Kimbrough, Ala., to Pensacola, Fla. Frisco tied these lines to its system by building a 152-mile connection from Aberdeen, Miss., to Kimbrough which opened on June 27, 1928. Frisco reached a traffic agreement with the Alabama, Tennessee & Northern that same year which gave it access to another port, at Mobile, Ala. Acquisition of AT&N operations came Dec. 28, 1948, but the company was not abolished as a separate corporation until 1971.

The Great Depression and a drought in the Southeast helped push Frisco into bankruptcy once again on May 16, 1933. Despite bankruptcy, improvements to Frisco's physical plant continued. For example, in 1945 Frisco made a line change on Dixon Hill, the westbound ruling grade between St. Louis and Springfield, reducing the grade from 2.3 to 1.6 percent. Frisco's last bankruptcy finally ended on Jan. 1, 1947, after 14 years.

On Dec. 10, 1939, Frisco had stepped into the "streamline" era of passenger service with the introduction of the *Firefly* between Kansas City, Tulsa and Oklahoma City. The train consisted of three heavyweight cars painted blue and silver and rebuilt to look streamlined. The mini-streamliner was pulled

FACING PAGE: The system map from a 1964 passenger timetable shows Frisco in somewhat larger-than-life proportions (a hallmark of maps found in the OFFICIAL GUIDE OF THE RAILWAYS). Nonetheless, SLSF was a critical addition to Burlington Northern, providing a direct route into the booming Southeastern U.S. This addition brought BN nearer to true transcon status than any other U.S. road. INSET: At the suggestion of President Clark Hungerford, all of Frisco's E-units were named for famous horses, giving the units an extra touch of nobility. E8 No. 2018, *Ponder*, suns itself beside Gulf, Mobile & Ohio's *Abraham Lincoln* at St. Louis in 1965. Other names in the corral included *Flying Ebony* (2012); timetable star *Winchester* (2005); *Twenty Grand* (2015); *Pensive* (2017) and—appropriately—*Big Red* (2020).—JIM BOYD

ABOVE: The mostly head-end consist of this morning arrival at St. Louis belies its true identity as Frisco's flagship passenger train, the *Meteor*. When inaugurated in 1902, the *Meteor* linked St. Louis and Tulsa, but eventually its realm was expanded with an extension beyond Tulsa to Oklahoma City and Lawton, Okla., and the addition of sections to Fort Smith, Ark., and Wichita, Kan. Like many railroads, Frisco was caught up in post-World War II euphoria and, expecting a postwar boom in travel, ordered lightweight equipment from Pullman-Standard to streamline the *Meteor*, which occurred on May 14, 1948. Alas, this scene reveals that postwar streamlining could not prevent the inevitable: Three streamlined cars— a coach, sleeper and diner—were more than sufficient to handle the scant passenger loads on this summer day in 1965; in a few weeks, the *Meteor* would be history.—JIM BOYD LEFT: In the days before bridge graffiti was widespread, a northbound freight off the Memphis line eases over a highway span soon to be doomed by an impending Interstate 44. In moments, the train will enter the St. Louis-Springfield main and terminate at Lindenwood Yard, St. Louis. It's 1965 and the black-and-yellow freight scheme still is in vogue—as is Alco power, as the trailing unit attests, but neither will last much longer.—JIM BOYD

In January 1975, Extra 429 East (compass north) has 45 cars in tow near Viburnum, Mo., on the "lead" branch in central Missouri. Many of the cars are filled with lead concentrate, returning to the mainline connection at Cuba from the lead mines near Buick, Mo. In the mid-70's the 43-mile "lead branch" was worked daily except Sunday with a turn originating at Lindenwood Yard near St. Louis. Note the concrete ties; when the branch was extended 32.7 miles from Keysville to Buick in 1967, Frisco installed concrete, rather than wood ties—a harbinger of BN practices to come. At Lead Junction, 13 miles south of Cuba, another branch led south 26 miles to Salem, Mo. That segment was abandoned in 1984, leaving only the newer line to Buick in place.—MARK NELSON

by shrouded, streamlined 4-6-2's, and was intended to compete with Santa Fe trains operating between the same cities. The train was cut back to Tulsa in 1949 and eliminated in the 1950's.

In October 1945, bankruptcy trustee Frank A. Thompson authorized the expenditure of $4.5 million to purchase new streamlined passenger cars in preparation for an expected postwar passenger boom. The order, placed with Pullman-Standard, would include 38 new cars—enough to re-equip the *Meteor* and cover Frisco's share of the *Texas Special* pool. The cars arrived in 1948, with the new streamlined *Meteor* making its debut between St. Louis and Oklahoma City two days before the streamlined *Texas Special*, on May 14, 1948. The *Texas Special* entered revenue service on May 16 operating between St. Louis and San Antonio.

Frisco offered other passenger services, of course. The joint Frisco-Southern *Kansas City-Florida Special* operated between Kansas City and Jacksonville, Fla., via Birmingham. Other memorable Frisco trains included the Kansas City-Birmingham *Sunnyland* (which later had a St. Louis-Memphis section), the Tulsa-Dallas *Black Gold*, and the *Will Rogers* between St. Louis and Oklahoma City.

IN THE STEAM ERA, Frisco was known for fine 4-8-2 and 4-8-4 locomotives, but the railroad was also an early proponent of the 4-6-2 "Pacific" wheel arrangement, and eventually owned 70 examples. Frisco's Pacific designs grew larger through the years, but by the 1920's and 1930's, growing traffic and heavier passenger cars required higher-capacity power like 4-6-4's and 4-8-2's. For freight service, Frisco acquired 60 2-10-2's between 1916 and 1918, and 33 2-8-2's of USRA design arrived in 1919.

Frisco also possessed some unusual steam power. In 1910, the company received seven Mallet 2-8-8-2's, built by American and intended for pusher service in areas with heavy grades. They were never popular, but did manage to stay on the roster into the 1930's. Another unusual locomotive were the 2-10-0 "Decapod" types. Twenty of these machines arrived after World War I.

With a need for bigger power, SLSF turned to Baldwin. In 1922, 15 4-8-2 "Mountain" types were ordered for passenger service, and 35 2-8-2's for freight operations. The 4-8-2's were well received, and more orders were placed for them: Five came in 1925, with ten more in 1926. In 1930, 20 more heavy 2-8-2's arrived to bolster freight service. With Frisco's 1933 bankruptcy and the Depression, there

SLSF 2001, *Ranger*, named for the horse of Revolutionary War hero General Henry "Light Horse Harry" Lee, may look like an E8, but it's actually a "horse" of a different color. The 2001 is an E7 that has been cosmetically altered to resemble an E8. The steed and its mate have just ushered the *Sunnyland* into Terminal Station, Birmingham, Ala., under skies appropriate to the train's name on April 20, 1964.—GEORGE BERISSO RIGHT: When Frisco acquired the Alabama, Tennessee & Northern in 1948, it inherited a GE 45-ton switcher and 11 Alco RS1's. The 300-h.p. GE was assigned to the carfloat operation on Blakely Island in Mobile, Ala., and worked there for 38 years, a record assignment for SLSF. Nicknamed "The Crab," it was retired in 1979 and replaced by an ex-BN SW1.—JIM BOYD

was little money to spare for new engines, so the railroad chose to rebuild what it had. Eleven 2-10-2's entered Springfield shops in 1936-37, emerging as 4-8-2's. Twenty-three more 2-10-2's were converted to 4-8-2's by 1942.

Freight traffic rebounded with the onset of World War II, and although Frisco was still in bankruptcy, 15 new 4-8-4's arrived from Baldwin in 1942. Like the 4-8-2's, these were handsome, powerful machines that helped Frisco live up to its reputation for fast freight service, but they also put in stints on passenger trains. Oil-burning 4-8-4's 4500-4502 were specially painted for *Meteor* service, with the train name on the tender and blue boiler jackets; the black freight engines had "FFF" on their tenders, for "Frisco Faster Freight." In 1943, ten more 4-8-4's arrived, the last new steam power purchased.

By Jan. 1, 1952, Frisco had only 26 steam loco-

motives left on the active roster, operating mostly out of Birmingham, Memphis and Amory, Miss. The final regular-service trip for a Frisco steam engine occurred when 2-8-2 4018 operated on a Birmingham-Bessemer, Ala., local freight, Feb. 29, 1952.

In the post-World War II years, Frisco entered a period of quiet prosperity under president Clark Hungerford, formerly of the Southern Railway. His regime included modernized passenger services and better track. In June, 1957, SLSF opened Tennessee Yard near Memphis—the first hump yard on the system. In 1959, the modernization and expansion of Cherokee Yard in Tulsa was completed; it included installation of a 40-track hump facility. In the early 1950's, Springfield yard was also modernized, and CTC began to be extended over much of the system.

Through much of its history, Frisco had a reputation for fast freight service. For example, in 1964 "hot" No. 138 was carded to make the 250-mile journey from Tennessee Yard in Memphis to Thomas Yard in Birmingham in just 5½ hours. The same year, the company expanded again with the acquisi-

tion of two connecting short lines. The 42-mile Northeast Oklahoma Railroad between Miami, Okla., and Carona, Kan., was purchased, as was the remaining trackage of the Okmulgee Northern Railway in Okmulgee, Okla.

The 1960's presented Frisco with the vexing question many railroads faced: what to do about its money-losing passenger services. The railroad had begun to cut back passenger service in the 1950's, ending its 42-year agreement with the Missouri-Kansas-Texas on Jan. 5, 1959, to jointly operate the *Texas Special*, due in part to Katy allowing its track and equipment to deteriorate.

Frisco's flagship, the *Meteor*, was not immune to reductions in service either. Tulsa and Ft. Smith sleepers were gone by 1965, as were food-service cars and the Lawton (Okla.) section. In 1965, SLSF threw in the towel by filing petitions with the ICC to discontinue all remaining passenger services, which were carrying only about 50 passengers on each train daily and losing close to $7 million per year.

The Commission allowed the company to elimi-

TOP: An F "B" unit is sandwiched by U30B 842 and two other GE's as crews exchange greetings at Oklahoma City before taking a train west on a baking summer afternoon in 1970.—F. L. Becht ABOVE: F's at the scrub rack in St. Louis, summer 1965.—Jim Boyd RIGHT: By the time this classic scene was recorded at Crystal City, Mo., on a sultry summer day in 1965, passenger service on the River Division was down to a single train, the St. Louis-Memphis *Sunnyland*. In less than three months, though, the little *Sunnyland* will wander no more.—Jim Boyd

Frisco's massive bridge across the Mississippi River at Memphis was 100 years old in 1992, the first rail bridge to span the river at Memphis. Viewed from the Arkansas side of the river, a westbound freight led by SD45's 930/917 and a GE heads downgrade from the river crossing to reach ground level on May 31, 1974.—DAVID M. JOHNSTON

nate eight of its twelve remaining trains, but required the road to operate a core service between Kansas City and Birmingham and between St. Louis and Oklahoma City. On Sept. 17, 1965, the *Meteor*, *Kansas City-Florida Special*, *Will Rogers* and *Sunnyland* began their last trips. The following day, the new St. Louis-Oklahoma City *Oklahoman* debuted, running on the day schedule of the old *Will Rogers*, while the new *Southland* held down Kansas City-Birmingham service.

Losses continued. In late 1966 the railroad again petitioned to end all passenger service. The *Oklahoman* made its last run May 14, 1967; the *Southland*'s termination on Dec. 8, 1967, made Frisco the largest freight-only railroad in the U.S. at the time.

St. Louis-San Francisco relied on agriculture for much of its business: By the time of BN acquisition talks, 24 percent of all its rail freight revenue came from transporting wheat, corn, cotton and processed

food. Even larger, however, were revenues from industrial traffic. As the 1960's and 1970's progressed, Northern industries began moving to the South, which usually had a more favorable tax and labor climate. Industrial traffic contributed to more of Frisco revenues. Auto/truck assembly plants, paper mills, lead and zinc mines and chemical plants were among the industries located along Frisco lines.

As a result, Frisco had become an especially attractive property for other railroads. CB&Q, Illinois Central and Gulf, Mobile & Ohio purchased Frisco stock in the 1960's, and Santa Fe and Southern both made overtures toward the carrier.

In 1973, Frisco had a brief brush with BN when subsidiary Fort Worth & Denver agreed to to buy 104 miles of Frisco subsidiary Quanah, Acme & Pacific. The "Quanah Route" operated between a Frisco/FW&D connection at Quanah, Texas, to a Santa Fe connection at Floydada, Texas. For many

years, QA&P served an important role as Frisco's western outlet to Santa Fe. FW&D wanted to buy the Quanah line to replace its Lubbock branch, which was blocked when a derailment in a tunnel (the last in Texas) caused it to collapse. The two parties cancelled the deal in 1974, and the FW&D branch was repaired. . . but QA&P became a BN property after the acquisition of the Frisco, and was fully integrated into BN on June 8, 1981.

Like CB&Q, Frisco was a leader in operating run-through and power-pool services with other roads. In the 1960's, among the longest were trains 37 and 437 run jointly with Santa Fe between Birmingham and Los Angeles. The two roads began a motive-power pooling arrangement on Jan. 10, 1962, that put Frisco power over Santa Fe and vice versa. By the late 1970's, Frisco was operating ten run-through trains daily, among them the QLA (Quanah-Los Angeles). QLA originated on the Seaboard Coast

Line at Hamlet, N.C. Frisco picked it up at Birmingham, and routed it quickly through Memphis, Springfield and Tulsa before handing it over to Santa Fe at Avard, Okla., which relayed it to L.A. Other pooling arrangements found Frisco power running through on UP (on trains such as the Memphis-North Platte *Northwest Forwarder*) and SCL (the *Florida Southeastern*, which went through to Miami).

In 1962, LOUIS W. MENK became Frisco's president, succeeding Clark Hungerford. At 44, Menk was among the youngest chief executives of any U.S. railroad. Under his administration, dispatching functions were consolidated at Springfield, making Frisco one of the first roads to combine this function at one location. Many of the road's offices were also relocated from St. Louis to Springfield.

It was during the Menk administration that Frisco altered its image. Concern over grade-crossing accidents led to a search for high-visibility colors for the diesel fleet. On Feb. 14, 1965, U25B 802 emerged from Springfield shops in mandarin orange and white colors, which became standard for the system.

Menk left the Frisco in September 1965 to head CB&Q and was succeeded by J. E. Gilliland. During Gilliland's term, Frisco made its last expansion. On Sept. 28, 1967, the company put into operation its new Missouri Mineral Belt line. The 32.7-mile branch was constructed from Keysville to Buick to furnish transportation for new lead mines then opening in the area.

Gilliland moved up to chairman and was succeeded by Richard Grayson, who had been employed by Frisco since 1941. Grayson was named president and chief executive officer in 1969, and added the title of chairman in 1973. He headed Frisco until the BN acquisition, then became BN's vice chairman and president of the Transportation Division.

The 1977 agreement Menk and Grayson signed to bring Frisco into BN's fold was a logical one. Historically, BN had been dependent on three commodities: coal, grain and forest products. While coal traffic grew steadily in the 1970's, other commodities were subject to downturns in demand and the economy. Frisco's industrial base and location in the booming Southeast would help BN develop a more-diverse traffic mix, and as an "end to end" merger, would also bring the big railroad into new territory. On Friday, Nov. 21, 1980, the St. Louis-San Francisco Railway disappeared into Burlington Northern.

FRISCO

ABOVE: Train 39 punches through Rolla, Mo., on June 14, 1975. Year-old GP38-2 444 leads the the 56-car train, which includes 34 loads of automobiles from Chrysler's Fenton plant near St. Louis.—MARK NELSON RIGHT: On the last full day of the Frisco, Nov. 20, 1980, a southbound en route from Cherokee Yard in Tulsa to Dallas/Fort Worth passes Tower 16 guarding the MP crossing at Sherman, Texas.—TOM POST FACING PAGE: One doesn't usually associate central Missouri with snow, but this Nov. 30, 1974, scene helps dispel that notion. Eastbound train 438, led by GP38AC 655, is descending Dixon Hill with 55 cars west of Arlington, Mo. The Gasconade River is visible in the valley.—MARK NELSON

CHAPTER 7

BN HEADS FOR THE 21ST CENTURY

CHANGE AND INNOVATION FOR A POST-FRISCO BN

The year 1980 was a watershed time for Burlington Northern. As the company celebrated its 10th year of operation, several changes took place which altered its face.

A new president arrived on June 1 in the person of Richard M. Bressler, then 49. Formerly executive vice president of energy giant Atlantic-Richfield, Bressler was the first BN leader hired from outside the company, rather than being promoted through the ranks. After taking office, Bressler made it clear that he wasn't satisfied with the return on investment the company was getting from the millions it had spent on its coal-hauling facilities. Increasing this return, and the productivity of the railroad in general, would be one of Bressler's top priorities.

In his first year at BN, Bressler addressed several changes. On Oct. 14, 1980, President Jimmy Carter signed into law the Staggers Rail Act of 1980. The long-awaited legislation deregulated the railroad industry, bearing on issues like abandonments, mergers, ratemaking and marketing. For example, the law allows a railroad to enter into a contract with a shipper, gearing price and service to the shipper's specific needs without reference to other shippers and carriers. Previously, railroads had to set rates jointly with other lines via rate bureaus.

The Staggers Act also put a time limit on abandonment applications. Within nine months, the ICC would have to rule on such applications; previously there had been no time limit. Shippers also could benefit from the new law. If another rail line could serve an industry by building a spur from a nearby line, they could do so, even if that line was already served by another carrier.

These may not seem like radical concepts, but for the railroad industry, which had been heavily regulated during most of its existence, this new freedom was like a breath of fresh air. Now lines like BN could be more selective about which shippers they would serve and how much they could charge them. The abandonment provisions proved useful when BN began a program of "downsizing" physical plant.

A little over one month after the Staggers Act became law, the acquisition of Frisco became reality, with SLSF being absorbed on Nov. 21, 1980. Frisco Chairman and President Richard C. Grayson became vice chairman and president of the Transportation Division, effective Jan. 1, 1981; Louis Menk remained chairman of BN, Inc., with Bressler as president. The new rail system was 31,420 miles long including subsidiaries Fort Worth & Denver and Colorado & Southern, making it the largest in the U.S. This included 17,697 miles of main lines and 13,623 miles of secondary mains and branch lines.

With the newly expanded system came a new transcontinental route. In late November 1980, new through Portland (Ore.)-Birmingham (Ala.) freights began service—the longest (3,076 miles) through freight operations over a single railroad in the U.S. Initially, these trains were symboled PBF (Portland-Birmingham Freight) and BPX (Birmingham-Portland Xpress); the symbols were later dropped in favor of Nos. 120 and 121. Their usual routing was Portland to Kansas City via Laurel, Mont., and Alliance, Neb., then over ex-Frisco rails to Birmingham.

As it had in 1970, BN faced the prospect of renumbering and repainting predecessor diesels. By March 1981, 430 Frisco units were restenciled with BN numbers, and all units were repainted in BN colors or retired by July 31, 1983.

The new company had an abundance of assets. To manage them, BN formed a holding company that had seven profit centers: the railroad, forest management, forest products manufacturing, energy, air-freight forwarding, trucking and real estate. The new management was particularly interested in further developing the non-rail assets, partly because at the time they were outperforming the railroad.

The holding company was incorporated in Delaware March 30, 1981, as Burlington Northern Holding Co., and on May 14, 1981, this company acquired Burlington Northern, Inc. At the same time, the *former* Burlington Northern, Inc. changed its name to Burlington Northern Railroad, with the holding company then adopting the BNI name. In August 1981, the offices of the holding company were moved to Seattle, to be closer to international and Pacific Rim markets.

Later in 1981, Louis Menk retired, with Bressler taking over the reins as chairman, president and

ABOVE: A change of face for Burlington Northern? In the decade following the 1980 BN acquisition of Frisco, the term change—as well as development, expansion, contraction, and innovation—was an understatement. This scene near Farrington, Wash., is illustrative of two of those points. The first involves motive power. A highly visible BN innovation was the "power by the hour" concept introduced in 1986 with the arrival of 100 EMD SD60's leased to Oakway, Inc. Painted in EMD blue and white, the SD60's are serviced by Electro Northern, a joint undertaking of EMD, BN and several shopcraft unions. These three colorful "Oakways" leading westbound train 101 descending Devils Canyon on May 17, 1987, don't belong to BN; rather, the railroad pays for the power the units generate on an hourly basis. The second point this scene depicts is the change in BN's route system, which expanded and contracted several times during the railroad's second decade. In this case, abandonment was eminent—the above photo was recorded during the last weeks of through-train operations on the Spokane-Pasco ex-SP&S line. This segment was laced with tunnels and huge trestles, and much of it was built through rocky areas that were unstable. The combination of rock slides, bridges and tunnels eventually proved to be too much of a maintenance headache for the railroad, and through operations ended on June 29, 1987.—BLAIR KOOISTRA FACING PAGE: A symbol of domestic containerization, another pioneering effort of BN.—STEVE GLISCHINSKI

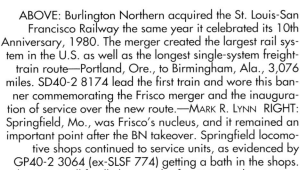

ABOVE: Burlington Northern acquired the St. Louis-San Francisco Railway the same year it celebrated its 10th Anniversary, 1980. The merger created the largest rail system in the U.S. as well as the longest single-system freight-train route—Portland, Ore., to Birmingham, Ala., 3,076 miles. SD40-2 8174 lead the first train and wore this banner commemorating the Frisco merger and the inauguration of service over the new route.—MARK R. LYNN RIGHT: Springfield, Mo., was Frisco's nucleus, and it remained an important point after the BN takeover. Springfield locomotive shops continued to service units, as evidenced by GP40-2 3064 (ex-SLSF 774) getting a bath in the shops. The 3064 will finally be awash of its Frisco colors in May 1983.—BOB SCHMIDT

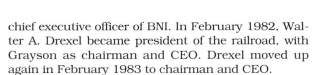

chief executive officer of BNI. In February 1982, Walter A. Drexel became president of the railroad, with Grayson as chairman and CEO. Drexel moved up again in February 1983 to chairman and CEO.

Darius Gaskins became president of the railroad in July 1985; Drexel went on to vice chair BNI in December 1985. Gaskins served as the railroad's president, chief executive and chief operating officer until Jan. 31, 1989. His term was marked by motive-power developments, line sales, innovation—and acrimonious relationships with labor unions. Other changes in top management of the railroad immediately after the Frisco merger put many former-SLSF managers in executive positions.

With corporate restructuring and the management changes that took place, something was lost. The new Burlington Northern Railroad was simply a subsidiary (the largest, in fact) of BNI. This was probably a logical business decision, but some of the "spirit" of the old railroad was gone: It just wasn't the same as when the primary business of the company

was railroading. This feeling was accentuated by some of the moves the new company made, reductions in the work force chief among them. The number of railroad employees shrunk from 57,300 in December 1980 to 49,800 by December 1981. By 1990 this was further reduced to less than 33,000. Although the "old" BN managers had been sensitive to properly integrate pre-merger properties and were concerned with the feelings of employees, new management was more "bottom-line" oriented—a common focus in corporate America in the 1980's, but one that did nothing to build employee morale.

There was little question some cuts were needed. Simply put, there were too many people handling too many jobs. For example, in Minneapolis, one of Northtown's switch jobs routinely came on duty at 3 p.m., but was "tied up" by 5:30 p.m.—yet the crew was paid for eight hours work, and there were two other jobs which handled the same work area within a 24-hour period. Cuts included closing locomotive and car shops (Livingston, Mont., and St. Cloud,

Minn., shut down in 1986) and excess yards and eliminating personnel that went with them. Other jobs were combined or centralized, such as dispatching. These and other changes moved the United Transportation Union in 1986 to accuse Gaskins of trying to abolish unions on the railroad.

Another action that drew the ire of labor took place the following year. In November 1987, the railroad granted (with ICC approval) its wholly owned subsidiary, the Winona Bridge Railway Company (WBRC), trackage rights over 1,860 miles of track from Winona Junction, Wis., to Seattle. At the time, WBRC owned but 1.7 miles of track, consisting of a bridge across the Mississippi River between Winona, Minn., and East Winona, Wis., but the company was not bound by any union contracts.

BN wanted to run two- and three-crewmember intermodal trains, with fewer crew-change stops, between St. Paul and Seattle. At the time, the railroad was already running reduced-crew intermodal trains (*Expediters*) in the Midwest and between Seattle and Portland, but on the GN/NP High Line route, the UTU had balked at implementing reduced crews. Winona Bridge would be a bargaining chip to gain concessions from the unions. BN maintained it would prefer to have its own personnel agree to new work rules rather than implement the WBRC plan, which would involve hiring separate crews. The unions stood fast and went to court, obtaining a court order in June 1988 enjoining BN from implementing the plan. Ultimately, BN softened and the Winona Bridge plan was quietly dropped. New crew-consist agreements reached in October 1991 allowed two-person crews on all trains along the southern two-thirds of the system, but the northern lines were not part of the agreement.

Although painful, some of the changes and the overall streamlining of BN in the 1980's helped the company survive competitive pressures and increase productivity. However, the manner in which changes were carried out often left bitter feelings between employees and employer. Happily though, by the end of the decade, new management was talking about a "kinder, gentler Burlington Northern."

MANY TRACKAGE CHANGES TOOK PLACE across BN's huge route system in the post-Frisco years. The company took advantage of the Staggers Act to shed miles of unprofitable branch lines at an accelerated pace. For example, in Washington state, BN abandoned only 141.39 miles of track during the 1970's versus 694.75 miles between 1980 and 1989, while another 325 miles were sold to regional Washington Central.

Nonetheless, there were expansions. In addition to Frisco trackage, the railroad picked up several former Milwaukee Road branch lines in Idaho, Washington and Montana when that road abandoned the West in 1980. BN also acquired Milwaukee's former main line over Snoqualmie Pass in Washington. Although intended to be an alternative to the Stampede Pass route, the Stevens Pass and Columbia River routes were deemed adequate and BN never ran a train over the line, abandoning it in 1987.

BN also briefly operated segments of the Rock Island in Colorado, Kansas and Illinois after that road ceased operations on March 23, 1980. Included were 34 miles of track from Peoria to Henry, Ill., and 202 miles of Rock's Chicago-Colorado Springs route from Phillipsburg, Kans., to Siebert, Colo. These operations were turned over to other roads in 1981.

BN's presence in South Dakota grew significantly during Milwaukee Road's retreat. South Dakota, faced with the loss of over 50 percent of its total

A fuel tender spliced by a pair of GP50's rides a Seattle-bound train at Diamond Bluff, Wis., in 1988. Fuel tenders were a notable, if short-lived, experiment on BN. The railroad converted company-service fuel-transport cars for high-speed operation, thereby eliminating fuel stops and enabling the huge carrier to purchase fuel where it was most cost effective—and bypassing areas where fuel was too expensive. The tenders could fuel diesels automatically as the train moved. Regular operation of fuel tenders began in April 1983, but by 1990 most had been relegated to helper districts.—STEVE GLISCHINSKI

operating rail mileage, developed a "core system" of lines designed to preserve rail service. The majority were purchased by the State and service restored in 1981 through an operating agreement with BN, including lines from Aberdeen through Mitchell to Sioux City, Iowa (265.5 miles), and from Sioux Falls to Chamberlain (168.5 miles).

In May 1981, Milwaukee Road filed to abandon its main line from Miles City, Mont., to Ortonville, Minn. This abandonment would have resulted in the closing of power plants at Big Stone City, S.D., and Ortonville. On Feb. 22, 1982, the South Dakota Railroad Authority purchased the line and approved a lease and operating agreement with BN to operate 479.9 miles of this line from Terry, Mont., (where it connects with the northern corridor coal main) to the Minnesota border. Operations began on April 29, 1982. BN now operates more miles of track in South Dakota than any other carrier.

On Dec. 31, 1981, C&S was officially merged into BN. At that time, subsidiary FW&D was extended from Texline, Texas, over the old C&S to Denver. The expanded FW&D was short-lived, as it was absorbed Dec. 31, 1982.

After a decade of expansion and contraction, BN mileage stood at 25,329 on Dec. 31, 1990, comprised of 15,946 miles of main lines, 6,418 miles of branch lines owned by the company, and 2,965 operated under trackage rights. The system originat-

ed 89 percent of all the tonnage it handled. The average haul for the railroad was 766 miles.

Changes also came to BN headquarters, which moved from its traditional home in St. Paul to Fort Worth. Hints of a move from St. Paul came as early as 1978 when BN began a study to determine the practicality of moving to escape the high costs of doing business in Minnesota, known for high corporate and personal income taxes. Chairman Menk, long a critic of the state's business climate, met several times with Minnesota's governor, but no action was taken by the State.

The Frisco acquisition and the formation of a holding company hastened the decision to leave Minnesota. The first move came with the departure of the holding company itself to Seattle in 1981. In 1983, BN moved its operating department to Kansas City. The company stated it wanted the department in a "more central location," but in reality some ex-Frisco executives felt little love for Minnesota's weather and tax situation and were determined to move their departments south.

Slowly and quietly, other departments were pulled out of Minnesota, and in 1983 BN sold the Frisco Building in St. Louis and began relocating those offices. In 1984, the marketing and coal departments moved to Fort Worth, leaving accounting and a few other functions in St. Paul. There was no question Texas offered advantages: no personal income tax,

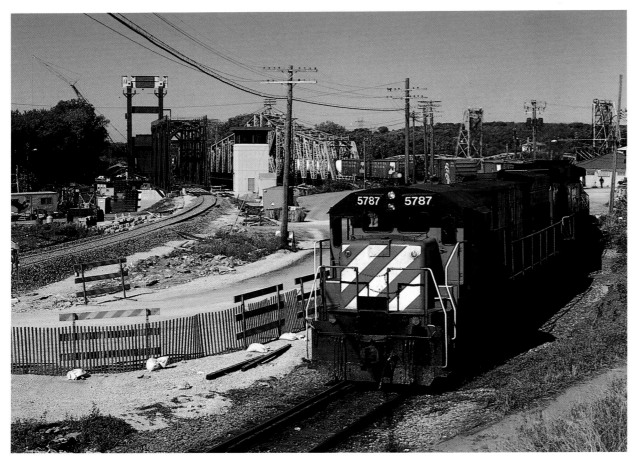

BN's locomotive experiments may have captured the limelight in the 1980's and 1990's, but more-routine improvements have resulted in overall physical-plant improvement. On Sept. 15, 1984, ex-Frisco U30B 5787 leads two uniquely BN units—SD40B 7600 and a cabless GE B30-7A—as they tip-toe off the St. Croix River bridge at Prescott, Wis., at the confluence of the St. Croix and Mississippi Rivers. To the left is a the new lift bridge under construction, which will replace the old CB&Q swing span bridge, permitting river traffic to move through the area and at the same time eliminating a 10 mph curve on the east approach to the river crossing.—STEVE GLISCHINSKI

low corporate taxes, a better business environment and, of course, better weather. By Jan. 1, 1985, the general offices of the company were officially listed as being in Fort Worth. For the first time, the "northern lines'" main offices were outside the Midwest.

Throughout the 1980's and into the 1990's, improvements in the physical plant continued. Although the huge coal-related projects were largely completed, other projects kept maintenance forces busy. In 1986, the company began installing concrete ties along heavily used lines, with the one millionth tie placed Sept. 29, 1988, near Reno, Wyo.

The use of welded rail and high-speed switches also increased dramatically. Many improvements were the result of efforts by Bill Glavin, BN's highly respected chief engineer.

MOTIVE-POWER INNOVATIONS were particularly dramatic in the post-Frisco years. In 1980, BN addressed high locomotive-fuel costs. Like motorists, BN felt the oil crises of the 1970's. In 1972, diesel fuel cost 9.88 cents a gallon; by the early 1980's, it was up to around $1 a gallon. Fuel cost was a huge issue: In 1990 BN used 593 million gallons of diesel fuel.

The company began conducting experiments on a variety of fronts, including studying a proposal to build a new generation of steam locomotives (the "ACE 3000," conceived by steam expert Ross Rowland, but never built), electrifying its coal lines, and developing a coal-burning diesel. Actual changes were less radical, but important nonetheless.

BN's first change in motive power was not related to fuel, but rather straight cost savings—a principal catalyst for BN to purchase cabless units. The first were from GE, an order of 53 3,000-h.p. B30-7A's that came in 1982; 67 more were delivered in 1983. The elimination of cabs saved BN $50,000 per unit.

Another unusual experiment was the fuel tender. Originally suggested by Soo Line employee Bud Bulgrin in a *Trains* Magazine editorial in 1972, the concept was first embraced by Amtrak, which converted E-units to carry fuel. The concept was simple: carry extra fuel to eliminate time-consuming refueling stops. Initially, fuel tenders were assigned to high-priority intermodal and merchandise trains between Chicago and Seattle, with five fuel stops eliminated.

Over 400 locomotives were modified to run with tenders, which eventually numbered 78. However, tenders limited access to other locomotives in consists, and the high-speed service began to cause structural problems for the cars. Fuel costs also declined, which combined with the other difficulties resulted in the elimination of tenders from regular mainline operation.

GP50 3156 featured an innovation less visible (and more successful) than the fuel tender: It was the first of 102 locomotives to be equipped with Rockwell International's Locomotive Analysis and Reporting System (LARS), which monitors 33 parameters of locomotive condition. Every 15 minutes this "snapshot" of information is sent from a LARS-equipped locomotive via digital data link to specified locomotive distribution, maintenance and service facilities, where it is accessed through desktop computers. LARS is part of Rockwell's ARES (Advanced Railroad Electronics System), which uses locomotive-mounted transponders that are tracked by 18 satellites orbiting 11,000 miles above the earth. ARES can fix a train's location within 150 feet and track its speed to within 1 mph—information that can be relayed reliably by satellite to the dispatcher in any weather condition. ARES could someday eliminate conventional train-control systems. ARES was first tested in the Twin Cities in 1985; testing then moved to the Iron Range where the locomotive fleet is relatively captive.

The railroad also began experimenting with alternative fuels in the 1980's. BN GP9 1961 was part of a project involving the use of natural gas as a locomotive fuel—a joint effort of Northern States Power, Northern Natural Gas and Northern Natural Resources Co. The Geep was modified at West Burlington Shops to burn the gas, which was supplied by a truck trailer on a flatcar carried behind the locomotive. The diesel could burn either natural gas or regular diesel fuel carried in the unit's fuel tanks. The 1961 made its first test runs in 1985, but the experiment was not entirely successful, partly because horsepower was reduced and because it was not economical on low-horsepower locomotives.

The next generation of natural-gas locomotives are high-horsepower mainline units. BN entered a partnership with Air Products & Chemicals of Allentown, Pa., to develop natural-gas locomotives, tenders and fueling stations. BN contracted with Energy Conversions, Inc., for the development of a gas-conversion kit for a locomotive engine. SD40-2 7890 was converted to burn either diesel fuel or refrigerated liquified methane, and was in the early throes of its tests as this volume went to press.

What is perhaps BN's most-radical locomotive development is the "power-by-the-hour" (PBH) concept, introduced in 1986. Under the arrangement, outside parties purchase new locomotives from their builders and turn them over to BN, with the railroad buying only the electrical power generated by the locomotives. The third-party owners contract with the builders to maintain the units and must meet pre-determined performance standards.

The first PBH units were 100 SD60's built by EMD and leased to Oakway, Inc., in 1986. Painted in EMD blue and white, the SD60's were maintained by Electro Northern, a joint undertaking of EMD, BN and several shopcraft unions. The units initially were based at Trinidad, Colo., but moved to the $4.5 million Electro Northern shop at Murray Yard in North Kansas City, Mo., in 1988.

At first, unions objected to the program, fearing it would jeopardize shop workers' jobs. BN was able to reach accord with unions by using the "shared facility" concept, first implemented with the arrival of 100 General Electric B39-8's in 1987-88, which are leased by LMX Corp.* The B39-8's are maintained by BN employees working under the direction of GE technicians. The 100 SD60M's added to the roster in

*Two of the units were deliberately wrecked by vandals on Montana Rail Link in October 1987 but were rebuilt as GECX 8000-8001 and returned to service. Two other units replaced them making a total of 102 power-by-the-hour GE's, although three other units were later wrecked and scrapped.

1990-91, are also maintained under a shared facility agreement at the Glendive (Mont.) shop, under the supervision of EMD management.

The B39-8's are leased to LMX and BN pays for the megawatt hours they generate, the same as the Oakway units. Both GE and EMD have a direct economic interest in the locomotives' performance through maintenance contracts, so it's in their best interests to ensure reliability. In 1991, PBH units were able to achieve an average of 85 to 95 days between mechanical failures (versus around 70 days for BN's conventional fleet in 1990, although BN's fleet was older). Although power-by-the-hour is a success reliability-wise, it required complicated legal and financial agreements, which is why BN reverted to conventional financing methods for the SD60M's.

With the arrival of new and PBH units, BN was able to downgrade many of its older diesels—nearing the end of their 20- to 30-year life expectancy—to secondary service. Rather than replace them with expensive new units, BN entered into "competitive remanufacturing." During 1988, the railroad, through bid arrangements, signed agreements to

lease or purchase 250 remanufactured locomotives, in many cases rebuilt from old locomotive hulks from other railroads. Rebuilt units featured updated technology, a 20-year life span and a three-year warranty—and they save BN 40 percent of the $1 million-plus cost of new locomotives.

Two companies initially competed to do the work: EMD at La Grange, Ill., and Morrison-Knudsen at Boise, Idaho. In 1990, VMV Enterprises at Paducah, Ky., entered the project. GP30's, GP35's and GP40's were selected to be rebuilt reusing as many of the original components as possible. The GP30's and GP35's are reworked as GP39-2's, while the GP40's become GP40-2's. The units receive new power assemblies, essentially new engines (except for the block and turbocharger) and rebuilt traction motors and trucks. An almost entirely new electrical system is installed, similar to that used in new locomotives. BN identifies the remanufactured units from MK, EMD and VMV with an "M", "E" or "V" after the GP39 or GP40 designation, hence "GP39M." The units performed so well they were used on priority

Text continued on page 92

This spring 1992 scene suggests that the fuel tender concept has resurfaced; in reality it depicts a new concept in locomotive fuel. SD40-2 7890 has been modified to burn both regular diesel fuel (carried in the normal underbody tanks) and/or refrigerated liquified methane (RLM), a purer version of liquified natural gas. The RLM is carried in special tank cars, such as the one seen here, which are insulated and pressurized—necessary for storing methane at temperatures below -260 degrees Fahrenheit to keep the fuel liquid. Work began on the 7890 at Coast Engine & Equipment in Tacoma in 1990, and the unit was released in 1992 sporting a special version of BN's "whiteface" paint scheme. The locomotive is expected to operate longer intervals before needing fuel, with better engine efficiency. The 7890 and its accompanying tender were taken on an informational tour to various communities along its intended assigned route (the northern corridor) early in 1992. A special fueling facility for the experimental duo was constructed at Staples, Minn.—STEVE GLISCHINSKI

A variation of the black/orange "tiger-stripe" scheme that appeared in 1985, white and orange stripes for a time graced GP50's 3110 and 3112. The former leads *Expediter 44* at Hager City, Wis., in 1989.—DAN POITRAS

LEFT: Certain E-units presented a challenge to BN painters. Some former CB&Q units had unpainted stainless-steel sides, which did not take paint well, so paint variations were invented that focused on the nose. Several versions were tried, including one scheme which had the units painted solid silver, with black-and-white nose stripes. BN eventually settled on a solid green nose with white nose stripes. Here, BN's *Denver Zephyr* exits Chicago in August 1970 behind the only E7 to receive full BN colors.—JIM HEUER FAR LEFT: The "white-face" scheme represents the BN of the '90's.—PAUL D. SCHNEIDER

*B*N's trademark color is "Cascade Green," indicative of the lush northern forest areas the railroad serves. In the 22 years since Burlington Northern was created, that color has remained the same, but there have been many variations in how it has been applied to the diesel locomotive fleet.

Upon merger, BN adopted two basic paint schemes, one for passenger units, the other for freight. At the time, most of the former were streamlined F and E-units, which received green with white nose stripes and, on the sides, a white stripe that angled downward sharply toward the cab end, thus resembling a "pistol grip." On F-units assigned to freight service, the white pistol-grip stripe was simply omitted.

In 1972, BN turned over its Chicago-Aurora commuter service to the West Suburban Mass Transit District, with all the equipment leased back to the BN for operation. Twenty-five E-units eventually were rebuilt (four weren't done until 1978) for this service by contractor Morrison-Knudsen. The rebuilt E's saw the revival of the BN pistol-grip scheme. At the suggestion of the Illinois Department of Trans-

portation, high-visibility orange "day-glo" nose stripes were added to the unit noses, replacing green between the white nose stripes.

The majority of BN freight units were painted in the standard scheme of green with white lettering and nose stripes and the BN emblem and name on the side of the cab. In early 1985, BN repainted SD40-2 8002 into an experimental scheme in an overall effort to increase visibility. The bulk of the 8002 remained Cascade green, but the whole face of the unit was reworked with orange and black striping. The sides of the unit were redone as well, with a large herald and lettering on the hood and the road number on the side of the cab. The unit was released from BN's Havelock Shop in Lincoln, Neb., on Feb. 5, 1985. This experimental design, which came to be known as the "tiger stripe" scheme, was chosen for BN's next order of new locomotives, 53 GP50's and three leased SD60's, all delivered by late 1985.

A new image seemed to be well on its way, but BN was not happy with the high cost of the tiger stripes. No other units were painted this way, and older units being repainted all appeared in the standard green and white. However, several variations on the striped-nose look were conducted during the late 1980's. For example, Livingston Rebuild Center repainted GP38-2 2100 with black-and-white stripes along the numberboard marquee and the top of the cab, with the standard green and white nose stripes continued onto the cab's lower front.

Still seeking to improve the visibility of its units, BN had by April 1989 chosen a new revision of its standard green-and-white livery. The cab front was painted solid white, but the nose striping was replaced with solid green with a large white BN herald—thus was born the "whiteface" scheme. The short-lived tiger-stripe scheme was consigned to history, and by late 1989, BN's Springfield (Mo.) shops and contractor Independent Locomotive Service of Bethel, Minn., began to give the tiger-stripe GP50's a "facelift," repainting the nose, frame and front wall only in the whiteface scheme.

Several paint variations occurred in the rush to obliterate the orange. In March 1989, GP50 3153 was released from the Livingston Rebuild Center in the full old scheme, one of the last units so painted. Yet, only seven months later, 3153 rolled out of Springfield with a white face, becoming the first GP50 to show the new scheme completely (versus a facelift only, as its sisters received).

Several other diesels have received special paint schemes. "Executive" F-units 1 and 2 received an entirely new scheme in October 1990, which combines a very dark green and cream striping with a black underframe, white roof and red pinstriping to give the units an almost European appearance. In March 1991, the railroad unveiled SD60M 1991, adorned in a special scheme in support of U.S. troops on duty in the Persian Gulf War. Special schemes have also been devised for propane-powered SD40-2's (page 92). A variety of units have worn special paint or emblems to commemorate events in BN territory. For example, GP38 2075 was painted by Pacific Division shop forces to celebrate BN's 20th Anniversary in 1990. The unit was named Pacific Pride and wore the emblems of each of the pre-merger roads, including Frisco.

SD45 6430, formerly GN 400, was the first production-model SD45, and was named Hustle Muscle by GN. BN retained the name, painting it in white letters on the side of the unit.

BN continues to refine its paint designs. The two orders of SD60M's, delivered in 1990-91, have the whiteface application altered to fit the unique contours of the units' wide noses. BN's SD60MAC's, delivered in 1992, wore a green scheme with a white stripe running the length of the unit to its white face, as well as BN and EMD logos on the cab, and green GM and BN logos on the white nose. In 1991, many whiteface units began appearing with a white separation stripe between the black and green at the top of the long hood, which has greatly improved the overall appearance of the locomotives.—Dan Poitras and Steve Glischinski

ABOVE: GP38-2 2100, featuring black and white stripes over the numberboard marquee and an extension of the green-and-white nose stripes onto the cab, leads two GP38E's (leased from EMD) at Canton, S.D., on a "Canton Turn" out of Sioux Falls, S.D., Jan. 30, 1990, on trackage owned by the State of South Dakota.—DAN POITRAS LEFT: In 1991, a new SD60M was painted in a special livery as a salute to U.S. forces serving in the Persian Gulf War. Originally scheduled to be the 9297, the SD60M was instead numbered 1991. Painted red, white and blue, the unit also includes the seal of the United States on its nose, and large circular decals with the words "Pulling For Freedom . . .Supporting Our Troops" adorn each side of the unit. Dedicated in Chicago on March 3, 1991, the locomotive was used frequently at community celebrations and special events; when not on tour, it was assigned to northern corridor coal trains.—TIM HENSCH

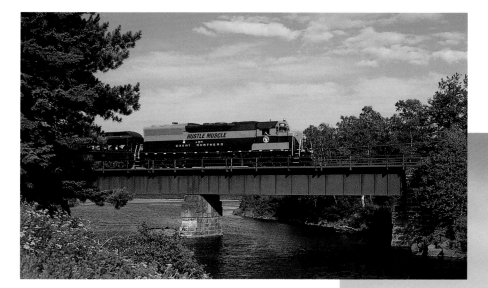

ABOVE: Behind its corporate facade, BN has a soft spot for its heritage, having generously donated locomotives, cabooses and other equipment to on-line museums and communities. Former GN SD45 400, the first production-model SD45, is an example. Built in May 1966 and named *Hustle Muscle* by GN, the 400 was donated to the Great Northern Historical Society after it was retired in 1985. In 1988, the locomotive was restored by BN shop forces at Grand Forks to full GN livery. The locomotive was restored to service in May 1990 and serves as back-up power on the North Shore Scenic Railroad, which operates out of the Lake Superior Museum of Transportation at Duluth to Two Harbors, Minn. On Aug. 10, 1990, the 400 hustles across the Knife River on former Duluth, Missabe & Iron Range trackage.—STEVE GLISCHINSKI

trains. By the end of 1991, 190 of the units had been delivered, 150 of which were leased and 40 purchased directly. In early 1992, the railroad sent 50 elderly GP9's to M-K for similar rebuilding.

Another ten old locomotives also saw a new lease on life, but with entirely different power plants. In 1988, BN sent four GP20's to Minneapolis-based Generation II Locomotive, a manufacturer established by Caterpillar dealer Ziegler, Inc. Generation II installed new Caterpillar diesel engines in the GP20's at its shop in Babbitt, Minn. Ziegler completely overhauled the units, with very little retained save for the carbody and trucks. The main reason for the "Cat" engine? Fuel savings. Unlike normal diesel engines, a Cat engine can be shut down in cold weather, thanks to engine design and a new cooling system which allows antifreeze to be used. The units have also shown substantial fuel savings and meet pollution emission standards, expected to get tougher in the future. The first "Cats" were delivered in 1989, with a total of ten rebuilt, the last arriving in 1990.

The next generation of new power the railroad experimented with was the alternating current SD60M's, dubbed "SD60MAC's." Unlike conventional diesels, which use direct current in their traction motors, the four SD60MAC's, delivered in 1992, employ a.c. traction motors whose chief benefit is lower maintenance costs. However, the units are electrically quite complex. Also, the new units have newly developed self-steering radial trucks, which reduce wheel wear and improve adhesion.

The units, Nos. 9500-9503, are a cooperative venture between BN, EMD and Siemens AG, GM's German-based partner which supplied the a.c. traction motor system. If successful, BN's SD60MAC's may be pioneers for a new generation of freight locomotive traction in North America.

In the late 1980's more changes came to the corporate hierarchy. Gerald Grinstein came to BN from Western Air Lines in 1985 as a member of the holding company's board of directors. In February 1989 he became chief operating officer of Burlington Northern Railroad. Grinstein, with his background in airline management, took a more cooperative approach on labor issues.

Grinstein's arrival was coincident with a major change in the company. On June 3, 1988, BN announced a restructuring that kept the railroad as the major component of the holding company, but spun off the other properties in a new subsidiary, Burlington Resources, Inc. (BR). BN's railroad would now stand alone as a pure railroad transportation company. The initial spinoff of BN's resources in 1981 was planned to help balance the cyclical nature of the railroad business. As it turned out, the railroad became one of the stronger units of BNI, with some of the other businesses suffering.

When the restructuring of the corporation was completed in December 1988, Grinstein became the president and CEO of BNI, with Bressler as chairman (he retired in 1990). Darius Gaskins resigned from the railroad on Jan. 31, 1989. Since the railroad became the principal business of BNI, Grinstein

assumed Gaskins duties heading both companies.

With BN directing all its energies to rail transportation, it put new emphasis on customer service. In 1989, rail service was divided into seven independent business/marketing units to serve the primary customers: agricultural commodities, automotive, food and consumer goods, forest products, industrial products, intermodal and coal. Thanks to this new emphasis, customer surveys consistently rank BN above other Class I railroads for customer service.

Coal continues to be the railroad's Number One commodity and the biggest revenue generator, accounting for 33 percent of BN's revenue in 1991. C&NW/UP's entry into the Powder River Basin in 1984 hurt the company's coal business greatly.

With a variety of run-through motive-power arrangements, BN power and trains are frequent sights on the trackage of other railroads. Here, four BN SD40-2's are *way* off line as they swing through the famous curve at Ludlow, Calif., on Santa Fe's Needles District through the Mojave Desert, July 31, 1989. In 1990, joint intermodal marketing efforts began with Santa Fe, allowing BN to provide service to Los Angeles and the Bay Area, with a single management team with employees from both railroads coordinating the effort.—JAMES A. SPEAKER

LEFT: BN greatly expanded its intermodal services throughout the 1980's, but one technology it did not embrace was that of the "RoadRailer," whereby truck trailers ride directly on flanged wheels, thus eliminating the need for flatcars. Grand Trunk Western and BN ran a joint RoadRailer test train to move auto parts from Flint, Mich., to Kansas City in July 1985, seen here at Cicero Yard, Chicago. GTW declined to get further involved, but BN liked the the test results and bought 220 RoadRailer units. At the time, GM was looking for a faster, more economical way to get auto parts from Detroit-area factories to its assembly plant at Wentzville, Mo., 40 miles west of St. Louis. BN implemented a Chicago-St. Louis RoadRailer run on Jan. 7, 1986, with the auto parts trucked from Michigan to Cicero Yard. Unfortunately, the economics of trucking the parts and making up trains at Cicero didn't work out, and GM turned to Norfolk Southern, which could handle most of the move by rail. NS went on to build a fleet of RoadRailer trains, while BN concentrated on double-stacks, containerization and conventional TOFC.—CHUCK BENTON

RIGHT: Two success stories for the post-Frisco BN were intermodal service and the remanufacturing of old locomotives into new, state-of-the-art units. Rebuilt GP30 2833, once Union Pacific 723 and now classified as a GP39M, passes a set of BN America double-stack containers at the Midway (Twin Cities) Hub Center.
ABOVE RIGHT: BN offers several gathering points, termed "Hub Centers," for motor carriers.—TWO PHOTOS, STEVE GLISCHINSKI

When UP/C&NW arrived in 1984, they undercut BN rates and won away several contracts. BN cut rates and won back some contracts, but intense competition continues to keep profit margins low.

On a typical day (Jan. 17, 1992) BN had 62 loaded trains en route to their destinations, 64 returning empty and 53 trains off-line for a total of 179 unit coal trains in operation that day. In 1991, nearly 9 percent of all electricity generated in the U.S. was produced from coal hauled by BN.

Burlington Northern is also the nation's largest grain carrier, handling 447,000 carloads in 1990, the same year it acquired 1,000 new covered hoppers for grain service. Five hundred more came in 1992, for a total of over 24,000 owned or leased.

During the 1980's, intermodal services grew

When is a BN coal train not a BN coal train? When it's running over regional railroad Montana Rail Link, with Burlington Northern power but MRL crews. At 8:58 p.m., only two minutes from sunset, westbound coal train No. 33/MRL 241-20 rumbles across the Clark Fork River bridge east of Clark Fork, Ida., on the first day of August 1991. Clark Fork is on the far western edge of the Mountain Time Zone accounting for the late hour of the photograph. This bridge marks the western end of a 1957 Northern Pacific line change necessitated by the construction of the Noxon Rapids Dam. This train was the 33rd trainload of Caballo Rojo coal from the Powder River Basin bound for Portland General Electric's plant at Castle, Ore., southwest of Hinkle. A mixture of UP and BN SD40-2's are bracketed by new SD60M's 9250-9251. In 1991 the use of the wide-nose units on this thrice-weekly coal move were their only regular assignment on the west end of the system.—BLAIR KOOISTRA

tremendously. The company began the *Expediter* intermodal concept on its former Frisco lines in 1985, the same year the first double-stack cars were operated in intermodal service. *Expediter*s used reduced (two-person) crews, were initially limited to 60 trailers and operated on truck-competitive schedules on routes under 850 miles. The *Expediter*s won new business away from motor carriers and was expanded to the competitive Chicago-Twin Cities corridor in early September 1986. It has since been expanded across much of the system.

By the end of 1991, 90 percent of all intermodal traffic moved in dedicated trains (an average of 50 trains daily) and accounted for 15 percent of the railroad's revenues, up from 7 percent in 1983. Much of this traffic is bound for overseas markets, but future

growth may be in the domestic market. To help capture this traffic, the company in 1989 established BN America, a domestic containerization program offering door-to-door service with double-stack technology.

Intermodal traffic was also enhanced by a joint marketing strategy with Santa Fe Railway. Through this agreement, reached in 1990, BN America was able to connect several cities on old Frisco lines to Los Angeles and the San Francisco Bay Area. A single management team with employees from both railroads coordinated these efforts, and BN power began running through on the Santa Fe to the coast. BN intermodal hubs have been expanded to off-line cities like Green Bay (Wis.), Detroit and Louisville. Twenty-nine of these hubs across the U.S. originated 825,545 intermodal loads in 1991.

BN's new service commitments also included precision scheduling, begun in January 1992. With certain exceptions, trains are scheduled to be within plus or minus 30 minutes of their published time at crew-change points. Coal, grain and potash unit trains were initially not scheduled, although some coal moves were to be included in mid-1992.

As BN entered the 1990's, it had survived 20 years of change, which included merging five rail systems together, deregulation, downsizing and corporate restructuring. Through it all, BN has emerged to become one of North America's premier rail carriers. It's impossible to predict what the future will be for the nation's largest railroad, but one fact is certain: James J. Hill's dream of a unified rail system in the Northwest has been fulfilled, and then some.

ABOVE: At Springdale, Ark., two Arkansas & Missouri shop workers scrub Alco Century 420 No. 58 (ex-Delaware & Hudson and Lehigh Valley) on Aug. 29, 1989. LEFT: One of the first BN branch lines to be turned over to a short line operator was one of its most famous, the 44-mile ex-GN line between Wayzata and Hutchinson, Minn. Shortline service began on Dec. 5, 1985, under the Dakota Rail banner. Less than two weeks after the Dakota Rail takeover, F7's 81A and 81C (once employed by Milwaukee Road for helper service in Tacoma, Wash.) trundle up to the BN interchange with four cars on Dec. 12, 1985. The ex-GN main line to Willmar and Breckenridge is visible to the right of the photo.—BOTH PHOTOS, STEVE GLISCHINSKI

"*If someone offers a decent price, all or part of [the BN] is for sale.*" That's what BN spokesman Howard Kallio told the Missoulian, a Montana daily newspaper, in 1987. What he was stating was a reality Class I railroads of the 1980's faced: They had too much mileage that failed to return an adequate return on investment.

Industry management frequently cited excessive labor costs, high taxes, government regulations and competition as reasons for many lines losing business. Not as frequently mentioned by railroads was lack of service, which forced shippers to turn to alternate modes of transport, usually trucks. As motor carriers took more business, more lines became less profitable.

Many lines, of course, were eventually abandoned, but others turned enough of a profit, or had constituencies that desired continued operation, so that the idea of selling lines to shortlines or new, larger "regional" railroads took hold. These smaller lines can usually operate with small, non-union crews and thus offer more-flexible, responsive service to shippers.

BN began to embrace this strategy by selling small line segments to shortlines. After the company in 1984 announced its intention to abandon the famous "Hutch" branch between Wayzata and Hutchinson, Minn., the McLeod County Rail Authority—which hoped to keep the line in operation—searched for options. They turned to Dakota Rail, which successfully operated a 37-mile ex-Milwaukee Road branch in South Dakota, which acquired the line in 1985.

From this modest beginning, BN switched into high gear. On Sept. 1, 1986, Tony Hannold, who owned the Alco-powered Maryland & Delaware, took over 145 miles of ex-Frisco trackage from Monett, Mo., to Fort Smith, Ark., including a 5.7-mile branch to Bentonville, Ark. Hannold's operation was named the Arkansas & Missouri Railroad.

Fifteen days after A&M began service, John Greene's Montana Western began operations in that state. MW operates between Butte and Garrison, Mont., over 40 miles of former NP track that was the route of the North Coast Limited and Amtrak's North Coast Hiawatha until 1979.

More startups followed. Nick Temple's Washington Central took over 149.3 miles of ex-NP main line from Kennewick to Cle Elum, Wash., on Oct. 13, 1986. WCRC also picked up several branches, all ex-NP: Yakima-Moxee City; Yakima-Naches; Gibbon-Granger; and Toppenish-White Swan. In December 1986, the railroad added over 100 miles of former NP and Milwaukee Road branches north of Connell. Total mileage is 325, all in the State of Washington.

In Minnesota, the Otter Tail Valley Railroad Company commenced service on Oct. 27, 1986. OTVR operated over 151 miles of former GN secondary main line from Moorhead (plus trackage rights into BN's yard at Dilworth) to Avon, Minn. In addition, the railroad operates ex-NP branches from Fergus Falls to Foxhome and Hoot Lake. OTVR's ex-GN main at one time or another hosted GN's Dakotan, Red River, Western Star and Winnipeg Limited streamliners. Ninety percent of OTVR's traffic is between Moorhead and Fergus Falls, so the eastern 96.6 miles of line from Fergus Falls to Avon was abandoned in 1991.

The year 1987 was another landmark for line sales, including the largest and most acrimonious, the spin-off to Montana Rail Link. With its excessive grades, the Northern Pacific main line across southern Montana was vastly inferior to the more northerly GN route. Consequently, the GN became BN's primary transcontinental line. With the emergence of Powder River coal, lines east of Huntley (12 miles east of Billings) became busier than ever. Local business was strong west of Billings but not enough to justify maintaining the entire route west to Sandpoint, where the ex-NP and GN main lines rejoined. BN formulated an alternative plan: rebuild the ex-GN line from Mossmain (12 miles west of Billings) through Great Falls to Shelby, to handle traffic from NP and ex-CB&Q routes in Wyoming north to the transcontinental main; the NP as a through route could then be closed. Unfortunately, the cost of rebuilding the Great Falls line turned out to be prohibitive, and the plan was dropped.

In view of BN's "sell the whole railroad" policy, Montana industrialist Dennis Washington began negotiations to purchase the former NP lines west of Jones Junction to Sandpoint. On Oct. 31, 1987, his new railroad, dubbed Montana Rail Link, began operations. The railroad included the 510-mile main line, the 94-mile alternate main between De Smet and Paradise via St. Regis, plus 217 miles of branches. The main was leased, rather than purchased, because of liens still held on the property by NP bondholders.

Before the sale, Montana had already been a troublespot for BN. Union relations were tense, thanks to cutbacks at several terminals, and state tax burdens were deemed excessive. With the MRL transaction, BN was able to rid itself of these problems, at least on the ex-NP route. Through trains entered MRL jurisdiction at Spokane (the regional has trackage rights from Sandpoint to Spokane) and returned to BN at Laurel. Since MRL connects with no other railroads, BN had a captive, low-cost

By far the largest of the carriers created by BN line sales to date is Montana Rail Link, which began operations Oct. 31, 1987. All of MRL's lines are former NP, with the main line leased from BN and the branch lines owned by the new railroad. MRL has been prosperous from its inception, so much so that its revenues qualify it as a Class I carrier by the ICC. This classification carries with it a considerable (and costly) amount of paperwork, so the road requested an exemption from its reporting requirements. Other than trains handled for BN, MRL runs its own symbol freights to serve on-line customers: westbound LM (Laurel-Missoula) and MS (Missoula-Spokane), and eastbound SM (Spokane-Missoula) and ML (Missoula-Laurel). Other than locals, these were some of the few trains to utilize MRL, rather than BN motive power. In June 1990, LM is blasting through Tobin, Mont., heading west to do battle with the the 2.2 percent grades of Mullan Pass. Helena is visible in the distance.—ROBERT S. KAPLAN

route for traffic bound from the Pacific Northwest to the Midwest and south.

Unions had opposed the transaction in the courts, but eventually the sale went through. Start-up of the new railroad went anything but smoothly, however. On Day One, two LMX GE's and a BN SD40-2 were set loose over Bozeman Pass, finally derailing on a curve. Nonetheless, MRL was here to stay, and operations quickly settled down. Based in Missoula, the railroad has a modern office building and a state-of-the-art dispatching system.

MRL wasn't the only sale in 1987. BN eliminated many of its North Dakota branchline burdens by selling its former NP lines to Red River Valley & Western. RRV&W took over operation of 667 miles of BN track, primarily in North Dakota, on July 19 and Aug. 29, 1987. Headquarters for the new line are in Breckenridge, Minn. RRV&W handles mainly grain traffic from this rich agricultural area.

On July 22, the Kiamichi Railroad Company took over 186 miles of former Frisco trackage from Lakeside, Okla., to Hope, Ark., plus a branch from Antlers, Okla., to Paris, Texas, 45 miles. Headquarters for the line are in Hugo, Okla., where these two lines cross. Traffic includes paper products, lumber, and chemicals. Kiamichi also receives a coal train from BN bound for Fort Towson, Okla.

Another ex-Frisco line was turned over to short-line Grainbelt Corporation on Aug. 31, 1987; the transaction included 186 miles of trackage in Oklahoma, stretching from Enid to Davidson, and some trackage rights on BN. The main commodity handled by Grainbelt is wheat, with chemicals, fertilizer and other products handled as well.

In Colorado, BN sold it's historic 14-mile branch between Leadville and Climax in November 1987. This is a line of many records: It was the last of Colorado & Southern's narrow-gauge lines to operate, being converted to standard gauge in August 1943. It then became the highest standard-gauge rail operation in the U.S.—the elevation at Climax is 11,400 feet. The branch was home to the last operating standard-gauge Class I steam locomotive in regular service, C&S 2-8-0 No. 641, which ran until Oct. 11, 1962. The branch was not connected to the rest of the C&S after the narrow-gauge abandonments, but did have a rail connection with the Rio Grande at Leadville. The chief source of traffic for the railroad was a molybdenum mine at Climax, which has closed. The tourist carrying Leadville,

Colorado & Southern began operations on the branch May 28, 1988, purchasing the line for $1.

So far, the strategy of selling off these lines has paid off, as most of the new carriers' business has grown, which translates into more interchange for BN. Recent labor agreements allowing the use of two-person crews eventually should pay off in lower labor costs, which may allow some lines now deemed marginal to become more cost effective. Only time will tell if BN will continue the practice of selling off its network piece by piece.

ABOVE: The spirit of NP's *North Coast Limited* lives on in the Pacific Northwest, in the form of Washington Central's *Spirit of Washington* dinner train. Like the *North Coast*, it features domes and an observation car—although neither is of NP heritage. WCRC, owned by Nick Temple, took over 149.3 miles of ex-NP main line from Kennewick to Cle Elum, Wash. on Oct. 13, 1986. In addition to the old main line, WCRC picked up several former NP branches, and in December 1986 the railroad added over 100 miles of former NP and Milwaukee Road lines north of Connell. The dinner train, established in 1989, generally ran out of Yakima, traveling west to Ellensburg or east to Prosser on a 3 1/2-hour round trip. Like the Red River Valley & Western, Washington Central has a fleet of ex-Santa Fe CF7's, one of which is in charge of a five-car dinner run at East Selah, Wash., on Aug. 17, 1991, heading west into the Yakima River Gorge. In 1992, the train was moved to Renton, Wash., operating on BN trackage.—OTTO P. DOBNICK

ABOVE LEFT: Shortlines often face the same tribulations that forced Class I's to sell trackage. Red River Valley & Western CF7's are forced to wait for a maintenance-of-way crew to straighten a sun kink east of Tuttle, N.D., on a blazing June day in 1988.—BUD BULGRIN

PART III

THE DIVISIONS OF BN

Teton, Mont. on the former Great Northern main line, Sept. 24, 1990.—SCOTT BONTZ

To effectively manage a railroad that encompassed over 23,000 miles of track in 17 states and two Canadian provinces (not including subsidiaries), BN in 1970 established six regions: Chicago, Omaha, Twin Cities, Billings, Seattle and Portland. The regions directly controlled operations and services in their territory, reporting to headquarters in St. Paul. An additional region, Springfield, was established with the addition of Frisco in 1980. Vice presidents were in charge of each region, which was further broken down by smaller divisions, overseen by a division general manager.

Over the years, divisions in the regions were consolidated or whole regions were eliminated entirely as the company cut costs, abandoned or sold trackage, and improved efficiencies. By the end of the 1980's, the regions had been pared to just two: Northern and Southern, encompassing several divisions. Finally, with the downsizing that many railroad managements went through in the past few years, the "extra" layer of management running the remaining regions was eliminated at the vice presidential level in 1990, with administrative work continuing into the first quarter of 1991. At this writing, BN is comprised of eight operating divisions: Pacific (headquartered in Seattle), Montana (Havre), Dakota (Fargo), Nebraska (Lincoln), and Denver, Galesburg, Springfield and Fort Worth (headquartered at their namesake cities).

To logically portray the photographic images of a company as large as BN, this portion of the book is arranged by division. Locations or segments of track covered appear within a division chapter as they exist in 1992, even though scenes may have been recorded when the location was in another or previous division. Where logical, references are made to the old regional structure as it existed back in the 1970's, before many abandonments and line sales took place. Maps further identify both past and present trackage of a division or region.

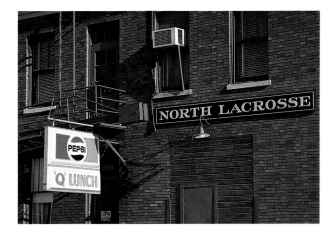

CHAPTER 8

GALESBURG DIVISION

THE "Q" IN GREEN

If any part of the railroad could be considered the "beginning" of BN's rail system, it would be the Galesburg Division, formerly part of the Chicago Region. Until the takeover of the Frisco in 1980, Chicago was as far east as BN rails reached—and these were historic rails, since it was one of the oldest parts of predecessor Burlington Route.

The Galesburg Division is comprised entirely of ex-CB&Q trackage. When today's division was under the management of the Chicago Region, there were three divisions under its jurisdiction: Chicago, Ottumwa and Hannibal. The Chicago Division's principal boundary cities were Chicago (east), Galesburg (south), and Hastings, Minn. (west and north).

The Hannibal Division, headquartered in the Missouri city of the same name, included all lines south of Galesburg, with the western boundary at St. Joseph, Mo., and the southern boundary at Paducah, Ky.—BN's only foray into the Bluegrass State.

The Ottumwa Division included the Galesburg-Pacific Junction (Iowa) main line through Illinois and Iowa, plus associated branches; the St. Joseph-Kansas City main, and the secondary line northeast out of St. Joseph into Iowa ending at Humeston, which once continued to a connection with the Chicago-Omaha main at Chariton. Today, the Galesburg Division includes all lines in Illinois, and stretches west to Creston, Iowa, and Birmingham, Mo., near Kansas City.

If the territory covered by the Galesburg Division is anything, it is diverse. It includes the triple-track Chicago-Aurora "speedway" and once had a network of branch lines in Iowa populated by diminutive SW1 switchers. BN's "other" source of coal, the fields of southern Illinois, are part of the Division, and before division and regional consolidations, the metropolitan areas of St. Louis and Kansas City were included as well. Major yards include Cicero in Chicago—a busy hump yard and intermodal terminal—and another hump yard at Galesburg, also home to the division's dispatchers. The former Burlington shop at West Burlington, Iowa, handles major locomotive rebuilding projects.

The Galesburg Division is *Expediter* territory. BN began the *Expediter* concept in September 1985 when it inaugurated intermodal train services that were short, fast and used two-man crews. Cicero Yard in Chicago is the Division's major intermodal hub, dispatching *Expediter*s to destinations as varied as the Twin Cities, St. Louis and Texas. Most of the traffic has been generated by siphoning business away from truckers, a happy reversal of the prevailing trend in railroading the last three decades.

The Galesburg Division's first 38 miles traverse Chicagoland's busy western suburbs. At Aurora, the main line splits, with the Twin Cities line heading northwest across the pleasant rolling farm country of northern Illinois. This was the old racetrack of the

*Zephyr*s, where Burlington trains frequently romped at speeds in excess of 90 mph.

From Aurora to Savanna the line is mainly single track controlled by CTC, and primarily double track beyond Savanna (a former crew-change point) up the Mississippi to the current crew base of North La Crosse, Wis. River running continues to St. Croix at Hastings, Minn., where joint track operation with Soo Line (former Milwaukee Road, an agreement dating from 1892) begins into the Twin Cities

Beyond Aurora and 125 miles to the southwest is Galesburg, a hub of CB&Q operations that continues to be an important point for BN. Lines radiate from Galesburg like wheel spokes: north to Savanna, south to St. Louis and southern Illinois, west to Kansas City and Omaha, and east to Chicago and Peoria.

The line to Omaha through Illinois and southern Iowa is little remarked, but its scenery is surprisingly diverse: while a great deal is flat prairie, in Iowa BN's main swings and curves through hills and crosses a variety of waterways with mainly ABS-controlled double track. In the 1970's, the southern Iowa route boasted several branch lines, which reached out from the main line to small towns with interesting names like Washington, Cumberland, Griswold and Clarinda, all of which are gone today.

South from Galesburg, St. Louis and Kansas City-bound trains travel a common route for 104

ABOVE: A hub in CB&Q days, Galesburg—population 32,000 and home of Knox College—remains central to Galesburg Division operations. Viewed from the roof of the Galesburg depot, CB&Q class S-4 4-6-4 3006 (Baldwin, 1930) stands silent on a June day in 1980 as an empty coal train passes, picked up from the Elgin, Joliet & Eastern at Eola Yard (near Aurora). The photo was taken during Galesburg Railroad Days, an annual community festival commemorating the city's railroad heritage.—STEVE SMEDLEY FACING

PAGE, TOP: La Crosse was home of the "Q Lunch," a railroad beanery in the old North La Crosse passenger depot/division office. For years, train crews and public alike congregated at the friendly cafe, until it closed in December 1987. In pre-Amtrak days, passenger trains stopped at a newer facility to the south on a new city bypass as well as at North LaCrosse. The bypass, constructed early in the 1940's, took freight and passenger trains off the downtown streets of La Crosse.—MIKE SCHAFER

Galesburg Division abandonments

Illinois (all ex-CB&Q)

Lewiston-Fairview, 15 miles, 1976
La Salle-L&S Junction, 15 miles, 1977
Nifa-West Batavia, 3 miles, 1977
Cambon-West Frankfort, 4 miles, 1978
Marblehead-East Hannibal, 10 miles, 1978
Buda-Lombardville, 7 miles, 1978
Alexis-North Henderson, 5 miles, 1978
Vermont-Rushville, 15 miles, 1980
Joy-Aledo, 6 miles, 1980
L&S Junction-Streator, 14 miles, 1980
White Hall-East Alton, 46 miles, 1980
Bushnell-Roseville, 16 miles, 1980
Herrin-Herrin Junction, 2 miles, 1980
Mendon-Quincy, 15 miles, 1981
Lombardville-Wyoming, 14 miles, 1981
Vermont-Astoria, 7 miles, 1981
Lass-Garden Plain, 6 miles, 1982
Earlville-Baker, 7 miles, 1982
Lewistown-Liverpool, 9 miles, 1982
Alpha-Woodhull, 4 miles, 1983

Rio-North Henderson, 4 miles, 1983
Elmwood-Wyoming, 26 miles, 1983
Concord-White Hall, 30 miles, 1983
Earlville-Sterling-Lyndon, 60 miles, 1984
Lewiston-Fairview, 4 miles, 1984
Quincy-Marblehead, 4 miles, 1984
Mendota-Denrock, 47 miles, 1985
Alpha-Aledo, 21 miles, 1986
Alton-West Alton, Mo. (Mississippi River bridge), 3 miles, 1988

In 1978, BN abandoned its Shattuc-East St. Louis trackage rights over Baltimore & Ohio in favor of rights over Missouri Pacific (now Union Pacific) from Toland to Lenox Tower (Mitchell).

From June 1980 to Sept. 30, 1981, BN operated Rock Island trackage between Peoria and Henry, 34 miles

Iowa (all ex-CB&Q)

Farragut-Riverton, 5 miles, 1971
Henderson-Carson, 7 miles, 1972
Randolph-Sidney, 10 miles, 1972
Chariton-Humeston, 17 miles, 1973
Corydon-Humeston, 13 miles, 1975
Lamoni-Mount Ayr, 20 miles, 1977
Mediapolis-Washington, 37 miles, 1980
Fort Madison-Stockport, 38 miles, 1980
Hastings-Randolph, 12 miles, 1980
Humeston-St. Joseph, Mo., 129 miles (39 miles in Iowa), 1980-81
Centerville-Alexandria, Mo., 85 miles (17 miles in Iowa), 1981
Villisca-Clarinda, 15 miles, 1981
Payne Junction-Nebraska City, Neb., 5 miles, 1982

Creston-Marysville, Mo., 59 miles (49 miles in Iowa), 1982
Henderson-Hastings, 10 miles, 1983
Elliott-Griswold, 5 miles, 1984
Red Oak-Elliot, 10 miles, 1985
Pacific Junction-Council Bluffs, 11 miles, 1985
Greenfield-Cumberland, 26 miles, 1986

Leased lines:

BN operates ex-Milwaukee Road main line Council Bluffs-Bayard, 98.7 miles, for owner Shippers Consortium, which purchased it from Milwaukee Road in 1980. Operations began Monday, Oct. 25, 1982.

Missouri

Tarkio-Westboro, ex-CB&Q, 7 miles, 1974
Amazonia-Savannah, ex-CB&Q, 6 miles, 1974
Maitland-Skidmore, ex-CB&Q, 6 miles, 1977
Maryville-Barnard, ex-CB&Q, 14 miles, 1978
Old Monroe-Mexico, ex-CB&Q, 65 miles, 1980
St. Joseph-Humeston, Iowa, ex-CB&Q, 129 miles (89.7 miles in Missouri), 1981
Albany Junction-Grant City, ex-CB&Q, 21 miles, 1981
West Quincy-Kirksville, ex-CB&Q, 67 miles, 1981
Alexandria-Centerville, Iowa, ex-CB&Q, 85 miles (68 miles in Missouri), 1981
Laclede-Unionville, ex-CB&Q, 53 miles, 1981
Cotter-Carrolton, ex-CB&Q, 12 miles, 1981
Bigelow-Maitland, ex-CB&Q, 14 miles, 1981
Maryville-Creston, Iowa, ex-CB&Q, 59 miles (16 miles in Missouri), 1982
Corning-Tarkio, ex-CB&Q, 15 miles, 1982
Kennett-Holcomb, ex-SLSF, 10 miles, 1982
Kennett-Senath, ex-SLSF, 6 miles, 1982
Willow Springs-Winona, ex-SLSF, 38 miles, 1983
Kissick-Ozark, ex-SLSF, 7 miles, 1983
Aurora-Mount Vernon, ex-SLSF, 11 miles, 1984
Lead Junction-Salem, ex-SLSF, 27 miles, 1984
Laclede-St. Joseph, ex-CB&Q, 92 miles, 1984
Carl Junction-J&G Junction, ex-SLSF, 8 miles, 1985
Hayti-Caruthersville, ex-SLSF, 8 miles, 1985
East Leavenworth-Leavenworth, ex-CB&Q, 2 miles, 1987
BV Junction-East Lynne, ex-SLSF, 41 miles, 1989
West Alton-Alton, Ill. (Mississippi River bridge), ex-CB&Q, 3 miles, 1989
Joplin-Webb City, ex-SLSF, 4 miles, 1991

Line sales:

To Arkansas & Missouri Railroad Co., Sept. 1, 1986:
Monett-Ft. Smith, Ark., ex-SLSF, 134 miles

MINNESOTA

WISCONSIN

IOWA

ILLINOIS

MISSOURI

KENTUCKY

GALESBURG DIVISION

	BN, current and active
	BN trackage rights on another railroad (owning road in parenthesis)
	BN, abandoned after 1970
	Ex-BN, sold to another operator

SCALE
0   50   100   Miles

miles to West Quincy, Mo., where St. Louis trains head south along the Mississippi. Another scenic river line, the St. Louis route passes through Hannibal, of Mark Twain fame, then West Alton to St. Louis. Kansas City traffic goes west at Mark, Mo., 98 miles to Brookfield where trains turn southwestward along the Centennial Cutoff to Birmingham. Constructed by CB&Q between 1949 and 1952, the Cutoff saved 22 miles over the old route to K.C. It included 48 miles of all-new line, substantial rebuilding of 28 miles of an existing branch, cost $16 million and was the largest new piece of railroad constructed after World War II until BN built the Orin coal line in Wyoming. The entire Galesburg-Birmingham route is single-track CTC, with two main tracks from Birmingham to North Kansas City, 16 miles of which are owned by Norfolk Southern (ex-Wabash).

Trains headed to southern Illinois leave Galesburg and travel the St. Louis/Kansas City route 29 miles to Bushnell, where they head south. At Concord, 16 miles south of Beardstown, a line once headed southwest to East Alton, Ill., where BN trains entered trackage rights to reach East St. Louis. BN also had trackage rights over the Baltimore & Ohio from Shattuc, Ill., to East St. Louis, primarily used by coal trains. In 1980-83 the Concord-East Alton route was abandoned and B&O trackage rights dropped in favor of rights over the joint Conrail-Missouri Pacific (now Union Pacific) route from Toland.

ABOVE: The big shoulders of Chicago—largest city on the entire Burlington Northern system—serve as the railroad's east end anchor (though not the road's easternmost point). A huge percentage of BN traffic out of Chicago is, of course, attributed to freight and intermodal, but there remains a significant slice of passenger traffic in the form of Chicago-Aurora suburban runs operated by BN under contract with Metra, Chicago's commuter-rail agency, and Amtrak. As empty "dinkies" (as commuter trains are known to Burlington crews) file into Union Station from 14th Street Yard to gather their payload, outbound suburban trains march away to the suburbs. In this May 1981 scene at 12th Street, the E-unit fleet remains clean and fit for another ten years of duties getting the "5:15" home at 5:15.—DENIS CONNELL RIGHT: Transfer runs radiate from Cicero Yard (mostly on trackage rights) to interchange with other lines. This SW1000 pair nosing across the Illinois Central/Amtrak/Metra (ex-GM&O) main at Brighton Park interlocking near downtown Chicago have pulled interchange at Conrail's Ashland Avenue Yard and are now heading back to Cicero at the end of a fine summer day in 1987.—MIKE SCHAFER

Burlington originally pushed into the southern Illinois coal fields to gain a source of steam locomotive coal for itself and its parent roads. At Neilson, BN uses UP (former Chicago & Eastern Illinois) rails for 16 miles to West Vienna. Just 22 miles later, trains swing onto Illinois Central's Paducah & Illinois Railroad at Burlington Junction for the 17-mile trip into Paducah. There is also a one-mile line from Burlington Junction to Metropolis, Ill., which declares itself "Home of Superman." Connections are made at Paducah with short line Paducah & Louisville. The single-track Bushnell-Paducah route is probably one of the Galesburg Division's most overlooked properties, what with other attractions like the triple-track main line into Chicago, and the Mississippi River route. But on its southern end, it runs through some rugged scenery.

Once the anchor in the Burlington route system serving "Everywhere West," the Galesburg Division continues in that role for Burlington Northern with strong intermodal traffic and heavy coal and merchandise tonnage.

LEFT: Birthplace of the Burlington was Turner Junction (now West Chicago) where the pioneer Aurora Branch Railroad terminated. In this 1976 scene, the way freight from Aurora has just dropped its waycar by the old depot (since moved and preserved) and has begun working local industries. West Chicago remains important to BN: General Mills is the biggest customer here, and there is interchange to C&NW, whose main is visible in the distance.—MARK LLANUZA

LOWER LEFT: BN's 14th Subdivision local to Ottawa, No. 11841, switches the U.S. Silica sand plant at Wedron, Ill., in a scene where the sand resembles snow. The crew will spend several hours switching this industry on the banks of the Fox River on this July day in 1991. The two locomotives are SD38-2's, part of a group of nine built in 1978 for Minnesota's Reserve Mining Co. Following Reserve's 1986 bankruptcy, the units went to GATX Leasing, from which BN leased the units beginning in 1987. Wedron is on the Streator Branch, which cuts south from the Aurora-Galesburg main at Montgomery, just outside Aurora. The line follows the Fox River to its mouth at the Illinois River in Ottawa, a popular destination for steam excursions in CB&Q days.—STEVE SMEDLEY

In a scene that aptly portrays the "feel" of the Burlington in Illinois, train 161 races through Earlville, Ill., on double track on Sept. 23, 1980; the short westbound has just passed its counterpart, No. 160, receding to the horizon where a westbound empty hopper train's headlight has just appeared. On the point of 161 is F45 6608, constructed in July 1969 as GN 435. The big cowl unit was returned to the lessor in 1984, ending up for a time on the Utah Railway, a coal-carrying shortline in its namesake state. The stately little Earlville depot was in CB&Q days a stop for such secondary trains as the *American Royal Zephyr* and *Ak-Sar-Ben Zephyr* as well as for selected BN runs for the short time the road operated intercity passenger trains.—STEVE SMEDLEY

We're at milepost 27 on famous Naperville Curve on Saturday, Feb. 29, 1992. There's no commuter rush today, but activity on the "speedway" this afternoon is hardly disappointing. A somewhat tardy eastbound *California Zephyr* on track 1 is accelerating from its Naperville stop as a merchandiser bird-dogs along track 2 in preparation for crossing to track 1 behind the *CZ*, thus clearing the center track for the westbound *California Zephyr*. Track 1 has a yellow indication—the "normal" aspect at this location—but shortly it will blink green for an oncoming westbound suburban train. BN's Chicago-Aurora corridor is often cited as one of the best railroad main lines in North America for train-watching. It features variety (BN, Southern Pacific, Amtrak and Metra, with foreign-road power from the likes of Grand Trunk Western and Santa Fe) and traffic density (over 100 movements during a 24-hour weekday) and is quite photogenic (quaint depots with flower gardens and a tree-lined right-of-way).—MIKE SCHAFER

The highest traffic density on BN—over 100 trains in a 24-hour period—can be found along the 38-mile three-track raceway between Chicago and Aurora, Ill. Known by a variety of names: the "east end" by BN employees; "The Land of the Burlingtons" by commuters, in reference to a 1969 CB&Q advertising campaign; and the "third rail" to some local train-watchers. Now the 1st Subdivision of the Galesburg Division, the "triple track" is a BN showcase for commuter, intermodal and merchandise train operations. Amtrak also puts in an appearance with four trains daily, and Southern Pacific exercises its trackage rights with Kansas City traffic.

Commuter service along this line has always been one of many firsts: the first "gallery"-style bilevel car in regular service (1950), the first all-air conditioned commuter fleet (also in 1950) and the most passengers carried on a single train (3,500,

carried in bilevels pulled by 4-8-4 No. 5632 during CB&Q's centennial in 1964).

Always a source of pride for the railroad, CB&Q considered the service of such importance that it formed the Suburban Services Department in 1969. Commuter service today is operated by BN under contract to Metra, Chicago's commuter-rail authority. The rebuilt E8 and E9 units (replaced by new F40PH-2M's) that formerly pulled the trains and the bilevel cars are owned by the West Suburban Mass Transit District, formed in 1970. BN provides the fastest scheduled service carrying the most passengers on a single line in Metra territory.

Fourteenth Street Yard, just west of Chicago Union Station (opened in 1925), is home to the commuter fleet (referred to as "dinkies" by crews) when not laying over at Hill Yard in Aurora. The yard is also the site of a new $20 million shop opened in 1988 to maintain the bilevels and their locomotives.

West of downtown is Cicero Yard and Clyde diesel facility, nucleus of BN's Chicago freight operations. The yard, which occupies 242 acres, was extensively updated by the Q in the 1950's. Its 42-track hump handles merchandise traffic, but the real story at Cicero is intermodal—it is one of BN's busiest terminals. BN moves merchandise, U.S. Mail, United Parcel Service and double-stack container traffic out of Cicero, as well as standard and TOFC/COFC intermodal business.

The chore of ensuring that the First Subdivision is operated safely and efficiently falls to dispatchers at Galesburg, who relocated from Cicero in 1986. Operations are controlled by a computerized dispatching machine. Maximum speed for passenger trains is 65 mph, freight 50.

BN track ownership begins near Roosevelt Road south of Union Station. At 14th Street, trains swing west on a 9-degree curve—tightest in the commuter district; no other curves exceed 2 degrees. At Union Avenue Tower, the two tracks expand to four briefly and junction with the South Branch wye and St. Charles Air Line, a connection to Illinois Central's lakefront line. Five miles west is Cicero Yard, where three-track operation begins. Track 1 is the farthest north and generally is reserved for westbounds; track 2 is the famous center track, used by express commuters, many intermodal and merchandise trains and Amtrak, all in either direction. Track 3 is the southernmost, generally used by eastbounds.

All three tracks are bidirectionally signaled, and

LEFT: Many of the 1st Subdivision's 38 miles wedges its way through the city's prestigious western suburbs. This is the "Land of the Burlingtons," where sturdy, tidy brick depots of CB&Q heritage still serve their original purpose as gateways for rail passengers. Freights, such as this eastbound at Riverside in 1972, mix freely with "varnish," thanks to bidirectional signaling, numerous crossovers and CTC control.—MIKE SCHAFER ABOVE: The Chicago-Aurora line is the most-comprehensive of Metra's ten trunk routes in terms of schedule frequency and availability of express service. Its retirement imminent, E9 9916 races through Riverside with a westbound "dinky" in October 1991.—DAVID ALLERSON

there are many crossovers—two reasons why this line above all other Metra commuter routes in Chicagoland has the most-comprehensive commuter schedule patterns. In 1990, BN operated 815,259 commuter train-miles, serving approximately 24,739 commuters each weekday. Along the line's long straight stretches, it is frequently possible to glance down the tracks at rush hour and see three headlights coming west at once!

The triple track skirts to the south of BN's north side Cicero "hub center" (as the railroad refers to its intermodal terminals) then heads straight as an arrow through La Vergne, Berwyn and Riverside, crossing intersecting railroads only at grade separation—the Chicago Central at La Vergne, the busy Indiana Harbor Belt at Congress Park and the Elgin, Joliet & Eastern at Eola, near Aurora.

One of the charms of the speedway is its stations. In many Burlington communities, the central business district is literally divided by the main line, with renovated downtown buildings facing the tracks. Many of these communities retain their hulking brick CB&Q depots that have been renovated to preserve their classic look. Examples include River-

side, Hinsdale, Downers Grove and Naperville. Several locations have received new structures.

The western end of the commuter district is anchored by Naperville and Aurora. Naperville in the 1960's was a small community surrounded by cornfields. Now, the rural countryside has been transformed into a wealthy, sprawling suburban area. Just east of the Amtrak/Metra depot is famous Naperville Curve, where in 1946 the Exposition Flyer failed to heed restrictive signal indications and smashed into the rear of the (standing) Advance Exposition Flyer. The resultant crash killed 45—and ushered in strict structural standards for lightweight passenger cars used on Burlington lines, which is why to this day cars from other Metra lines cannot be mixed with those built to special specifications for Burlington service.

West of Naperville the tracks pass Naperville Auto Reload Center, which unloads shipments of imported cars that have arrived on BN, and also loads American-made vehicles for shipment.

The main crosses the Du Page River into Eola, where a small yard straddles the main line and the EJ&E crosses overhead; connecting tracks allow

interchange with BN, and this is to be the transfer point for a planned circumferential suburban passenger service that would use EJ&E tracks. Locals, work trains and switchers that work the yard and Naperville reload are based here. Some BN through freights also stop to pick up or set out.

From West Eola interlocking, the two tracks now used by commuter trains split to the north, while two freight/Amtrak mains parallel them two miles into Aurora. The freight tracks take a grade elevation through downtown, while dinkies gradually descend into Hill Yard and the new Aurora Transportation Center, rebuilt from Q's historic Aurora roundhouse and shop complex, where the first Vista-Dome car was built (1945). The old downtown Aurora depot saw its last train on Dec. 7, 1986.

In 1987, BN cut the triple track to double from West Eola into Aurora and closed RO Tower, where the main divides for Galesburg and the Twin Cities. Commuter trains tie up nights and weekends at Hill Yard. Amtrak, intermodal and merchandise trains simply cruise by, bound for other points, leaving behind the Land of the Burlingtons and its incredible fleet of trains.

LEFT: Following ferocious blizzards in January 1979, BN was forced to bring rotary snowplows, usually stationed farther west, to clear Illinois branch lines. On Jan. 27, BN's rare Bros plow 972556 (with blades parallel to the rails), along with an F7 to provide the rotary with power, are pushed by a pair of SD9's as it clears the Earlville-Rock Falls branch. BELOW: Crewmen watch carefully as the plow, built for the U.S. Army and sold—unused—to GN in 1954, inches its way toward Rock Falls. This blizzard was so intense that Santa Fe was forced to move a rotary in from Albuquerque to clear its branch to Pekin, Ill.—BOTH PHOTOS, JOE McMILLAN

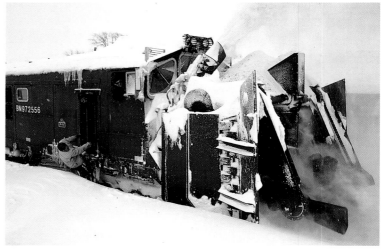

LEFT: BN's route to the southern Illinois coal fields and Paducah, Ky., may be one of the road's more unremarked main lines, perhaps because it angles off through remote areas of Illinois, avoiding major population centers. Only one daily freight operates each way between Galesburg and Paducah, Ky, over the 9th Subdivision, although there is quite a bit of coal traffic generated by mines with classic names like "Orient No. 6" and "Old Ben No. 26." CB&Q first penetrated southern Illinois in 1909, when the Q obtained trackage rights over 16 miles of the Chicago & Eastern Illinois between Neilson (Marion) and West Vienna, from which new construction brought the railhead into Metropolis, on the Ohio River, Oct. 15, 1910. The line continued on to Paducah, Ky. offering the Q access to the coal fields as well as a gateway to the Southeast, in particular with the Nashville, Chattanooga & St. Louis. Exercising the C&EI trackage rights, a quintet of SD7 and SD9's led by SD7 6045 sets the windows of the old depot at Goreville, Ill., shuddering as they drag 98 hopper cars through town on a 10-degree February day in 1972.—DON CRIMMIN

ABOVE: An empty coal train led by SD40-2 7845 creeps north across the Illinois River Bridge of the Peoria & Pekin Union at Peoria in the spring of 1985. The train had been dumped the previous day at the Chicago & Illinois Midland's rail-to-water terminal at Havana, Ill., where the coal is transloaded to barges for the trip upriver to Chicago-area power plants. BN and C&IM swap empty trains for loaded ones on P&PU's double-track CTC main line near Creve Coeur, Ill., just across the river and below East Peoria. C&IM relays the coal trains to and from Havana, 38 miles.—STEVE SMEDLEY

FACING PAGE: Billowing thunderheads crown an evening vignette of bigtime railroading in smalltown mid-America in July 1981. A GE U30C and two EMD's storm west with a coal train through Albia, Iowa, junction point of the Des Moines branch with the Galesburg-Omaha main line. The BN main is separated through Albia, with the eastbound on the south side of town and the westbound on the north.—MIKE SCHAFER LEFT: Until 1980, BN based a 600-h.p. SW1 at Fort Madison, Iowa, to work the 53-mile branch to Stockport. Light rail and fragile bridges dictated the use of the lightweight switcher to reach one of the line's main customers, a cement supplier at Stockport. On March 9, 1980, the Stockport Job trundles along near Houghton, Iowa. The branch was abandoned later that year.—ALLEN RIDER

RIGHT: Although the Rochelle (Ill.) switcher—GP38-2 2292, ex-SLSF 437—has been put to bed for the night, blazing depot lights seem to indicate the freight agent is working late on this Sept. 9, 1986. The handsome brick-and-stucco depot where passengers once congregated to await their appointed *Zephyr* boarding times is typical of many ex-Q depots. Rochelle's importance in agricultural products, principally canning, still warrants two locomotives to be based here to switch local industry, the main line west (working a sand plant at Oregon and the Mount Morris branch) and the nearby branch to Rockford. In Q days, railroad-owned Burlington Trailways buses linked Rockford with Rochelle and Mendota, with buses scheduled to connect with various Burlington passenger trains. *Zephyr* services were heavily advertised in Rockford newspapers, and the city generated a substantial number of passengers, but they had to travel 25 miles to Rochelle or 50 miles to Mendota to board trains.—LLOYD RINEHART, LIGHTING ASSISTANCE BY MARK BROMAN AND MARK JONES

ABOVE RIGHT: As granger roads blanketing the Midwest, BN and Milwaukee Road crossed paths at numerous locales. Among the more-well-known was at Savanna, Ill., where BN's river line intersected Milwaukee Road's Chicago-Omaha/Kansas City route on the south side of town. On a crisp August morning in 1980, Savanna tower has given the go-ahead for back-to-back SD40-2's to tread southward across Milwaukee's double track. For both carriers, Savanna was once a crew-change point. Milwaukee had a major yard and—partially visible at right in this scene—locomotive terminal while BN fielded somewhat more-modest facilities.—JERRY PYFER ABOVE: Probably the most famous boat to ply the Mississippi in modern times is the *Delta Queen*, which, together with sister ship *Mississippi Queen*, are the last paddle-wheel steamboats carrying overnight passengers. A stroll on the *DQ*'s deck netted this interesting view of eastbound BN traffic near Savanna in 1980.—JERRY PYFER RIGHT: Gingerly treading on what could be thin ice, the photographer took advantage of a rare clear winter afternoon to record a stack train skating north along the Mississippi near Savanna in January 1990.—H. MICHAEL YUHAS

RIGHT: An eagle's-eye view of the BN river line at La Crosse (from Granddad Bluff) catches an eastbound angling around the east side of the city on a clear spring day in 1980. BN's North La Crosse facilities are visible in the far distance as is the Grand Crossing interlocking tower where BN intersects the Milwaukee Road/Amtrak Chicago-Twin Cities main. Originally, CB&Q's River Line passed through downtown La Crosse on a congested right-of-way that included 29 grade crossings and a stretch of street running through the downtown area. In 1940, a new bypass opened, complete with a handsome stone passenger depot that served until Amtrak; it stood just south of the location of the train in this scene. The bypass allowed *Zephyr* running times to be reduced by 15 minutes, thus making the north-bound *Morning Zephyr* the fastest train in the U.S. in terms of end-to-end running time. BELOW: All along the River Line, the BN crosses several Mississippi tributaries. North of La Crosse, a westbound speeds across the Black River on an April afternoon in 1980.—BOTH PHOTOS, MIKE SCHAFER

MORRIS HOBSON
BN engineer, La Crosse, Wis.

*B*urlington Northern's 427-mile former-CB&Q route between Chicago and St. Paul is a scenic delight. For 286 miles, from Savanna, Ill., to St. Paul, the railroad follows the contours of the Mississippi River. Burlington advertised this route to potential passengers as "Where Nature Smiles 300 Miles." The passenger trains are gone, but there are upwards of 30 freights that now ply the line; let's take a ride on one between La Crosse and Northtown Yard at Minneapolis, the Third Subdivision of the Galesburg Division.

Our journey begins at North La Crosse, a crew-change point. La Crosse itself is a beautiful city, nestled deep in the Mississippi River Valley. It is also home to preserved Burlington 4-6-4 4000, displayed in Copeland Park. This cold January evening we are aboard westbound train 241, a Galesburg-Northtown drag freight. In late 1991, BN instituted precision scheduling of its trains for manifest and intermodal traffic, with trains targeted to stay within a 30-minute window of arrival and departure times. Unfortunately, tonight's 241 is running about eight hours off its new schedule. With no speed-restricted cars, we are allowed a maximum of 60 mph over the subdivision, with tonight's 4,195-ton train of 38 loads, 17 empties, two SD40-2's and a dead SD40-2 in tow.

We depart the yard heading north, passing frozen Lake Onalaska, then head uphill toward the 1,500-foot bridge over the Black River. From the bridge, we begin a slight downgrade on our 22-mile flight toward East Winona, location of a passing siding and the interchange with Green Bay & Western. Our route is double track nearly all the way to St. Paul, with a few short stretches of single-track CTC.

At East Winona siding, we hold for No. 34, an auto-rack train bound for Cicero Yard, Chicago. Number 241's importance for local blocking shows as we make a 19-car set out and pick up 24 cars off the GB&W interchange following our meet with 34. In 1991, BN opened an intermodal terminal in Green Bay, with GB&W handling double-stack cars to and from East Winona.

After completing our work, we head toward the Twin Cities again, reaching double track at Winona Junction. There was once a depot here, with passengers for Winona proper met by a "Burlington bus" which carried them across the Mississippi to the Burlington depot in the Minnesota city; C&NW's Dakota

At 7:20 p.m., Aug. 29, 1989, the Mississippi River bluffs reflect the evening sun as St. Louis-Northtown *Expediter* 45 leaves the rails of the Galesburg Division behind at St. Croix interlocking near Hastings, Minn. Trailing Oakway SD60 9068 are 37 cars weighing 2,200 tons, cruising west on ex-CB&Q track 2 on joint BN/Soo trackage.—MIKE CLEARY

Division also crossed the Burlington at grade here.

East Winona reminds me of the great flood of 1965. In the spring of that year, rising waters washed out much of the CB&Q roadbed, including the GB&W crossing—and also the East Winona depot, which was never seen again. A temporary connecting track was built at Winona Junction so Burlington trains could use North Western to detour around the washouts. Just north of La Crosse, another temporary connection allowed Q trains to return to home rails.

We pass the Winona Junction detector with a "no defects" hail, then inspect three eastbound merchandisers highballing by in rapid succession. Near Fountain City we notice the site of a wreck which occurred in 1991. Backwash from a tow boat stranded on a sand bar undermined the right-of-way, and a freight hit the washout. The lead units made it over the damaged track before derailing, but the trailing unit, "Cat" engine 2000, and 29 cars landed in the river.

Leaving Fountain City, we cut across prairie for the next 16 miles to Alma. Grain elevators at the small town of Cochrane appear. Our train cruises into Alma, site of a power plant, and as we travel past Lock & Dam No. 4, I catch a glimpse of the Burlington Hotel—one of two that existed along our route.

Next, after Nelson, we head across a three-mile stretch of Mississippi backwaters leading to the former Milwaukee Road diamond at Trevino. The Milwaukee line from Chippewa Falls crossed the Q at grade here and then bridged the Mississippi on a pontoon [floating] bridge. The bridge was retired in 1952, and Milwaukee then began using trackage rights on our line from Winona to Trevino.

After crossing the clear waters of the Chippewa River on a single-track bridge, we curve into Pepin where the Mississippi widens to form Lake Pepin, birthplace of water skiing. For many crews, this part of the trip is the most enjoyable. During summer and fall nights, a full moon reflecting off the waters of Lake Pepin, broken occasionally by the white lights of anchored boats, is a sight to behold. In autumn, the view is even more spectacular with the colorful hues of leaves. Winter is not without its beauty either. The lake gradually freezes over, and bald eagles follow the formation of the ice, with the leading edge providing a place for them to swoop down and snatch fish.

After Bay City we head inland for 11 miles through Hager City to Diamond Bluff, where the tracks snuggle up to the river again for ten miles into Prescott. Here, the rails bridge the St. Croix River on single

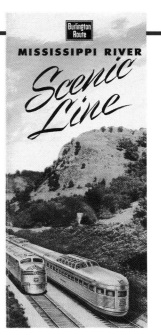

ABOVE: Crew's view from an eastbound freight near Hastings.—PAT MALONE ABOVE RIGHT: After the *Twin Zephyrs* received domes in 1947, Burlington issued a brochure describing its river route.—COLLECTION OF STEVE GLISCHINSKI

track and pass into Minnesota. A new lift bridge was installed here in 1984, replacing a swing span built in 1910. From Burns, the west side of the bridge where two main tracks begin, it's only three miles to St. Croix, where BN and Soo Line joint track begins.

Prior to the new bridge and the installation of CTC, a tower controlled St. Croix interlocking. Once past St. Croix, we enter the Twin Cities terminal, affectionately referred to by crews as the "Zoo." On eastbound trips, we sometimes were delayed several hours in the Zoo. Hunger often overtook us, so we'd radio the St. Croix operator, who would telephone a food order to the Pilot's Wheel restaurant in Prescott. When the swing bridge and a 10-mph curve through Prescott were still in place, the tracks curved right by the "Wheel" where we would slow down, grab the chicken or burgers and hand off the money, "on the fly."

Leaving St. Croix westbound, there are two separate main tracks. Number 1 (owned by Soo, formerly Milwaukee Road) heads up the bluffs on a steep 3½-mile grade. Number 2 (owned by BN) normally is the westward track. It is longer, hugging the river for five miles before curving away into Newport, where the two mains rejoin. BN dispatchers normally route us up track 1. Entering Newport we usually radio the BN

west hump dispatcher at Northtown, who gives us permission to use the main track from Mississippi Street in St. Paul to University Avenue in Minneapolis.

From Newport, we pass Soo's St. Paul Yard and the ex-CB&Q Daytons Bluff facility before we encounter the river once again at Hoffman Avenue, east of downtown St. Paul. At Division Street, we turn past the old leads to St. Paul Union Depot, then enter ex-NP trackage. The tracks pass through short tunnels under the former GN and C&NW mains at Westminster Street, all the while climbing a steep grade, emerging at the Mississippi Street crossovers. The top of the grade is at the old NP Como car shops. From Como it's a quick seven-mile trip to University Avenue and Northtown Yard, where our journey ends.

Running on the River Line is a great experience. Thanks to double track and the new precision scheduling, delays are minimal. The line is also rich with history: Old heads talk of "slow to 100 mph" orders and tell of silk trains that had priority over even the hottest passenger schedules. Just as exciting for me, however, are running double-stack and Expediter trains. It may not be the Morning Zephyr, but for me they are stirring reminders of the old high-speed Burlington tradition.

CHAPTER 9

DAKOTA DIVISION

THE HEART OF BN COUNTRY

For many years the "heart" of Burlington Northern was in the Twin Cities Region, most of which exists today as part of the Dakota Division, with headquarters in Fargo, N.D. Even though BN's corporate headquarters has moved from St. Paul to Fort Worth, it's difficult not to accept the upper Midwest as BN's heart and home. Three of the predecessor roads all had a large presence in the Twin Cities, with many yards and engine terminals. When BN was formed, the showcase Northtown Yard was built, which streamlined operations and eliminated most duplicate facilities—a textbook case in how the merger could be effective.

There are other arguments to make the case of the Dakota Division being BN's nucleus. Traffic was, and remains, diverse and heavy. Some of the heaviest tonnage is taconite lugged out of the iron range country of northern Minnesota to Lake Superior boats. Grain is another strong commodity. Fingerlike grain branch extensions protrude north from the former GN in North Dakota, serving as conduits to the main line, and major grain staging terminals are located at Willmar and Breckenridge. The division is also the final destination for many coal trains, with several on-line power plants, plus the Midwest Energy coal transloading terminal at Superior, Wis.

The divisional realignment in what was the Twin Cities Region is a good example of the complexity of tracing BN's divisions. Until 1991, much of the old Twin Cities Region was encompassed in the Lakes Division, itself an amalgamation of parts of the old Minnesota and Wisconsin divisions. In August 1991, the Lakes Division was eliminated, with other divisional boundaries extended. The Denver Division was extended east to Ravenna, Neb., from Alliance, formerly a part of the Nebraska Division. The Nebraska Division then came north to Aberdeen, S.D., and east to Willmar, Minn., taking parts of the Lakes Division. The Montana Division was expanded to include Minot, N.D. (on the old GN), Bismarck (NP) and Mobridge, S.D. (old Milwaukee Road), all once part of the Dakota Division. The eastern boundary of the Dakota Division was then expanded to include the Twin Cities and Twin Ports terminal areas.

Although the Twin Cities metro area has a population over two million, the area west of the Twin Cities is sparsely populated. Between Minneapolis and Seattle, the next city encountered with a population of over 100,000 is Spokane, Wash.—1,400 miles distant.

The area served by the Dakota Division is largely flatland, although northeastern Minnesota is covered with lakes and forests. As the railroad heads farther west, things flatten out considerably, but thanks to many rivers and streams, there are some large valleys which must be bridged—and some of the bridge structures are spectacular.

Besides the Twin Cities, the Dakota Division has two other busy terminals, both encompassing two cities in close proximity. Duluth, Minn., and Superior, Wis. (often referred to as the "Twin Ports"), is an area worthy of a book itself. The BN merger drasti-

cally reduced the number of yards, docks and interlocking towers that helped make the area a virtual maze of track. Yet the two cities are still filled with rail activity, made all the more fascinating by the presence of huge lake boats and ocean-going ships (referred to as "salties"). BN delivers a great deal of traffic to these vessels, including taconite, coal and grain, and it all comes through the Twin Ports. The steep hills in and around the area give you the feeling you're in San Francisco rather than only 150 miles from the Canadian border.

The other city pair—Fargo, N.D./Moorhead, Minn.—serves as a junction point for several former GN and NP routes, making it one of BN's busiest. The old GN main from Breckenridge to Grand Forks, the secondary line for the Surrey Cut-Off, and the former NP which serves as BN's main transcontinental route are among the rail lines passing through the terminal. BN's main yard is the former NP facility at Dilworth, three miles east of Moorhead.

Eastern gateway for the Dakota Division is at St. Croix interlocking at Hastings, Minn., where trains from/to Chicago and Galesburg come off the Galesburg Division. The other eastern terminus is at Superior (although a former NP branch once reached another 63 miles into the Badger State to reach Ashland), while the western outskirts are at Mandan (a 1,000-mile inspection point for coal trains) and Minot, N.D. A fourth state, South Dakota, is also represented, thanks to the former GN branches to Aberdeen and Huron, plus the Milwaukee branches

ABOVE: Serving as the eastern anchor in the mostly rural, seemingly infinite prairie country that dominates the Dakota Division are the Twin Cities of Minneapolis and St. Paul, Minn. Formerly corporate home for BN, the carrier still maintains a high profile here, at least in terms of train operations: Green diesels continuously thread the complex Twin Cities Terminal trackage with coal trains, ore Extras, grain trains and merchandise freights. Morning sun bathes downtown St. Paul on June 7, 1987, as the photographer, perched high on Daytons Bluff just east of downtown, records an eastbound BN coal train heading out of town for a trip down the Mississippi (background). No green on this train, though; leased Oakway units, led by SD60 9052, are in charge today. The state capitol can be seen at right in the background, and a portion of St. Paul Union Depot is visible directly behind the first span of the highway bridge over the Mississippi. This was the city that was home to James J. Hill, father of Burlington Northern.—MIKE CLEARY FACING PAGE, TOP: Fargo, N.D., serves as headquarters for the Dakota Division; nearby Dilworth Yard is a focal point for several ex-NP and GN routes.—STEVE GLISCHINSKI

LEFT: James J. Hill allowed only one structure on the GN to bear his name: the bridge across the Mississippi River in Minneapolis. The 2,300-foot span, better known as Stone Arch Bridge, took 19 months to build, in 1883-84; the first revenue train crossed the bridge on April 16, 1884. In 1965, Mississippi floods caused one arch to sink as a train passed over, closing the structure while the arch was reinforced with concrete. The sag can be detected just below the second and third units in this scene of an eastbound coal train on Sept. 21, 1979. Amtrak used the bridge to reach GN Station in Minneapolis. On April 25, 1981, the Duluth-bound *North Star* became the last regularly scheduled passenger train to cross it, after which passenger trains were rerouted; coal trains used it until 1982.—STEVE GLISCHINSKI BELOW: One of BN's earliest redevelopments was the redesign and reconstruction of Northtown Yard at Minneapolis. BN's largest classification facility, Northtown officially opened for business in October 1976 following piecemeal reconstruction. The yard originally was an NP facility. This view looks east on the evening of Jan. 25, 1975, toward the new hump. The hump tower is on the right, with the diesel shop, which opened that same year, hidden behind the hump to the left.—GERALD A. HOOK

and main line from Mobridge to Ortonville added in 1980 and 1982.

Today's Dakota Division encompasses three former divisions: the Minnesota, based in Minneapolis; Wisconsin, headquartered in Superior; and the old Dakota, which had offices in Fargo, where they remain today. All dispatching functions have been consolidated at the "White House" at Northtown (a white, windowless brick building adjacent to the yard). Before the consolidations, there were dispatchers offices at Superior, Grand Forks (moved in 1977) and Minot (moved in February 1984) in addition to Minneapolis.

In addition to the prime transcontinental route which slices right through the middle of the division, there are other main lines of note. The Seventh Subdivision between Coon Creek (seven miles west of Northtown) and Boylston, near Superior, sees not just BN trains, but also those of Soo Line and C&NW, both of which have trackage rights over this former GN route.

More ex-GN trackage heads west from Superior to Carlton, where the line splits, with one route heading for Staples. This ex-NP line, part of the Fourth Subdivision, is "dark" (unsignaled) territory, yet sees heavy traffic with coal trains destined for the Midwest Energy Terminal in Superior. There is also a large paper mill serviced by BN at Brainerd. Until

1969, NP ran RDC's over this route, referred to affectionately as the "Staples streetcars" which connected the Twin Ports to the *Mainstreeter* and *North Coast Limited* at Staples.

The 5th Subdivision heads northwest out of Carlton and serves as a prime route for ore traffic. At Brookston, the 6th Subdivision ore line heads north to the iron range, circling through the mining areas before returning to the 5th Sub main line at Gunn, near Grand Rapids. West of Gunn there is no ore, and the line passes through Indian reservations and other sparsely populated areas. Traffic on this part of the railroad is made up largely of coal trains destined for Minnesota Power & Light at Cohasset, and a Soo Line local which runs via BN trackage rights from Bemidji to Superior. Most of the general freight traffic on this line is paper-related, with large mills at Cloquet, Grand Rapids and Bemidji.

Another ex-GN "coal line" heads west from Minneapolis to Willmar, Breckenridge and Moorhead. This was the "Big G's" main line until the merger, when through traffic shifted to the NP. Today, it is the Ninth Subdivision, serving as a conduit for coal trains coming off the northern corridor at Moorhead, as well as numerous potash and grain moves. Trains from as far away as Tulsa, Kansas City and Lincoln come onto this line from the Nebraska Division at Willmar, moving northward via Sioux City, Iowa. Daily manifest freights operate in each direction between Northtown and Grand Forks via Willmar, as do through freights originating in Pasco, Wash.

In old Milwaukee Road territory, another coal train can be found—one of the few that do not originate in the Powder River Basin. Instead, these trains bring coal from the Knife River Coal Company lignite coal mine at Gascoyne, N.D., east 350 miles to the power plant at Big Stone City, S.D. The entire operation is a holdover from Milwaukee days. Keeping this plant open and supplied with coal is one of the primary reasons the State of South Dakota helped preserve this line, which also provides an outlet for South Dakota grain to reach Pacific Northwest ports.

For sheer volume of trains on the Dakota Division, the 22 miles of former NP from Fargo/Moorhead to Surrey Junction Switch at Casselton is not to be missed. This line, part of the 10th Subdivision, sees not only transcontinental traffic destined to/from the Surrey Cut-Off, but an immense number of coal trains off the northern corridor. It's not unusual for the dispatchers in Minneapolis to line up trains in "fleets" to get them through this funnel, first in one direction, then the other. Things aren't

BN's "bread and butter," coal and grain, are represented by the open and covered hoppers waiting for their next call from the transfer yard at the Northtown complex in Minneapolis. SW1000 No. 380 (rostered as an "SW10" on BN) is in charge of a switch job based out of Northtown's 35th Avenue yard tower. The locomotive is moving a cut of cars past BN's Grove Yard and the former NP passenger main, which led to GN's Minneapolis passenger station. The Minneapolis skyline, dominated by the IDS building, looms in the distance.—BRUCE GUSTAFSON

119

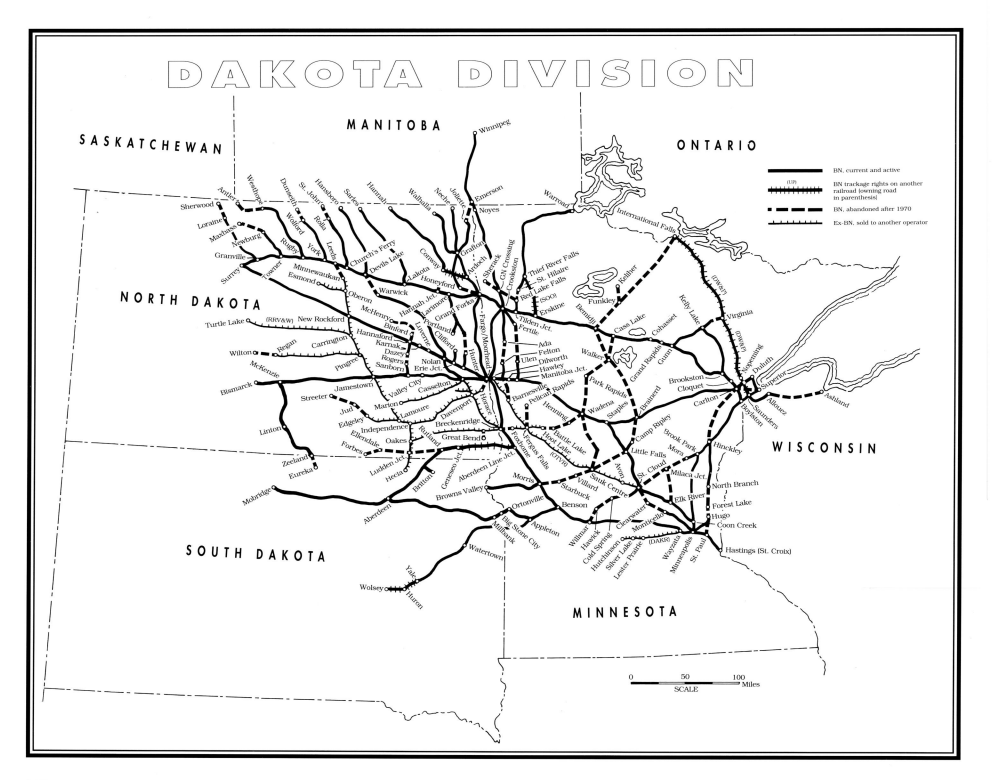

DAKOTA DIVISION

SASKATCHEWAN

MANITOBA

ONTARIO

NORTH DAKOTA

SOUTH DAKOTA

MINNESOTA

WISCONSIN

Winnipeg
Emerson
Noyes
Warroad
International Falls

Antler
Westhope
Sherwood
Loraine
Maxbass
Newburg
Granville
Surrey
Dunseith
St. John
Wolford
Rolla
Hansboro
Sarles
Hannah
Walhalla
Neche
Jolette

Rugby
York
Leeds
Church's Ferry
Devils Lake
Towner
Minnewaukan
Esmond
Oberon
Warwick
Lakota
Honeyford
Conway
Grafton
Ardoch
Sherack
GN Crossing
Crookston
Thief River Falls
St. Hilaire
Red Lake Falls
Erskine
(SOO)
Kelliher
Funkley
Bemidji
Cass Lake

Turtle Lake
(RRV&W) New Rockford
McHenry
Hannah Jct.
Larimore
Grand Forks
Tilden Jct.
Fertile
Fargo/Moorhead
Ada
Felton
Ulen
Dilworth
Hawley
Manitoba Jct.

Wilton
Regan
Carrington
Hannaford
Binford
Karnak
Dazey
Rogers
Sanborn
Nolan
Erie Jct.
Hunter
Portland
Clifford
Luverne

McKenzie
Bismarck
Streeter
Jamestown
Pingree
Valley City
Casselton
Horace
Barnesville
Pelican Rapids
Henning
Wadena
Staples
Brainerd
Carlton

Walker
Park Rapids
Grand Rapids
Gunn
Brookston
Cloquet

Kelly Lake
Cohasset
Virginia
Nopeming
Duluth
Superior
Ashland
Allouez
Saunders
Boylston

Linton
Jud
Marion
Lamoure
Davenport
Edgeley
Independence
Oakes
Rutland
Breckenridge
Great Bend

Zeeland
Eureka
Forbes
Ellendale
Hecla
Ludden Jct.
Geneseo Jct.
Britton
Aberdeen Line Jct.

Mobridge
Aberdeen
Browns Valley
Morris
Villard
Starbuck
Benson
Ortonville
Appleton
Big Stone City
Millbank

Fergus Falls
Foxhome
Hoot Lake (OTVR)
Battle Lake
Little Falls
Camp Ripley
Brook Park
Mora
Hinckley
North Branch
Forest Lake
Hugo
Coon Creek
Hastings (St. Croix)

Sauk Centre
Avon
St. Cloud
Milaca Jct.
Elk River
Clearwater
Monticello
Wayzata
Minneapolis
St. Paul

Willmar
Hawick
Cold Spring
Hutchinson
Silver Lake
Lester Prairie
(DAKR)

Watertown
Wolsey
Yale
Huron

Legend

— BN, current and active

(UP) BN trackage rights on another railroad (owning road in parenthesis)

- - - BN, abandoned after 1970

Ex-BN, sold to another operator

0   50   100
SCALE   Miles

Dakota Division abandonments and additions

Manitoba
Emerson Junction-U.S. Border, ex-NP, 3 miles, 1980

Minnesota
Princeton-Milaca, ex-GN, 13 miles, 1972
Little Falls-Villard, ex-NP, 51 miles, 1972
Park Rapids-Cass Lake, ex-GN, 49 miles, 1972
Red Lake Falls-Sherack, ex-NP, 31 miles, 1972
Carthage(Grand Forks)-Crookston, ex-NP, 24 miles, 1973
Downer-Glyndon, ex-GN, 9 miles, 1974
Henning-Wadena, ex-NP, 16 miles, 1975
Monticello-Clearwater, ex-GN, 12 miles, 1975
Wrenshall-Superior (Wis.), ex-NP, 15 miles, 1975
Sauk Centre-Long Prairie, ex-GN, 18 miles, 1976
Riverside Junction-New Duluth, ex-NP, 4 miles, 1976 (this
    line donated to City of Duluth and operated as the Lake
    Superior & Mississippi tourist line)
Carlton-West Duluth, ex-NP, 15 miles, 1976 (included Mil
    waukee Road trackage rights)
Hinckley-Moose Lake, ex-NP, 32 miles, 1977
Battle Lake-Henning, ex-NP, 16 miles, 1978
Moose Lake-Carlton, ex-NP, 22 miles, 1980
Foxhome-Breckenridge, ex-NP, 12 miles, 1980
Funkley-Kelliher, ex-NP, 11 miles, 1980
Pelican Rapids-Fergus Falls, ex-GN, 21 miles, 1981
Barnesville-Downer, ex-GN, 4 miles, 1981
Starbuck-Villard, ex-NP, 15 miles, 1981
Brainerd (Davis Spur)-Camp Ripley, ex-NP, 20 miles, 1981
Key West-East Grand Forks, ex-NP, 10 miles, 1982
White Bear Lake-Stillwater, ex-NP, 12 miles, 1982 (first 6
    miles from Stillwater to Duluth Jct. donated to
    Minnesota Transportation Museum for operation as
    Stillwater & St. Paul tourist line)
Wadena-Long Prairie, ex-GN, 37 miles, 1983
Hoot Lake-Battle Lake, ex-NP, 16 miles, 1983
Morris-Starbuck, ex-NP, 19 miles, 1983
Fertile-Ulen, 31 miles, 1983
St. Cloud-Mora, ex-GN, 45 miles, 1983
St. Cloud-Clearwater, ex-GN, 8 miles, 1983
Wadena-Park Rapids, ex-GN, 34 miles, 1984
St. Clair Junction-Chisholm, ex-NP, 2 miles, 1984
Elk River-Princeton, ex-GN, 19 miles, 1984
Emmert Junction-Dormer Jct., ex-GN, 11 miles, 1984
Wacootah Siding-Virginia, ex-NP, 2 miles, 1984
Hopkins Junction-Hopkins, ex-GN, 3 miles, 1984
Carlton-Wrenshall, ex-NP, 5 miles, 1984
Brainerd to International Falls, ex-NP, 194 miles, 1985
Hawick-Willmar, ex-GN, 21 miles, 1985
Red Lake Falls-St. Hillaire, ex-GN, 11 miles, 1985
Forest Lake-Hugo, ex-NP, 7 miles, 1987
St. Paul-M&D Jct. (White Bear Lake), ex-NP, 7 miles, 1987
Hawick-Cold Spring, ex-GN, 19 miles, 1988
Forest Lake-North Branch, ex-NP, 17 miles, 1989
Ada-Felton, ex-GN, 13 miles, 1990

Ex-NP Cuyuna Iron Range Lines, joint with Soo Line,
abandoned 1987:
Deerwood-Trommald, 10 miles
Huntington Junction-Riverton, 2 miles
Ironton-Cuyuna, 5 miles

Trackage leased to Dakota Rail, Aug. 20, 1985:
Wayzata-Hutchinson, ex-GN, 44 miles

To Otter Tail Valley Railroad, October 27, 1986:
Moorhead-Avon, ex-NP, 171 miles (Fergus Falls-Avon 97-mile
    segment abandoned by OTVR, 1991)
Fergus Falls-Foxhome, ex-NP, 12 miles
Fergus Falls-Hoot Lake, ex-NP, 1.5 miles

North Dakota
Maxbass-Dunning, ex-GN, 5 miles, 1972
Rutland-Ludden Junction, ex-GN, 30 miles, 1974
Neche-Canadian Border, ex-GN, 1 mile, 1976
Blanchard-Mayville, ex-GN, 12 miles, 1976
Minnewauken-Brinsmade, 7 miles, 1976
Brinsmade-Leeds, ex-NP, 10 miles, 1977
Jamestown-Kloze, ex-Midland Continental, 6 miles, 1979
Ellendale-Forbes, ex-GN, 13 miles, 1980
Devils Lake-Warwick, ex-GN, 21 miles, 1980
Joliette-Pembina, ex-NP, 12 miles, 1980
Fairview Junction-Great Bend, ex-NP, 9 miles, 1981
Binford-McHenry, ex-GN, 12 miles, 1981
Newburg-Dunning, ex-GN, 6 miles, 1981
Golva-Montana Border, ex-NP, 7 miles, 1981
Wolford-Dunseith, ex-GN, 23 miles, 1982
Casselton-Amenia, ex-GN, 6 miles, 1982
Rolla-St. John, ex-GN, 7 miles, 1982

Grand Forks-Honeyford, ex-NP, 17 miles, 1983
Edgeley-Streeter, 39 miles, ex-NP, 1983
Ludden Junction-Ellendale, ex-GN, 20 miles, 1984
Beach-Golva, ex-NP, 13 miles, 1984
Truax-Truax Junction, ex-NP, 7 miles, 1984
Regan-Wilton, ex-NP, 12 miles, 1984
Loraine-Sherwood, ex-GN, 8 miles, 1984
Zap-Killdeer, ex-NP, 41 miles, 1984
Zeeland-South Dakota border (Eureka), ex-Milwaukee Road,
    6 miles, 1985
Westhope-Antler, ex-GN, 13 miles, 1985
Hunter-Blanchard, ex-GN, 10 miles, 1985
Mandan-Mott, ex-NP, 99 miles, 1986
Rogers-Dazey, ex-NP, 8 miles, 1988
Fargo-Horace, ex-NP, 8 miles, 1988
East Fairview-Watford City, ex-GN, 37 miles, 1992

Lines sold to Red River Valley & Western, July 19 and Aug.
29, 1987 (all ex-NP except Breckenrige-Wahpeton [Brushvale]-
Casselton-Chaffee, ex-GN):
East Breckenridge, Minn.-Wahpeton, N.D.-Brushvale, Minn.,
    12 miles
Wahpeton-Oakes, 74 miles
Oakes-Minnewaukan, 160 miles
Oberon-Esmond, 28 miles
Carrington-Turtle Lake, 85 miles
Pingree-Regan, 81 miles
LaMoure-Edgeley, 21 miles
Wahpeton-Casselton, 55 miles
Casselton-Marion, 60 miles
Chaffee Junction-Chaffee, 12 miles
Horace-Independence, 72 miles

BN also transferred 12.6 miles of trackage rights to RRV&W
over the Soo Line from Sheldon to Lucca.

South Dakota
Hayti-Watertown, ex-GN, 16 miles, 1972
Yankton-milepost 4.1, ex-GN, 4 miles, 1976
Minnekahta-Hot Springs, ex-CB&Q, 12 miles, 1977
Wentworth-Hayti, ex-GN, 49 miles, 1980
Yankton-Irene, ex-GN, 17 miles, 1981
Hill City-Keystone, ex-CB&Q, 9 miles, 1981
Sioux Falls-Irene, ex-GN, 41 miles, 1981
Eureka-Linton, ND, 49 miles, purchased from Milwaukee
    Road 1980; Eureka-Zeeland, N.D., 19 miles,
    abandoned 1985
Madison-Wentworth, 8 miles, purchased from Milwaukee
    Road, 1981
Custer-Deadwood, ex-CB&Q, 66 miles, 1983
Kirk-Lead, ex-CB&Q, 3 miles, 1983
Edgemont-Custer, ex-CB&Q, 42 miles, 1986

Former Milwaukee Road lines acquired by State of South
Dakota and operated by BN beginning in 1981.
Acquired by S.D. 1980:
Jarrett Junction-Britton, 5 miles
Mitchell-Sioux City, 137 miles
Mitchell-Aberdeen, 129 miles
Canton-Mitchell, 80 miles
Mitchell-Chamberlain, 68 miles (operation taken over by
    Dakota Southern Railway, May 15, 1987)
Canton-Sioux Falls, 21 miles

Acquired by S. D. 1982:
East Wye Switch (Elk Point)-Canton 50 miles (operation on
    this line turned over to D&I railroad on Nov. 1, 1986,
    D&I also operates over BN line from Sioux City to East
    Wye Switch and Canton to Sioux Falls)
Terry, Mont.-Ortonville, Minn. (state line), 480 miles
Beresford Junction (Hawarden)-Beresford, ex-C&NW, 17
    miles, acquired by State of South Dakota 1980 and
    operation begun by BN in 1981; operation turned over to
    D&I Railroad Nov. 1, 1986.

Sold to Dakota, Minnesota & Eastern Railroad, 1991:
Huron-Yale, ex-GN, 13 miles (BN retains operating rights)

Wisconsin
State Line-Central Avenue, ex-NP, 10 miles, 1975
Minnesota and Wisconsin drawbridges between Superior and
    Duluth, ex-NP, 2 miles, 1984 (bridges locked open noon,
    June 1, 1984)
Superior-Ashland, ex-NP, 63 miles, 1985 (last run from
    Superior to Poplar, Aug. 22, 1985)
Boylston-Dedham, ex-GN, 6 miles, 1988 (line relocated to for-
    mer Soo Line right-of-way and new connection track)
Winona Bridge (Winona Bridge Terminal Co.) 1 mile, 1990—
    destroyed by fire 1989

ABOVE: Before the 1987 sale of 648 miles of North Dakota and Minnesota trackage to Red River Valley & Western, GP9-powered local freights were common sights on North Dakota branch lines. On the former NP Fargo & Southwestern branch, a typically short local heads east past the grain elevator at Jud, N.D., in a classic North Dakota scene on May 16, 1978. Unfortunately, it was dozens of little lines like these that filled abandonment (or sale) lists like that at left.—JOHN BJORKLUND

quite so busy on the GN lines out of Grand Forks. This city is largely bypassed by BN's main routes, thanks to the Surrey Cut-Off. Between Fargo, Grand Forks and Minot there isn't much through traffic, although Amtrak's *Empire Builder* continues to traverse these lines. Grand Forks does see coal trains and also serves as a hub of secondary and branch-line train activity.

Trains from the Dakota Division also head north into Canada, using the 90-mile 22nd Subdivision line from Crookston to the Canadian border at Noyes, Minn. Once at the border, BN interchanges cars to Canadian National, with which the railroad has a haulage agreement to take them into Winnipeg. BN's Canadian subsidiary, Burlington Northern Manitoba, Ltd., owns freight terminals in Winnipeg and still holds seldom-used trackage rights over CN between that city and the international boundary at Emerson. BNML even has its own motive power, painted BN colors but carrying its own number and small "BNML" initials on the cab.

From the clear, blue "10,000 lakes" of Minnesota to the gently rolling prairies of the Dakotas, transcontinental trains roll across this huge expanse of the Middle West. The Dakota Division serves as the bridge between the metroplex of Chicago and the vastness of the Montana Division, which takes the trains on to the mountains.

LEFT: Passing through the tunnel under Westminster Tower in St. Paul is eastbound intermodal train 4YA, bound for Chicago on Dec. 27, 1988. GP50 3120 is riding ex-NP rails, while the tower above the train is on former GN trackage, used primarily by passenger trains until Amtrak. As late as September 1961, 36 passenger trains of five railroads passed Westminster Tower each weekday. It was the last interlocking tower still extant in the Twin Cities, thanks to a new role housing signal equipment.—DAN POITRAS
ABOVE: Between Division Street in St. Paul and the ex-NP Como Car Shops, six miles to the west, westbound trains face a gradual uphill climb. Before track changes permitted higher-speed operations and trains could get a "run" at the hill, BN assigned two units, usually Geeps, to assist heavy westbound trains upgrade. In September 1979, a westbound led by U25B 5422 is being helped up the grade by a pair of GP10's, emerging from the tunnel at Westminster Street.—STEVE GLISCHINSKI

On Dec.12, 1986, one of the heaviest loads ever carried by rail crosses the ex-NP Grassy Point Drawbridge between Duluth, Minn., and Superior, Wis., behind GP10 1400 and GP20 2037. The train is moving a 750-ton reactor, built by Japan Steel Works, out of the Twin Ports to an oil refinery owned by Newgrade Energy, Inc. of Regina, Sask. The load weighed 1,509,150 pounds and is being carried on a special Schnabel car built by Krupp for CE Power Systems to carry large loads such as this. The car has 36 wheels, is 303 feet long and weighs 740,800 pounds. The move pictured actually began Dec. 10 when Soo pulled the reactor out of the Duluth Port Terminal one mile to interchange with BN. BN took the car to interchange with CP Rail, moving at 15 mph during daylight hours only. Highway overpasses, switch stands and crossing signals all had to be checked to ensure they did not foul the unique wide swing of the car.—ROBERT C. ANDERSON

The Lake Superior Terminal & Transfer Co. in Superior, Wis., was just another of the hundreds of small terminal railroads that once thrived in cities throughout the U.S. Organized in 1884, it was owned by NP, GN, Omaha Road (Chicago & North Western) and Duluth, South Shore & Atlantic (after 1961, Soo Line). LST&T toiled in obscurity through most of its existence, but after 1967 it gained in prominence, primarily because the little line's locomotives retained Great Northern's classic Omaha orange and Pullman green paint scheme. BN became the majority owner (owning 66.67 percent) of LST&T after the merger, and eventually took over servicing the Transfer's six units (five NW2's and an SW1200) at its ex-GN Belknap Street roundhouse, closing the LST&T roundhouse a block away. But BN never touched the units' paint, and they retained their GN styling until BN took over switching duties in Superior in 1985, ending LST&T operations. LST&T switchers clumped along on unsteady track among old waterfront warehouses, passing lake boats waiting to be loaded, or in storage. LST&T NW2 104 passes the *John Sherwin* stored on the Superior waterfront in the final days of the road's independent operation in June 1985. The 806-foot lake boat was built in 1958 for the Interlake Steamship Company, managed by Pickands Mather & Co.—ROBERT M. BALL

LEFT: Train NT 400, an "all-rail" ore train destined for Granite City, Ill., has just left the National Steel Pellet Co. plant at Keewatin, Minn., on July 4, 1977. The train includes many of the 70-ton ore cars—which could carry about 60 tons of taconite pellets (versus 70 tons of natural ore)—that BN has replaced with 100-ton cars. U28C 5652 leads the way; GE's were common power on ore runs in the late 1970's.—ROBERT C. ANDERSON FACING PAGE: "Big Sky Blue" SD7's switch GN's ore dock at Allouez, Wis., in May 1969. Superior was one of the last terminals with power still painted in GN colors.—RON LUNDSTROM

about 55 percent of U.S. production in the mid-20th Century. Natural ore was easy and cheap to mine in open pits, but with the decline in supply, the railroads faced the prospect of losing the ore business, and northeastern Minnesota, whose economy was closely tied to iron ore mining, faced economic depression. Their savior turned out to be taconite, a flint-like, low-grade iron-bearing rock found in abundant supply in the region. Although initially not thought to be commercially viable, researchers at the University of Minnesota Mines Experiment Station in Minneapolis developed a method of upgrading and pelletizing the rock that made the ore more attractive to steel companies.

Taconite has several qualities that give it an advantage over natural ore. The consistency of natural ore approximates that of dirt, which tends to "cake up" in blast furnaces. Taconite, after molded into pellets, reduces more quickly and uniformly to molten iron. For railroads, the introduction of taconite pellets made transportation easier: The pellets do not freeze easily, like natural ore did, which required expensive thawing operations during cold-weather months. Since pellets are easy to stockpile at lakeside storage facilities, railroads began year-round operations between the pellet plants and lake ports; previously operations were severely curtailed when Great Lakes harbors froze over.

In the 1950's, Reserve Mining Company and Erie Mining Company constructed large plants on the eastern Mesabi Range that proved the success of the taconite process. In 1966, two taconite plants were built along GN lines, both operated by the Hanna Mining Company. The Butler Plant was constructed near Nashwauk and began production in March 1967. The National Steel Plant near Keewatin, began production in August 1967.

In 1976, the Hibtac Plant opened near Hibbing;

Some of the heaviest tonnage handled by Burlington Northern originates in northeastern Minnesota, where the railroad serves as a "conveyor belt" between two taconite-producing plants on the Mesabi Iron Range and the ore docks at Allouez (Superior), Wis. At Superior, ore is transloaded into lake boats for shipment to steel mills in Indiana, Ontario and Michigan. BN also operates all-rail ore movements, primarily from National Steel at Keewatin, Minn., to Granite City Steel, Granite City, Ill.

BN-served ore plants are located on the western part of the Mesabi Iron Range, which covers an area approximately 100 miles long and 1 1/2 to 3 miles wide, with iron formations extending to a depth of 600 feet. Predecessor Great Northern was one of the larger ore carriers in the Lake Superior mining district. GN operations centered at Kelly Lake, while Northern Pacific serviced the smaller Cuyuna Iron

Range in the area of Crosby/Ironton, which it served jointly with the Soo Line.

For GN, the movement of iron ore was among the heaviest tonnage carried in terms of sheer weight, and during World War II, when arms and aircraft production were at their zenith, millions of tons of ore were handled. The Cuyuna Range did not see the kind of tonnage ore movements the Missabe Range did, with the ore being relatively low-grade. After the war, heavy traffic continued, with the peak year being 1953, when over 35 million tons were handled by the two companies. Curiously, neither railroad assigned its largest steam power to ore movements, although GN did assign some of its 2-6-8-0 and 2-8-8-0 articulateds.

World War II and the postwar boom years greatly accelerated the depletion of known high-grade natural iron ore deposits in Minnesota, which supplied

BN built a six-mile spur from Kelly Lake to serve the facility. The Butler Plant shut down permanently in 1985, due to the bankruptcy of Wheeling-Pittsburgh Steel. Hibtac and National remain as the only two taconite plants served by BN. The pellets from Hibtac go primarily to Burns Harbor, Ind. (Bethlehem Steel) and Hamilton, Ont. (Stelco Steel). National Pellets go primarily to Great Lakes Steel (Detroit) and to Granite City.

Natural ore movements are now non-existent, as are all mining operations once served by NP and Soo Line on the Cuyuna Range. NP's Superior ore dock, built in 1913, now sits abandoned, with all BN operations centering at the ex-GN facility in Allouez, Wis. Because of the varied chemical and physical properties of the natural ore (there were about 55 different grades), the ores were blended at the dock to attain the most-suitable grade for a particular blast furnace by mixing cars of different grades of ore and dumping them into dock pockets for the appropriate boat. The last natural ore was shipped through Allouez in 1979.

In 1966, GN spent $8 million to construct a pellet-handling facility adjacent to its ore docks which included on-land car dumpers, storage facilities and conveyor belts to the docks. Under BN, the company spent more than $60 million to handle more pellets and construct a shiploading facility; no longer do locomotives switch cars on top of the ponderous docks—conveyor belts and concrete silos handle this work today.

GN had four conventional-design ore docks at Allouez which were once the largest of their kind in the world. Dock No.1, last used in 1988, lasted the longest. Dock 2 was taken out of service in 1980, and Dock 3 was the last timber dock on the Great lakes when it was dismantled in 1965. Dock 4, built in 1911, was taken out of service in 1974.

BN's "ore country" encompasses all ex-GN trackage, stretching west from Superior through Carlton to Brookston, where trains destined for Hibtac or National swing north to Kelly Lake. At Hibtac, trains can make a loop and return via the same route, but no such loop exists at National, so trains continue west to the junction point of Gunn, east of Grand Rapids, where they turn back east toward Brookston and Superior, completing a huge circle.

Iron-ore movements on GN lines were in the hands of F-units since the end of steam in the 1950's, while NP lines were handled by Alco and EMD road-switchers. F's continued to be the power of preference the first couple of years after the merger, but were gradually replaced by GP35/38's, SD45's and later the ubiquitous SD40-2's and SD60M's, which handle pellet trains today. SD40-2's regularly assigned to ore service served as testbeds for BN's experimental ARES satellite dispatching technology (see Chapter 7). BN has also updated its pellet-carrying car fleet, taking delivery of hundreds of new 100-ton ore cars during the 1970's and 1980's.

Burlington Northern pellet trains (as well as coal trains) are operated as true unit trains, with consists remaining intact for complete trips. This, combined with the remoteness and beauty of the area, make BN's pellet-train operations among its most fascinating.—Steve Glischinski and Robert C. Anderson

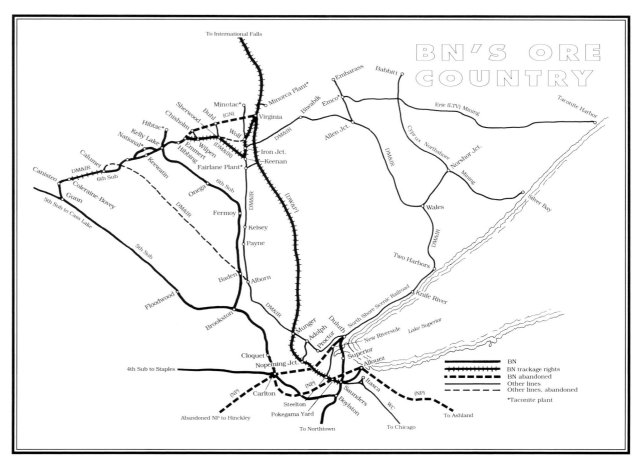

GN owned 10 of the 13 examples of EMD's unique NW5 road-switcher, and this fleet remained intact right into 1979, when one was sold. The units were designed for branch-line service with Blomberg trucks, a steam boiler for passenger service and light weight: only 216,000 pounds. In the 1970's, the 1000-h.p. NW5's found a home on branch and secondary lines in Minnesota and North Dakota; by 1981 six NW5's were assigned to the Twin Cities Region. The 986 and 990 were based in St. Cloud, Minn., with the remaining four assigned to Grand Forks, N.D. Two of these units were used on the ex-NP Oakes (N.D.) branch west out of Breckenridge, Minn. The NW5's came to this line after BN abandoned its ex-GN line from Rutland, N.D., to Ludden Junction, where it crossed C&NW's Oakes branch at grade en route to Ellendale and Forbes. A new connection to the C&NW was built and the line east of Ludden was torn up. BN continued to serve Forbes by using the Breckenridge-Oakes branch, then heading south on C&NW to Ludden Junction and west to Forbes. Since C&NW's line was in very poor shape (C&NW was using sure-footed Alco RSD4's and 5's on the line at the time), BN brought in its lightest power other than SW1's: the NW5's. The NW5-powered local operated six days a week: on Mondays and Thursdays it ran west from Breckenridge to Oakes; on Tuesdays and Fridays it would make a round trip to Ellendale and/or Forbes (the Ellendale-Forbes line was abandoned in 1980), and on Wednesdays and Saturdays the train would return to Breckenridge. On Feb. 14, 1981, the 992 and 995 are heading east for home, passing the wye at Fairview Junction, N.D., where a seven-mile branch headed south to Great Bend.—STEVE GLISCHINSKI

BELOW: Ten years after the BN merger, an eastbound coal train is cruising through Taylor, N.D., on the ex-NP northern corridor main July 9, 1980. Behind the lead BN units are three Milwaukee Road SD40-2's, part of a pool arrangement between the Milwaukee and BN. To serve the Wisconsin Power plant near Portage, Wis., a coal train originated in the Powder River Basin and traveled Milwaukee Road rails east of Miles City, Mont. Both BN and Milwaukee power ran through to the plant, with the result that both roads' locomotives appeared on the other to equalize motive-power horsepower hours. This trackage is now part of the Montana Division.—JOHN BJORKLUND

RIGHT: On Feb. 2, 1982, GP20 2009 is pushing—and pushing and pushing—a plow through a snow-covered cut on the Wayzata-Hutchinson (Minn.) branch at Silver Lake. The previous day the train crew had begun their journey at Willmar, running east on the main line to Wayzata with the 2009 and GP9 1808, then headed west on the branch with 14 cars for Hutchinson. The train tied up for the night at Lester Prairie, assaulting the Silver Lake cut the next day. The 2009 and plow cut off from the rest of the train and took numerous runs at the drifted snow. It took several hours before the plow was finally able to break through, grab the rest of the consist and reach Hutchinson, eight miles west. BN sold this line to Dakota Rail, Inc. on Dec. 1, 1985.—STEVE GLISCHINSKI

ABOVE: On the ex-GN branch between Watertown and Huron, S.D., signposts and telegraph poles seem to outnumber trees as a wayfreight pokes along at Yale on May 18, 1978. The 13-mile segment from Yale into Huron was sold to the Dakota, Minnesota & Eastern—a regional spinoff formed in 1986 from former C&NW lines—in 1991, with BN retaining operating rights. DM&E utilizes trackage rights for the remaining 57 miles from Yale into Watertown.—JOHN BJORKLUND

ABOVE: Triple SD40-2's hustle west near Hawley, Minn., in June 1986, with train 103. At the time, this was a Chicago-Seattle run, replacing old train 97. In 20 miles, the train will pause for a crew change at Dilworth. In the Hawley area the tracks swing north and south to follow the course of the Buffalo River through a series of cuts and fills which permit trains to maintain high speed and avoid grade crossings. LEFT: The old NP depot at Staples, Minn., is the backdrop for SD60M 9230, ready to depart east with a coal Extra for Northern States Power's Sherco generating plant at Becker, Minn., on March 25, 1990. Staples is the first division point west of the Twin Cities on the ex-NP main, as well as the junction with the Fourth Subdivision main to Carlton. Coal trains bound for Becker and the Midwest Energy Terminal in Superior frequent Staples, still a passenger stop for Amtrak's *Empire Builder*—BOTH PHOTOS, MIKE CLEARY

On Independence Day, 1980, another in the constant parade of BN coal trains marches over the Valley City bridge across the valley of the Sheyenne River.—JOHN BJORKLUND

North Dakota. Just the name conjures up images of a flat, barren prairie landscape, buffeted by an endless wind. Although this image is certainly correct for many parts of the "Peace Garden State," there is another side. Interlaced throughout North Dakota are streams and rivers that have cut deep valleys into the landscape—rivers and valleys that later challenged the builders of GN and NP. To cross these natural boundaries, they built bridges. Big ones.

There are four large steel trestles that offer a variety of photo opportunities. At Valley City, 58 rail miles west of Fargo on the ex-NP main line, a 3,737-foot-long bridge crosses the valley of the Sheyenne River. At its highest point, the bridge looms 160-feet above the river. Access to this span is easy: The city park under the south end is an excellent vantage point.

Just 30 miles north of Valley City is the small community of Luverne, located along the former-GN Fargo-Minot Surrey Cut-Off. Just west of Luverne, builders of the Cut-Off faced the same obstacle NP had to the south: the Sheyenne River valley. To cross the valley, they constructed a 2,741-foot-long steel bridge. Since the Cut-Off is on BN's transcontinental freight route, Luverne trestle does not suffer from a lack of traffic.

Just west of Surrey, where the Cut-Off joins the original main line, is the one-time GN hub of Minot. About three miles west is the Gasman Coulee Bridge, probably the most famous of North Dakota bridges. GN and even BN used the bridge as a location for publicity photos many times. At 1,792 feet long and 117 feet high, Gasman Coulee entered service in January 1899, replacing a huge wood structure.

About 110 miles south of Minot is Bismarck, the state capital. Bismarck stands on the east side of the Missouri River, which separates it from the City of Mandan, on the west bank. Connecting the two is the former NP main line, which crosses the Missouri on a 1,500-foot-long, 70-foot-high bridge. Completed Oct. 27, 1882, the bridge cost more than $1 million, but saved NP the time and expense of ferrying trains across the river in summer and building tracks across the ice on the frozen river in winter. The high bluffs on the Bismarck side of the bridge make photographing eastbound trains easy. With the elimination of the Lakes Division in 1991, the Dakota Division and Montana Divisions were extended eastward. As a result, this bridge is now a part of the Montana Division.

There are many other smaller bridges on the BN, plus interesting country around the Badlands that help dispel the image of North Dakota as being just "flat prairie."

CHAPTER 10

MONTANA DIVISION

ACROSS THE "BIG SKY"

If you long for the wide-open country of the "wild West," the Montana Division offers it. From the flatlands of South Dakota to the mountains of Marias Pass, the Montana Division passes through some of the least populated, but most-beautiful areas of Western U.S.

Although the name of the division would seem to indicate it serves mountainous territory (Montana is Spanish for "mountain"), hundreds of miles of track running across seemingly endless prairies is probably a truer picture of the majority of the division. Major commodities originated on this division include lumber, grain, wood chips, aluminum and, of course, the ever-present coal.

The Montana is one of BN's larger divisions in terms of sheer distance from one end to the other. Between Minot, N.D., and Boyer siding in Sandpoint, Idaho, the transcontinental main stretches for 869 miles—all under the juridiction of this one division. It wasn't always this way, of course. When BN was utilizing the regional concept, Montana was divided: the Billings Region managed mainly ex-NP lines from Sandpoint to Jamestown, N.D., while the Seattle Region took care of the GN main across northern Montana. Dispatcher's and regional offices for ex-NP territory were in Billings. As of the 1990's, these offices were gone, with dispatchers functions divided between Minneapolis, which handles trains as far as Jones Junction on the ex-NP northern corridor and Bainville on the ex-GN "High Line." Seattle-based dispatchers oversee operations west of Bainville.

Burlington Northern's presence in Montana used to be far greater, but it diminished with the 1987 sale/lease of former NP lines west of Jones Junction to Montana Rail Link. Although BN no longer controls these lines, it still runs trains over them—in a sense: Eighty percent of MRL's trains are BN's that the regional forwards between Laurel and Spokane. BN does retain the stretch of track over strategic Mullan Pass from Helena to Phosphate, and the railroad continues to dispatch and maintain this route as its 6th Subdivision. The Mullan Pass line was retained to preserve access to another former NP property, the 60-mile Butte-Garrison line, which was sold to shortline Montana Western in 1986, and to serve the Cominco phosphate mine at Phosphate. With the MRL and MW line sales, the Montana Division now consists mainly of former GN routes.

A glance at a map finds the Missouri River serving as a natural boundary for the Montana Division's eastern edge, flowing through the cities of Minot and Bismarck, N.D., and Mobridge, S.D. (a contraction of "Missouri Bridge" which the railroad crossed here) where the former mains of GN, NP and Milwaukee Road leave the Dakota Division and head west.

These three main lines form the bulk of the division's mileage. At Mobridge, the former Milwaukee line heads west 282 miles to a connection with the former NP at Terry, Mont. This was once part of Milwaukee's legendary Pacific Coast extension, but don't look for it west of Terry—nearly all of it is abandoned. BN took over operation of the line east of

Terry in 1982 after the State of South Dakota bought it to preserve the only main line across the northern part of the state. This route is equipped with CTC from Aberdeen (on the Dakota Division) to Hettinger (controlled from an ancient machine at Northtown), with the last 151 miles to Terry under ABS (Automatic Block Signal) control.

The Mandan-Jones Junction northern corridor line formerly was BN's (and NP's) Yellowstone Division, while the western lines now part of MRL were a part of the Rocky Mountain Division. Mandan, across the Missouri River from North Dakota's capital city of Bismarck, is the eastern end of the division and a 1,000-mile inspection point for all northern-corridor coal trains, so a major coal-car repair facility was located there. From Mandan, the 7th Subdivision main heads into the rugged and scenic Badlands of North Dakota and Montana. This area is often overshadowed by the scenic beauty on the western end of the division, but it has a charm all its own, with deep ravines and high buttes. It also has grades up to 1.5 percent—grades that caused NP to develop 2-8-8-4 "Yellowstone" steam locomotives. It was to conquer the 210-mile up-and-down profile from Bismarck to Glendive, not the Rockies, that these huge machines were purchased.

West from Glendive (home base for BN's SD60M fleet) the 8th Subdivision follows the Yellowstone River for 209 miles to Jones Junction, where ownership switches to MRL through Billings and Laurel. BN trains have trackage rights over MRL to Laurel to

Great Northern often took advantage of the scenery in and around Glacier Park to photograph passenger and freight trains for publicity purposes. One of the favored locations were the crossovers (sinced moved by BN) about one mile west of the summit of Marias Pass. From U.S. Highway 2, company photographers could capture dramatic views of trains snaking through an S-curve with mountain peaks jutting into a seemingly endless Montana sky. Photographer Poitras repeats the view, with tiger-striped, fuel tender-equipped GP50's heading priority intermodal train No. 1 on Sept. 13, 1988.—DAN POITRAS FACING PAGE, TOP : Marias sign, relocated to Essex, Mont.—MIKE SCHAFER

retain access to the former CB&Q lines that connect there, as well as the former GN line to Great Falls.

Two coal branches head south from the main line between Glendive and Jones Junction. The first extends south 39 miles from Nichols Wye to mines at Colstrip and Big Sky. Big Sky, owned by Peabody Coal, began operations in 1969. At Colstrip, spurs head east and west to serve Rosebud 1 and Rosebud 2 mines, owned by Western Energy. At Sarpy Junction, another branch swings south 35 miles to Kuehn and the Absaloka (Sarpy Creek) Mine, owned by Westmoreland Resources, which has been ship-ping coal since 1974.

Easily the backbone of today's Montana Division are the 1st, 2nd and 3rd subdivisions, the former GN main across the state's northern edge, dubbed the "High Line" after the merger. These subdivisions uti-lize mostly single-track CTC control over their entire

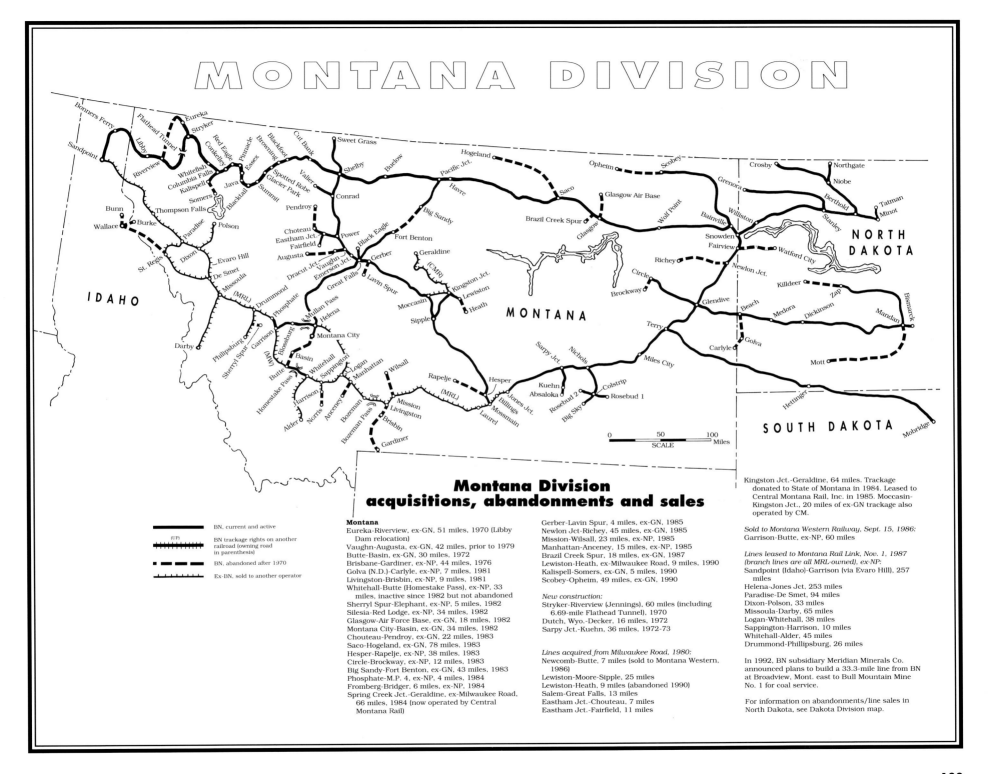

MONTANA DIVISION

Montana Division
acquisitions, abandonments and sales

Legend:
- BN, current and active
- (UP) BN trackage rights on another railroad (owning road in parenthesis)
- BN, abandoned after 1970
- Ex-BN, sold to another operator

Montana

Eureka-Riverview, ex-GN, 51 miles, 1970 (Libby Dam relocation)
Vaughn-Augusta, ex-GN, 42 miles, prior to 1979
Butte-Basin, ex-GN, 30 miles, 1972
Brisbane-Gardiner, ex-NP, 44 miles, 1976
Golva (N.D.)-Carlyle, ex-NP, 7 miles, 1981
Livingston-Brisbin, ex-NP, 9 miles, 1981
Whitehall-Butte (Homestake Pass), ex-NP, 33 miles, inactive since 1982 but not abandoned
Sherryl Spur-Elephant, ex-NP, 5 miles, 1982
Silesia-Red Lodge, ex-NP, 34 miles, 1982
Glasgow-Air Force Base, ex-GN, 18 miles, 1982
Montana City-Basin, ex-GN, 34 miles, 1982
Chouteau-Pendroy, ex-GN, 22 miles, 1983
Saco-Hogeland, ex-GN, 78 miles, 1983
Hesper-Rapelje, ex-NP, 38 miles, 1983
Circle-Brockway, ex-NP, 12 miles, 1983
Big Sandy-Fort Benton, ex-GN, 43 miles, 1983
Phosphate-M.P. 4, ex-NP, 4 miles, 1984
Fromberg-Bridger, 6 miles, ex-NP, 1984
Spring Creek Jct.-Geraldine, ex-Milwaukee Road, 66 miles, 1984 (now operated by Central Montana Rail)

Gerber-Lavin Spur, 4 miles, ex-GN, 1985
Newlon Jct-Richey, 45 miles, ex-GN, 1985
Mission-Wilsall, 23 miles, ex-NP, 1985
Manhattan-Anceney, 15 miles, ex-NP, 1985
Brazil Creek Spur, 18 miles, ex-GN, 1987
Lewiston-Heath, ex-Milwaukee Road, 9 miles, 1990
Kalispell-Somers, ex-GN, 5 miles, 1990
Scobey-Opheim, 49 miles, ex-GN, 1990

New construction:
Stryker-Riverview (Jennings), 60 miles (including 6.69-mile Flathead Tunnel), 1970
Dutch, Wyo.-Decker, 16 miles, 1972
Sarpy Jct.-Kuehn, 36 miles, 1972-73

Lines acquired from Milwaukee Road, 1980:
Newcomb-Butte, 7 miles (sold to Montana Western, 1986)
Lewiston-Moore-Sipple, 25 miles
Lewiston-Heath, 9 miles (abandoned 1990)
Salem-Great Falls, 13 miles
Eastham Jct.-Chouteau, 7 miles
Eastham Jct.-Fairfield, 11 miles

Kingston Jct.-Geraldine, 64 miles. Trackage donated to State of Montana in 1984. Leased to Central Montana Rail, Inc. in 1985. Moccasin-Kingston Jct., 20 miles of ex-GN trackage also operated by CM.

Sold to Montana Western Railway, Sept. 15, 1986:
Garrison-Butte, ex-NP, 60 miles

Lines leased to Montana Rail Link, Nov. 1, 1987 (branch lines are all MRL-owned), ex-NP:
Sandpoint (Idaho)-Garrison (via Evaro Hill), 257 miles
Helena-Jones Jct., 253 miles
Paradise-De Smet, 94 miles
Dixon-Polson, 33 miles
Missoula-Darby, 65 miles
Logan-Whitehall, 38 miles
Sappington-Harrison, 10 miles
Whitehall-Alder, 45 miles
Drummond-Phillipsburg, 26 miles

In 1992, BN subsidiary Meridian Minerals Co. announced plans to build a 33.3-mile line from BN at Broadview, Mont. east to Bull Mountain Mine No. 1 for coal service.

For information on abandonments/line sales in North Dakota, see Dakota Division map.

LEFT: BN and MRL trains climbing Mullan Pass westbound generally require helpers. Westbound helpers are based in Helena, and cut off the train at the summit at Blossburg or 8.4 miles west at Elliston, where eastbound trains take on the additional units. On July 9, 1979, three GE's apply 9,100 horsepower to a westbound near Skyline, Mont., on the looping eastern approach to Mullan. ABOVE: To conquer the Divide at Mullan, NP constructed a 3,896-foot tunnel. On March 2, 1949, the tunnel caved in, causing all traffic to be temporarily re-routed over Homestake Pass. Taking advantage of an opportunity, NP lowered the tunnel floor to eliminate an operating restriction against high loads and re-opened the bore Dec. 7, 1949. Photographer John Bjorklund first visited the tunnel in 1949 at age nine when his father, Walter R. Bjorklund, was in charge of its reconstruction. On his first return to the area to photograph trains, Bjorklund captured U33C 5711 emiting a torrent of smoke as it emerged from Mullan's west portal at Blossburg, Mont., on July 20, 1973.—THREE PHOTOS, JOHN BJORKLUND

distance, except for short stretches of double-track ABS at Williston and Columbia Falls.

Leaving Minot, the 1st Subdivision heads west over the Gassman Coulee bridge and across mainly prairie to Havre, home of the Montana Division. Over this subdivision, Amtrak's *Empire Builder* can cruise up to its maximum speed of 79 mph and keep the speedometer pegged there for miles. These lines were put down in GN's 1887 545-mile race across the prairies to Great Falls.

The 28th Subdivision heads south at Snowden 78 miles along the Yellowstone to connect with the former NP main at Glendive. This line is a combination of NP and GN branches: GN owned the Snowden-Sidney section, while NP operated from Sidney into Glendive. At Fairview another largely unremarked former GN branch headed east 37 miles into North Dakota, to the town of Watford City. . . unremarked, except that this branch had the only railroad tunnel in North Dakota. The line was abandoned in 1992.

Just west of Havre, at Pacific Junction, another branch heads south 31 miles to Big Sandy. Now the 18th Subdivision, this line used to be a through route from Havre to Great Falls and until 1960 was used by GN's *Western Star*. Until 1971, the Havre-Great Falls segment had daily passenger service in the form of the only Rail Diesel Car that saw service on BN; it connected at Havre with the *Western Star*.

Havre marks the beginning of the 2nd Subdivision, which continues west across the prairies but develops a more undulating profile. Havre is important to BN: It is a 1,000-mile inspection point and has a major refueling facility for transcontinental traffic. The city is at an elevation of 2,484 feet, but near Buelow the tracks reach an elevation of 3,413. West of Havre, at Cut Bank, trains cross Cut Bank Creek on 1,200-foot GN bridge No. 1090.8. At Blackfoot, the tracks begin their final climb toward the mountains, although there is a short downgrade between Spotted Robe and East Glacier Park. Just 13 miles later, westbound trains roll over the summit of the Continental Divide at an elevation of just 5,213 feet. For 60 miles, the main line passes along the southern boundary of Glacier National Park.

Leaving the west boundary of the park, the tracks cross the Flathead River and pass through Conkelley, end of the 2nd Subdivision and the beginning of double-track operation into Whitefish. West of there to Boyer (Sandpoint), Idaho, the main line is a part of the 3rd Subdivision. At Whitefish, trains pause for crew changes; the tracks then parallel Whitefish Lake heading northwest to Stryker. Here trains head

onto the 60-mile new line necessitated by the construction of Libby Dam. This line through the wilderness includes the 6.69-mile Flathead Tunnel. A 23-mile section of the old main line, from Stryker to Eureka, was retained to preserve service to that community.

Rejoining the old main at Riverview (Jennings), the tracks head along the waters of the Kootenai River for 64 scenic miles, cruising through another five tunnels before reaching Bonners Ferry, Idaho. Here, westbound trains begin an 11-mile climb to Naples, passing through two tunnels, with the Selkirk Mountains as a backdrop. The grade levels out for the final 21 miles into Boyer and Sandpoint. Trains cross the two miles of new track built to connect the GN with NP, then it's onto the "funnel" and the Pacific Division for the last lap into Spokane.

There are other main lines on the Montana Division as well. The former GN line from Mossmain (Laurel), Mont., heads northwest 223 miles to Great Falls. Now the 5th Subdivision, this line has five tunnels and innumerable bridges. In the early 1980's, the railroad examined extensively upgrading this line as a way of bypassing the western part of the old NP and routing traffic up to the High Line connection at Shelby. Eventually, the project proved to be far more

A Montana sunrise greats a westbound freight splitting the ex-NP General Railway Signal Company semaphores east of Helena, Mont., in October 1984. At 8 a.m. the train will arrive in the Montana capital city, preparing to head west to conquer the curves and grades of Mullan Pass. Situated on the eastern slope of the Rockies, Helena was founded in 1864 when gold was discovered in Last Chance Gulch, now one of the main streets in the city. NP service to Helena began June 15, 1883; the trackage east of Helena has been operated by Montana Rail Link since October 1987.—
JOHN BJORKLUND

expensive than originally estimated, and was abandoned in favor of selling NP's western lines to MRL.

One hundred twenty-two miles west of Mossmain, a 25-mile branch leaves the main line at Sipple and heads into Lewiston. This branch was acquired in 1980 from the Milwaukee Road. Thirteen miles west, another railroad connects with BN: Central Montana Rail, Inc. CM operates the original GN branch from Moccasin to Kingston Junction, then heads north-

west over former Milwaukee Road track to Geraldine, a total of 84 miles. BN operated this trackage from 1980 to 1984, when it was donated to the State of Montana. Central Montana Rail was formed to lease the line to carry grain, resuming service in 1985.

The 4th Subdivision extends 98 miles from Great Falls to Shelby. Just west of Great Falls, at Emerson Junction, the Milwaukee Road headed onto the GN, and the two roads jointly operated the eight miles of track to Vaughn in an agreement dating from 1938. At that city, a 41-mile branch to Augusta (abandoned in the 1970's) left the main, and GN/Milwaukee operation continued six miles down the branch to Dracut Junction, where Milwaukee trains went their own way to Choteau and Agawam.

There are other branch lines that feed into the 4th Subdivision as well, including a 28-mile line to Eastham Junction and Choteau, the last seven miles of which were also jointly operated with the Milwaukee. At Eastham Junction, the 13th Subdivision branch

heads south 11 miles to Fairfield; this is another line picked up from the Milwaukee in 1980. At Valier Junction, a 17-mile branch extends to Valier, once part of shortline Montana Western Railway. Shelby is the 4th Sub junction with the High Line; it then continues north to the Canadian border to handle traffic from the Canadian Pacific at Sweet Grass.

Another important branch heads southwest from Great Falls 95 miles down to Montana's capital city of Helena through Wolf Creek Canon, linking up with the 6th Subdivision main over Mullan Pass to Garrison and Phosphate. This line over Mullan's 2.2 and 1.4 percent grades is also used by Montana Rail Link, which runs most of the trains there.

The Montana Division has witnessed some radical changes during the course of BN's existence. Despite the emergence of Montana Rail Link and BN's program of abandoning superfluous lines, Burlington Northern remains a prime force in rail transportation in "Big Sky Country."

ABOVE: A loaded grain train behind SD40-2 6816 waits for Amtrak 7 (No. 1007 on BN), the westbound *Empire Builder* to make the station stop at Whitefish, Mont., before following the passenger train west toward Flathead Tunnel. Situated at an altitude of 3,040 feet above sea level, the beautiful chalet-style depot houses BN offices in its upper floors.—MARK R. LYNN RIGHT: The central Montana city of Great Falls is at the southern boundry of an area referred to as the "Golden Triangle," an area bordered by GN lines that stretched south from Havre to Great Falls, then north to the main line at Shelby and east back to Havre. Between 1951 and 1960, the GN's Chicago-Pacific Coast *Western Star* served two legs of the triangle, leaving the main line at Havre to serve Great Falls, returning to the main at Shelby. The center of this triangle is some of the most-fertile grain growing territory in Montana. In March, 1986 the Great Falls-Fort Benton turn is about to cross the Missouri River with only five cars in tow behind five units. Great Falls was built around the five great falls of the Missouri River, which flows north and eastward from the city. The discovery of gold at the latter city in 1862 made the town an important overland connection for Missouri River steamers, playing a significant role in the opening of the Northwest.—G. W. GROSS, COLLECTION OF ALLEN RIDER

Since 1929, the *Empire Builder* has been serving Montana. Just west of Browning, Mont., Amtrak's Superliner-equipped version of the *Builder* cruises east in May 1991 through wide-open Montana "Big Sky Country." The train has spent the first part of the morning winding through Glacier Park and will spend the rest of the day racing across the high prairies of eastern Montana and North Dakota. The *Empire Builder* has long been synonymous with Glacier Park, although it only began stop-ping at Glacier Park stations in 1968 (the *Western Star* was Great Northern's flag-ship serving the east and west entrances of Glacier). Ironically, scheduling require-ments for the *Builder* today and in GN days usually have put the train through the park in late afternoon or early evening westbound and early morning eastbound—often in darkness. The *Builder* was Amtrak's first long-distance train to be regularly assigned double-deck Superliner cars, beginning Oct. 28, 1979.—BILL FRANCIK

*G*reat Northern was always closely associated with Montana's Glacier National Park, established in 1910. The railway helped build the first highways, hotels and chalets for the new park between 1911 and 1927—including the 155-room Glacier Park Hotel (1913) and the even-larger Many Glacier Hotel (1915), and actively promoted train travel to the area. GN even modified its logo to include the words "See America First" and "Glacier National Park." Some of GN's hotels still house park visitors, but they are no longer railroad-owned.

Glacier Park is still a popular travel destination, with Amtrak's *Empire Builder* making three stops for visitors, at East Glacier (summer only), Essex and Belton (West Glacier). In GN days, the *Western Star* served the Park—the *Builder* just cruised right through. The railroad even arranged for Blackfeet Indians (who once controlled the land that is now the park) to meet passenger trains at East Glacier in the summer. Beginning with the 1968 summer season, the *Builder* began stopping at Glacier, giving passengers a choice of two trains.

GN first surveyed the area that would become the national park in 1889. Engineer John F. Stevens discovered the low-grade crossing of the Rockies at Marias Pass in December 1889. On Dec. 11, he spent the night in the pass walking in circles to keep from freezing to death in subzero temperatures. The route through Marias gave GN a definite competitive edge—it could conquer the Rockies at an elevation of 5,213 feet, the lowest rail crossing of the Rockies in the U.S. GN laid the rails over the Pass in 1891 on its march to the Pacific.

Over the years, GN made many improvements to the line through the Rockies. One of the biggest was undertaken near Red Eagle between 1942 and 1945. The project included heavy rock cuts and fills and three new tunnels, which eliminated 30 curves. In the 1960's, GN extensively reworked its mountain crossing with more line changes that eliminated several curves. In 1967-68, CTC was extended from Blackfoot through the Park to Conkelley.

Heavy freight traffic and beautiful scenery make Glacier Park one of the most visited locations for BN observers. Its popularity is aided by its accessibility —unlike many railroad mountain crossings, BN's route through the Rockies is paralleled throughout by a major highway, U.S. 2.

Westbound trains face a one percent grade for

ABOVE: Not long after the tourist season has ended, winter snows cover Glacier Park with a white blanket that doesn't depart until late spring. BN, of course, continues to operate all year long, which means it must battle "Old Man Winter" to get its trains over Marias. In a swirling February 1988 blizzard, the diesel units on this westbound BN manifest at the summit are slowly turning white as the wet snow sticks to the carbodies.—MIKE SCHAFER FACING PAGE: About a dozen photographers were poised atop the portal of tunnel No. 4 near Belton, Mont., during the October 1991 "Alta-Mont" (Alberta-Montana) "Railfan Weekend", hosted by the Izaac Walton Inn at Essex, to record this view of BN train 33. After a 45-minute wait, with the sun rapidly receding behind the mountains, the quietness was interrupted by the screaming of dynamic brakes in full retardation as the train burst out of tunnel 3.9 into the last rays of sunlight.—PHIL GOSNEY

eight miles from Browning (headquarters for the Blackfeet Indian Reservation) to Spotted Robe, then descend a one percent into Glacier Park station after crossing the bridge over Two Medicine Creek, scene of countless GN publicity photos. Leaving East Glacier station, westbounds climb a 1.2 percent grade to Summit station, reached at milepost 1149.8 (measured from St. Paul), where two main tracks carry trains down the next 14 miles to Java East on a 1.8 percent grade. The S-curve at Marias was another famous GN photo location (page 000).

From Summit, the railroad climbs above U.S. 2, passing the station of Blacktail. In the seven-mile stretch between Blacktail and Java, the railroad

passes through nine snowsheds. The railroad bridges Highway 2, then crosses two steel trestles: over the confluence of the Flathead River and Java Creek, and across Sheep Creek. After crossing the bridges two main tracks are again in use, passing through another snowshed to enter Essex. The town was known as Walton for a few years after 1926, and the grade to Summit is sometimes referred to as "Essex Hill" or "Walton Hill." Essex has long been the home base for Marias Pass helper units. Next to the BN yard in Essex is the Izaak Walton Inn, built by GN in 1939 for tourists and to house crews. The railroad-motif Inn still welcomes visitors year round.

Three miles west of Essex, single track resumes

at Pinnacle, where U.S. 2 goes over the top of the tracks, and the main line ducks through tunnels 2 and 3, after which it is single track for the next four miles to Paola. Both road and railroad parallel the Middle Fork of the Flathead River, which is one reason the route can maintain such a low-level crossing of the Rockies. But being close to the waters can have its drawbacks, as GN found out in 1964.

In a 36-hour period in June of that year, some 16 inches of rain fell along the Continental Divide. By the time it was over, the most destructive flood in Montana history had washed away almost eight miles of railroad, as well as other rail facilities in the 60 miles west of Marias. Crews worked around the clock to restore the line to service and, amazingly, were able to do so in just 21 days.

Highway 2 continues to parallel the BN from Red Eagle to the west end of Glacier Park, 10 miles. In this stretch, the line passes through four more short tunnels and the highway is elevated above the tracks, offering some great "down on" views of trains and the river. BN tracks leave Glacier Park at Belton (West Glacier).

For over 100 years, trains have been using this scenic crossing of the Continental Divide. Hopefully, a century from now, Burlington Northern trains will still be a familiar sight for Glacier Park visitors.

CHAPTER 11

PACIFIC DIVISION

WHEATFIELDS TO MOUNTAINS

If there is any question as to why BN chose Cascade green as its trademark color, a visit to the Pacific Division will answer it. This part of the Northwest encompasses the lush forest areas of the Cascade Mountains in Washington and Oregon, as well as the scenic panhandle of Idaho. Today's Pacific Division encompasses all lines in Washington, Oregon, California, British Columbia and Idaho, with the exception of the ex-GN main east of Sandpoint, Idaho.

The Emerald City of Seattle is home to the Pacific Division. Dispatchers are located in Seattle, from which they handle all BN operations not only on the Pacific Division, but the Montana Division west of Bainville and Mossmain (Laurel), Mont. Terminal operations abound, with bustling yards at Spokane, Pasco, Seattle, Tacoma and the two Vancouvers—Washington and British Columbia.

Spokane, population 190,000, is one of the busiest terminals, serving as a funnel for both Portland and Seattle traffic. There are separate facilities at the company's main yard in Spokane, distinguished as Yardley, which encompasses the freight yard, and Parkwater, the engine terminal. At Pasco, Wash., the 1955-built NP hump yard was completely rebuilt shortly after the merger. One of Pasco's main functions is blocking manifest traffic for eastern and southeastern destinations.

The ex-SP&S facilities at Vancouver, Wash., serve the Portland terminal area, although the locomotive shop was closed in 1987 and demolished. Seattle is

home to busy Balmer Yard and Interbay Engine Terminal. Intermodal freight is handled at the ex-NP Stacy Street Yard south of downtown, as well as a new terminal at South Seattle, near Boeing Field. Rivaling Seattle for intermodal traffic is Tacoma.

Although the Pacific Division includes forest and mountain areas, it also encompasses semi-arid regions in central Washington and Oregon. Most of eastern Washington is covered by irrigated wheatfields, while central Washington grows more potatoes than the entire state of Maine. Both are among the commodities carried by BN. Other traffic carried on the division includes lumber, paper, wood chips, plywood and of course, intermodal freight. Portland, Tacoma and Seattle are major ports for both Japanese and Korean automobiles, and imported bauxite ore for aluminum smelters along the Columbia River is also handled.

The GN main line is the route of choice through the Cascades. It includes the "new" 7.79-mile Cascade Tunnel, the longest in the western hemisphere when it opened in 1929. That record was broken in 1989 when Canadian Pacific opened its 9.1-mile Mount McDonald Tunnel through the Canadian Rockies. The new Cascade Tunnel route was lower, straighter and shorter with no snowsheds. Its opening permitted the abandonment of 18 miles of old line, which including snowsheds, trestles and the original Cascade Tunnel. At the same time, GN opened the Chumstick Cutoff, which eliminated many miles of steep grades through Tumwater

Canyon west of Leavenworth, Wash. Electric operations were then extended to Skykomish and Wenatchee and new, more powerful locomotives purchased; electrification was abandoned in 1956.

The 144-mile ex-NP Spokane-Pasco line, now the 7th Subdivision, was extensively rebuilt with welded rail and CTC-signaling to replace the paralleling SP&S route in 1987. The 7th Sub's rollercoaster grades are far inferior to the relatively level SP&S profile, but the latter was rife with expense-to-maintain tunnels and trestles. The grades have proven a hindrance, especially over Providence Hill east of Connell, Wash., and traffic jams have become a problem. West of Pasco, the ex-SP&S line to Portland follows the Columbia River on a water-level route.

The agricultural areas in eastern Washington and the Idaho panhandle—known as the "Inland Empire"—were served with an extensive network of branch lines of both GN and NP heritage, many of which have been trimmed or turned over to Washington Central for operation. Probably the most unique operation on the Pacific Division is the Camas Prairie Railroad in Idaho, jointly owned and operated with Union Pacific. The Camas Prairie never owned any right-of-way, locomotives or rolling stock. It operates 243 miles of trackage using equipment and crews supplied by BN (NP before merger) and UP. This railroad features some of the most spectacular rail engineering feats on the continent, particularly on the 67-mile Grangeville Branch southeast of Lewiston, Idaho, where the Camas Prairie navigates beautiful

ABOVE: The diverse geography of the Pacific Northwest sometimes exudes a beauty of almost surrealistic quality, as evidenced in this panorama along the Columbia River Gorge at Maryhill, Wash., in September 1991. GP39-2 2776 and an SD40-2 pilot eastbound merchandise under the haunting loom of Mount Hood—at 11,235 feet the highest point in Oregon. This is BN's ex-SP&S Portland-Pasco main line (some might say its most scenic) along the north bank of the Columbia. FACING PAGE, TOP: Oakway SD60 9025 is about to dive through a short tunnel west of Bingen, Wash., with an eastbound along the Columbia River in 1989.—BOTH PHOTOS, JIM THOMAS

Lapwai Canyon with 14 miles of three percent grades and 17 bridges. Operations since 1984 have seen motive power supplied by UP and cabooses by BN.

No review of the Pacific Division would be complete without mention of the "funnel" between Sandpoint and Spokane. Now the 1st Subdivision, this 68-mile ex-NP line through northern Idaho's Purcell Trench has grown to become one of the busiest BN line's in the Northwest. When BN was formed, this route was chosen to handle transcontinental traffic between Sandpoint and Spokane (the GN route was avoided because of a steep grade between Spokane and Hillyard and the twisting line through Scotia Canyon), and a new connection was built at Boyer Siding in Sandpoint. Today, trains operating between the terminals at Portland, Seattle and Pasco and eastern points on the former GN and Montana Rail Link all must negotiate this bottleneck, under control of the "Boyer West" Seattle dispatcher.

From Seattle to Portland, trains follow the 4th Subdivision. This NP trackage in pre-merger days was also used by GN, as well as Union Pacific south of Tacoma, and until 1980, Milwaukee Road trains used the line to reach Portland as a condition of the BN merger. Today the 4th Subdivision's trackage is busier than ever, including three Amtrak trains in each direction. Trains north of Centralia are under the control of the "Centralia North" dispatcher, while trackage south of that city is controlled by the "Centralia South" dispatcher. There is also a Seattle terminal dispatcher who handles traffic from Black River (where UP crosses the BN) into Seattle.

A former Great Northern line puts BN trains into British Columbia. The 9th Subdivision strikes northward 122 miles from Everett to Vancouver, B.C., skirting Puget Sound near Bellingham and Blaine.

There are other routes into Canada as well. The Kettle Falls-San Poil branch swings north across the border through Grand Forks, B.C., before turning back south into the U.S. Another branch heads north out of Kettle Falls to a CP connection at Troup Junction and Nelson, B.C.; but the portion of this line from Salmo, B.C., to Nelson, 35 miles, at this writing is up for abandonment.

BN trains continue to serve the old Oregon Trunk south from Wishram, Wash., on the Pasco-Portland line, through the Deschutes River Canyon of Oregon, today the 8th Subdivision. This "Inside Gateway" was an important route for BN and WP in the first decade after the merger, but this joint operation ended in 1982 when the UP/WP merger was imminent. Traffic declined with the loss of the run-

ABOVE: At the starting line, train 93 readies for its departure from Seattle on Oct. 2, 1991. Often in railroad circles there are references to "junk" trains, but No. 93 really lives up to its name. The train hauls solid waste from a transfer station in downtown Seattle south to Vancouver and east up the Columbia River to a massive landfill operated by Rabanco near Roosevelt, Wash. UP also moves "trash trains" from the Seattle area up the Columbia River.—BLAIR KOOISTRA
RIGHT: In a June 1983 self portrait, operator Paul Schneider descends the steps of North Portal Tower in Seattle to pick up a package from a southbound freight lead by GP38 2076, one of the first new units received by the railroad. North Portal, three miles south of Balmer Yard, guarded the north entrance to the tunnel under downtown that leads to King Street passenger station.—PAUL D. SCHNEIDER

RIGHT: Spring breakup is well under way in Spokane in March 1985 as the regular Sunday afternoon drag freight for Pasco, train 671 heavy with wood chips, lumber and grain, leaves downtown behind and vaults across the Latah Creek Bridge. The bridge was constructed in 1971-72 as part of BN's multi-million dollar line change to tie the former GN, NP and SP&S lines together in the Spokane area.—BLAIR KOOISTRA BELOW: Three LMX B39-8's lead train 3, the old *Pacific Zip*, as it negotiates the 8,000-foot bridge over Pend Oreille Lake at 7:30 a.m., July 6, 1991. The rear of the train is still trailing through Sandpoint Junction, where MRL and BN routes divide. Number 3 is entering the 1st Subdivision "funnel" connecting Sandpoint with Spokane. In the 1960's, NP spent millions to upgrade this trackage. In 1964-65, NP affected a five-mile line relocation that eliminated a 1,169-foot viaduct (near the scene of a *North Coast Limited* derailment in 1962), a 435-foot tunnel and 276 degrees of curvature. It also cut nearly two miles from the route and cost approximately $3 million. So many trains operate over this line that double tracking has been discussed. NP once had double track from Marshall, Wash., through Spokane to Athol, Idaho. The second main was removed before World War II from Irvin (E. Spokane) to Athol, Idaho. Later, the six miles of second mainfrom Marshall to Empire was removed, with the old second track through Empire becoming a two-mile long passing track.—STEVE GLISCHINSKI

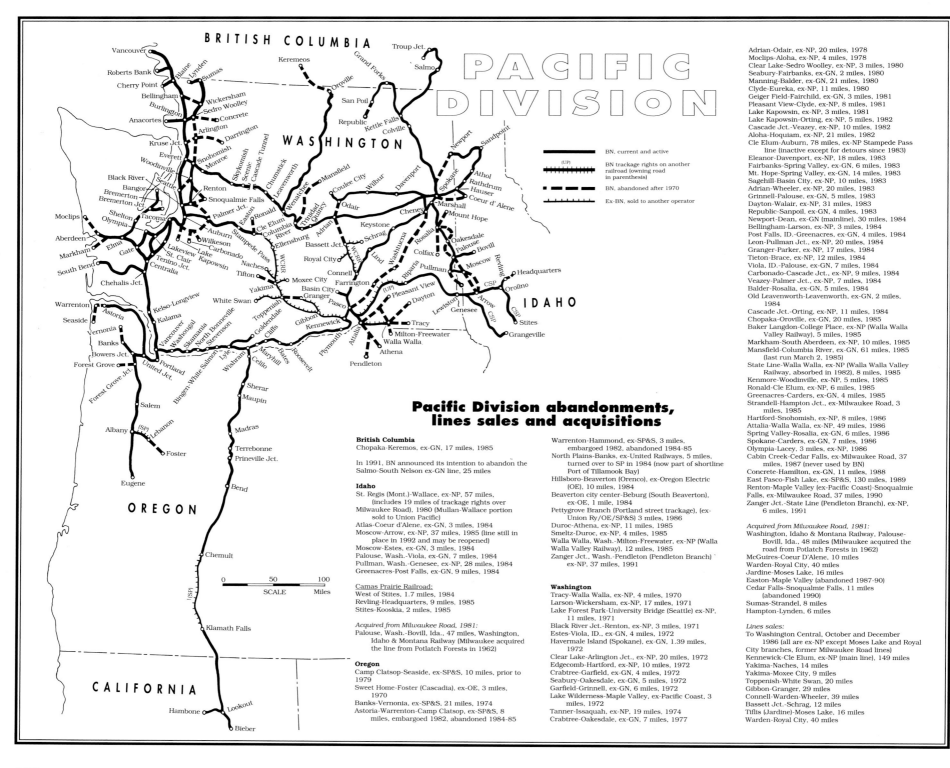

PACIFIC DIVISION

BRITISH COLUMBIA · WASHINGTON · IDAHO · OREGON · CALIFORNIA

Legend

- ▬▬▬ BN, current and active
- (UP) ┼┼┼┼ BN trackage rights on another railroad (owning road in parenthesis)
- ▬ ▬ ▬ BN, abandoned after 1970
- ┤┤┤┤ Ex-BN, sold to another operator

Adrian-Odair, ex-NP, 20 miles, 1978
Moclips-Aloha, ex-NP, 4 miles, 1978
Clear Lake-Sedro Woolley, ex-NP, 3 miles, 1980
Seabury-Fairbanks, ex-GN, 2 miles, 1980
Manning-Balder, ex-GN, 21 miles, 1980
Clyde-Eureka, ex-NP, 11 miles, 1980
Geiger Field-Fairchild, ex-GN, 3 miles, 1981
Pleasant View-Clyde, ex-NP, 8 miles, 1981
Lake Kapowsin, ex-NP, 3 miles, 1981
Lake Kapowsin-Orting, ex-NP, 5 miles, 1982
Cascade Jct.-Veazey, ex-NP, 10 miles, 1982
Aloha-Hoquiam, ex-NP, 21 miles, 1982
Cle Elum-Auburn, 78 miles, ex-NP Stampede Pass line (inactive except for detours since 1983)
Eleanor-Davenport, ex-NP, 18 miles, 1983
Fairbanks-Spring Valley, ex-GN, 6 miles, 1983
Mt. Hope-Spring Valley, ex-GN, 14 miles, 1983
Sagehill-Basin City, ex-NP, 10 miles, 1983
Adrian-Wheeler, ex-NP, 20 miles, 1983
Grinnell-Palouse, ex-GN, 5 miles, 1983
Dayton-Walair, ex-NP, 31 miles, 1983
Republic-Sanpoil, ex-GN, 4 miles, 1983
Newport-Dean, ex-GN (mainline), 30 miles, 1984
Bellingham-Larson, ex-NP, 3 miles, 1984
Post Falls, ID.-Greenacres, ex-GN, 4 miles, 1984
Leon-Pullman Jct., ex-NP, 20 miles, 1984
Granger-Parker, ex-NP, 17 miles, 1984
Tieton-Brace, ex-NP, 12 miles, 1984
Viola, ID.-Palouse, ex-GN, 7 miles, 1984
Carbonado-Cascade Jct., ex-NP, 9 miles, 1984
Veazey-Palmer Jct., ex-NP, 7 miles, 1984
Balder-Rosalia, ex-GN, 5 miles, 1984
Old Leavenworth-Leavenworth, ex-GN, 2 miles, 1984
Cascade Jct.-Orting, ex-NP, 11 miles, 1984
Chopaka-Oroville, ex-GN, 20 miles, 1985
Baker Langdon-College Place, ex-NP (Walla Walla Valley Railway), 5 miles, 1985
Markham-South Aberdeen, ex-NP, 10 miles, 1985
Mansfield-Columbia River, ex-GN, 61 miles, 1985 (last run March 2, 1985)
State Line-Walla Walla, ex-NP (Walla Walla Valley Railway, absorbed in 1982), 8 miles, 1985
Kenmore-Woodinville, ex-NP, 5 miles, 1985
Ronald-Cle Elum, ex-NP, 6 miles, 1985
Greenacres-Carders, ex-GN, 4 miles, 1985
Strandell-Hampton Jct., ex-Milwaukee Road, 3 miles, 1985
Hartford-Snohomish, ex-NP, 8 miles, 1986
Attalia-Walla Walla, ex-NP, 49 miles, 1986
Spring Valley-Rosalia, ex-GN, 6 miles, 1986
Spokane-Carders, ex-GN, 7 miles, 1986
Olympia-Lacey, 3 miles, ex-NP, 1986
Cabin Creek-Cedar Falls, ex-Milwaukee Road, 37 miles, 1987 (never used by BN)
Concrete-Hamilton, ex-GN, 11 miles, 1988
East Pasco-Fish Lake, ex-SP&S, 130 miles, 1989
Renton-Maple Valley (ex-Pacific Coast)-Snoqualmie Falls, ex-Milwaukee Road, 37 miles, 1990
Zanger Jct.-State Line (Pendleton Branch), ex-NP, 6 miles, 1991

Acquired from Milwaukee Road, 1981:
Washington, Idaho & Montana Railway, Palouse-Bovill, Ida., 48 miles (Milwaukee acquired the road from Potlatch Forests in 1962)
McGuires-Coeur D'Alene, 10 miles
Warden-Royal City, 40 miles
Jardine-Moses Lake, 16 miles
Easton-Maple Valley (abandoned 1987-90)
Cedar Falls-Snoqualmie Falls, 11 miles (abandoned 1990)
Sumas-Strandel, 8 miles
Hampton-Lynden, 6 miles

Lines sales:
To Washington Central, October and December 1986 (all are ex-NP except Moses Lake and Royal City branches, former Milwaukee Road lines)
Kennewick-Cle Elum, ex-NP (main line), 149 miles
Yakima-Naches, 14 miles
Yakima-Moxee City, 9 miles
Toppenish-White Swan, 20 miles
Gibbon-Granger, 29 miles
Connell-Warden-Wheeler, 39 miles
Bassett Jct.-Schrag, 12 miles
Tiflis (Jardine)-Moses Lake, 16 miles
Warden-Royal City, 40 miles

Pacific Division abandonments, lines sales and acquisitions

British Columbia
Chopaka-Keremos, ex-GN, 17 miles, 1985

In 1991, BN announced its intention to abandon the Salmo-South Nelson ex-GN line, 25 miles

Idaho
St. Regis (Mont.)-Wallace, ex-NP, 57 miles, (includes 19 miles of trackage rights over Milwaukee Road), 1980 (Mullan-Wallace portion sold to Union Pacific)
Atlas-Coeur d'Alene, ex-GN, 3 miles, 1984
Moscow-Arrow, ex-NP, 37 miles, 1985 (line still in place in 1992 and may be reopened)
Moscow-Estes, ex-GN, 3 miles, 1984
Palouse, Wash.-Viola, ex-GN, 7 miles, 1984
Pullman, Wash.-Genesee, ex-NP, 28 miles, 1984
Greenacres-Post Falls, ex-GN, 9 miles, 1984

Camas Prairie Railroad:
West of Stites, 1.7 miles, 1984
Revling-Headquarters, 9 miles, 1985
Stites-Kooskia, 2 miles, 1985

Acquired from Milwaukee Road, 1981:
Palouse, Wash.-Bovill, Ida., 47 miles, Washington, Idaho & Montana Railway (Milwaukee acquired the line from Potlatch Forests in 1962)

Oregon
Camp Clatsop-Seaside, ex-SP&S, 10 miles, prior to 1979
Sweet Home-Foster (Cascadia), ex-OE, 3 miles, 1970
Banks-Vernonia, ex-SP&S, 21 miles, 1974
Astoria-Warrenton-Camp Clatsop, ex-SP&S, 8 miles, embargoed 1982, abandoned 1984-85

Warrenton-Hammond, ex-SP&S, 3 miles, embargoed 1982, abandoned 1984-85
North Plains-Banks, ex-United Railways, 5 miles, turned over to SP in 1984 (now part of shortline Port of Tillamook Bay)
Hillsboro-Beaverton (Orenco), ex-Oregon Electric (OE), 10 miles, 1984
Beaverton city center-Beburg (South Beaverton), ex-OE, 1 mile, 1984
Pettygrove Branch (Portland street trackage), (ex-Union Ry/OE/SP&S) 3 miles, 1986
Duroc-Athena, ex-NP, 11 miles, 1985
Smeltz-Duroc, ex-NP, 4 miles, 1985
Walla Walla, Wash.-Milton-Freewater, ex-NP (Walla Walla Valley Railway), 12 miles, 1985
Zanger Jct., Wash.-Pendleton (Pendleton Branch) ex-NP, 37 miles, 1991

Washington
Tracy-Walla Walla, ex-NP, 4 miles, 1970
Larson-Wickersham, ex-NP, 17 miles, 1971
Lake Forest Park-University Bridge (Seattle) ex-NP, 11 miles, 1971
Black River Jct.-Renton, ex-NP, 3 miles, 1971
Estes-Viola, ID., ex-GN, 4 miles, 1972
Havermale Island (Spokane), ex-GN, 1.39 miles, 1972
Clear Lake-Arlington Jct., ex-NP, 20 miles, 1972
Edgecomb-Hartford, ex-NP, 10 miles, 1972
Crabtree-Garfield, ex-GN, 4 miles, 1972
Seabury-Oakesdale, ex-GN, 5 miles, 1972
Garfield-Grinnell, ex-GN, 6 miles, 1972
Lake Wilderness-Maple Valley, ex-Pacific Coast, 3 miles, 1972
Tanner-Issaquah, ex-NP, 19 miles, 1974
Crabtree-Oakesdale, ex-GN, 7 miles, 1977

through movements, but this scenic line still sees BN and UP trains rolling across the massive Crooked River Gorge bridge near Terrebonne, Ore., which at 320 feet was the second-highest railroad bridge in North America when opened in 1911. Another longer bridge, built by OT, can be found in Madras.

NP maintained a network of branch lines east of Centralia, Wash., to serve various lumber industries which continued to see service under BN. The "Gate Line" headed west from Centralia 14 miles to Gate, where it intersected the "Grays Harbor Line" from St. Clair and Olympia. It then continued west to Elma, Aberdeen (also a junction point for branch lines to Cosmopolis and Markham), and along Grays Harbor to the Pacific Ocean at Moclips (this was abandoned west of Hoquaim in 1978 and 1982). At Elma, yet another branch reached north to Shelton; beyond that point to U.S. Navy facilities at Bremerton and Bangor, the line was owned by the U.S. Government, with maintenance and operation by NP. Today the Centralia-Aberdeen line is BN's 21st Subdivision (also used by UP), while the Elma-Bangor line is the 22nd Sub. To the south of these lines is another NP branch, extending 56 miles from Chehalis Junction to South Bend, operated as the 23rd Subdivision.

In Oregon, historic branch lines serve former SP&S and Oregon Electric (OE) territory. From Willbridge, near Portland, the 24th Subdivision reaches 95 miles to Astoria. This was the old SP&S' 1st Subdivision of its Portland Division, better known as the Astoria Branch. It once extended west to Seaside and Holladay along the Oregon coast, and also included a 3.8-mile branch from Warrenton to Fort Stevens. The Astoria branch was one of the last to be served by SP&S's Alco FA fleet, as was the former OE main line through Albany to Eugene, operated as BN's 25th Subdivision. The OE, incorporated in 1906, as well as the former Oregon Trunk survived as "paper railroads" until May 1, 1981 when the two were joined becoming a new subsidiary, Burlington Northern Oregon-Washington.

Mountains, wide rivers and semi-arid terrain are all part of the Pacific Division's profile. Thanks to the continued expansion of trade with Pacific Rim countries, and the rich agricultural bounty of the area, the trains which cruise through the strange and wonderful geography of the Pacific Division promise to grow longer and more frequent.

Trains on BN's former GN main from Spokane to Wenatchee, the 2nd Subdivision of the Pacific Division, head west from Spokane across the Latah Creek Bridge and climb through Indian Canyon on one percent grades. The scenery changes dramatically a short distance west of the Spokane, as forest-covered hills give way to the rolling wheatfields of the Columbia Plateau. Along the way to Wenatchee, trains follow a series of coulees to keep grades to a minimum. East of Trinidad, Wash., is Trinidad Loop, a 10-degree, five-minute horseshoe curve. The loop is entirely downgrade westbound, as the tracks descend toward the Columbia River from Quincy to Columbia River siding. It's a different story for eastbounds, as this intermodal train demonstrates on Sept. 19, 1984. The train is coiling its way upgrade through the series of S-curves the railroad uses to escape the the Columbia River Gorge, heading toward the Loop at Trinidad.—D. B. HARROP

FACING PAGE: The photographer endured a three-hour wait to capture this view of grain Extra 8021 West crossing the ex-SP&S Bouvey Canyon bridge near Farrington, Wash., in the last rays of sunlight at 6:30 p.m., May 16, 1987. Within a few minutes, the sound of hundreds of wheels banging over jointed rails had disappeared, and a pleasant day along the slack waters of the Snake River was history. Silence reins here today, since this former main line has been abandoned. ABOVE: Traffic diverted from the old SP&S main line between Spokane and Pasco was shifted to a mostly NP routing between the two cities. Daily from early summer to well into winter, the former NP main line is jammed with grain trains, empty and loaded, coming to and from grain terminals in Portland, Kalama, Tacoma and Seattle. Hustling 109 empty grain pool cars eastward, SD40-2's 6831/8120 negotiate the S-curves along Sprague Lake at M.P. 45.5 (from Spokane) near Keystone, Wash. at 5:37 p.m., September 21, 1991.—TWO PHOTOS, BLAIR KOOISTRA

RIGHT: One of the busiest stretches of railroad in the Northwest is the "funnel" between Sandpoint and Spokane. Most through traffic running on the BN between points on the east and southeast end of the railroad and the Pacific Northwest must traverse this section of ex-NP line. Having found a "window" in the funnel's intense traffic flow, SD40-2 6811 and mates slice through the snowy countryside at Rathdrum, Idaho, with westbound grain on Christmas Eve day 1988.—BRUCE KELLY

ABOVE: The Army Corps of Engineers has constructed four dams along the Columbia between Pasco and Portland since the 1930's, resulting in the significant rebuilding of the old SP&S main. East of Maryhill, the huge John Day Dam serves as the backdrop for GP35's 2504/2556/2579 bringing 107 grain loads west on May 29, 1988.—SCOTT O' DELL

Burlington Northern has many lines that parallel water, particularly in the West. Perhaps BN's best-known "water level route" (with apologies to the late New York Central) is the ex-SP&S line through the Columbia River Gorge between Pasco, Wash., and Portland, Ore.

SP&S was one of the better-engineered railroads in the Northwest. Thanks to the mighty Columbia River, which has been cutting through the basalt cliffs for thousands of years, tracklayers were able to build a waterside route that never exceeds 0.2 percent. Not that the SP&S had it easy: Crews still had to carve 13 tunnels through rock outcroppings and cliffs between Portland and Pasco.

To see operations on the old SP&S main through the Columbia River Gorge, start at Pasco, BN's launch point for westbound trains on the 126-mile 6th Subdivision to Wishram, formerly SP&S's 2nd Subdivision. Leaving Pasco, trains head across the

nearly mile-long ex-NP bridge over the Columbia River to Kennewick and SP&S Junction, where Washington Central's ex-NP main heads north and west. From this point, the railroad heads southwest into mostly inaccessible territory, beginning its river running about five miles east of Kennewick. Forty miles later, it emerges into "civilization" again at Plymouth. Just east of town is McNary Dam, where the Corps of Engineers had to relocate the tracks to make way for the dam project, completed in 1956. At Plymouth, State Route 14—the Lewis & Clark Highway—begins to parallel the tracks. West at Bates, towering cliffs move in close to the tracks, allowing great views of trains, cliffs and river. The John Day Dam is passed near the short spur at Cliffs, then its a short, five-mile dash into Maryhill where at the state park former GN 4-8-2 No. 2507 is displayed.

From Maryhill, it's eight miles into the old divi-

An ample locomotive consist—three LMX B39-8's and a BN unit—blazes eastbound along the Columbia River near Roosevelt, Wash., during the waning hours of a November day in 1989. The Columbia forms most of the boundary between southern Washington and northern Oregon, and railroads flank both sides of the river east from Portland—UP on the south bank in Oregon and BN on the north in Washington. The Gorge was one of many scenic selling points in pre-Amtrak days for UP's *City of Portland* and SP&S's leg of the *Empire Builder* and *North Coast Limited.*—JIM THOMAS

sion point of Wishram. To enter the yard, trains must pass through tunnel No. 12. The highway is high above the town on its east approach, offering a panoramic view of the yard and tunnel. Wishram was a classic rail town, but time and change have caught up with it. The old depot and its beanery have been replaced by a new structure. The enginehouse which used to service Alco FA's and Centurys, and many yard tracks, are all gone. Wishram remains a crew-change point and Amtrak stop, but SP&S veterans probably shake their heads at what's happened to the town.

West of Wishram, trains enter the Pacific Division's 5th Subdivision (old SP&S 1st Sub) for the trip to Vancouver and Portland. Just west of the yard, the old Oregon Trunk (now the 8th Subdivision) cuts off and heads across the Columbia on the 4,197-foot Celilo Bridge. West of Wishram, the scenery begins to change again. The cliffs are still

there, but they begin to be covered with green foliage (mostly poison oak!) and evergreen trees as the Columbia, and the railroad, cut through the Cascade Range. Twelve miles west of Wishram, highway 197 crosses over to The Dalles, Ore. The 197 bridge, plus another leading to The Dalles Dam, offer excellent vantage points for photography.

There are five tunnels in the vicinity of Lyle, where the only branch off the Columbia River line heads north along the Klickitat River to Goldendale. West of Lyle, the 5th Sub passes Bingen (another Amtrak stop) and through five more tunnels. In the 11 miles from Stevenson to Skamania, the tracks pass under the Bridge of the Gods, linking Washington and Oregon at a narrow gorge, then pass through yet another tunnel at North Bonneville, which was constructed in 1977 when the line was relocated for a new power house for Bonneville Dam. The Dam itself was opened in 1943 and cost

over $81,000,000. Along the way to Washougal (the name means "rushing water"), the tracks pass 840-foot high Beacon Rock, where Lewis and Clark camped in 1804, and cruise through the 2,369-foot tunnel under Cape Horn, a large rock outcropping that rises straight up from the river.

At Vancouver, Wash., the line joins the Portland-Seattle main at the picturesque Amtrak depot and turns south to cross the Columbia on a 2,806-foot span. Portland was platted in 1845 on 640-acres owned by Amos Lovejoy of Boston and Francis Pettygrove, of Portland, Maine. A coin was tossed to name the settlement, and Pettygrove won.

The Columbia River line gets the lion's share of BN's heavy trains—grain, automobiles, coal, general merchandise—because the line is water level. Easy access, river running, sheer cliffs and tunnels make the Columbia River route a must-see on any visit to the Northwest.

The era of the Alco locomotive lasted through BN's first 10 years, thanks largely to the motive-power policies of predecessors SP&S and NP. Just after the merger, NP Alco power (mainly RS11's and RS3's, older switchers were retired by 1973) were regrouped and dispatched to the Pacific Northwest, where they were looked after by the Alco-skilled mechanics at the former SP&S diesel shop in Vancouver, Wash. SP&S's final Alco order was for a pair of C415's and four C636's, delivered in late 1968. This was the second order for the big Centurys; six had been delivered the previous March. The brutish, 3,600-h.p., six-axle units made for some impressive action. Three of the behemoths charge through Willbridge, Ore., in 1974, looking fine in the green-and-white livery of their second owner.—GREG STADTER

BELOW: Once upon a time, nearly every major U.S. city worth its salt had its own union station. Tacoma's opened on May 1, 1911; the city had waited for a new station ever since it had been chosen as NP's western terminus in 1873. Trains of NP, GN, UP and—after 1971— Amtrak used the station, and BN continued to use the building for offices, with dispatchers located in the building until 1981. In 1984, Amtrak opened a new station nearby, and the last train departed TUS on June 14, 1984. On July 16, 1979, GP30's 2220 and 2200 and a pair of F-units lead a northbound freight past the depot.—JOHN BJORKLUND

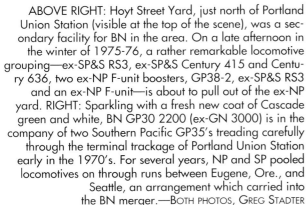

ABOVE RIGHT: Hoyt Street Yard, just north of Portland Union Station (visible at the top of the scene), was a secondary facility for BN in the area. On a late afternoon in the winter of 1975-76, a rather remarkable locomotive grouping—ex-SP&S RS3, ex-SP&S Century 415 and Century 636, two ex-NP F-unit boosters, GP38-2, ex-SP&S RS3 and an ex-NP F-unit—is about to pull out of the ex-NP yard. RIGHT: Sparkling with a fresh new coat of Cascade green and white, BN GP30 2200 (ex-GN 3000) is in the company of two Southern Pacific GP35's treading carefully through the terminal trackage of Portland Union Station early in the 1970's. For several years, NP and SP pooled locomotives on through runs between Eugene, Ore., and Seattle, an arrangement which carried into the BN merger.—BOTH PHOTOS, GREG STADTER

151

ABOVE: Railroading in the Pacific Northwest is synonymous with water and bridges. BN was well over a year old when this scene of big bridges and brawny locomotives was recorded at Celilo, Ore., in August 1972. Two BN Alco C636's and a former NP SD45—all still in predecessor livery—are taking a Portland-originated train across the Columbia River and back into Oregon from Washington for a trip down the Deschutes River line as a Portland-bound UP freight slides by underneath. The Celilo Bridge, which opened Jan. 5, 1912, allows BN trains access to the ex-Oregon Trunk line to Bend, as well as the former GN line to the Western Pacific at Beiber, Calif. In 1957, the new Dalles Dam created a reservoir which necessitated construction of a new lift span on the original bridge.—GEORGE BERRISO RIGHT: Farther down the OT line and five years later, BN Extra 1977 West cruises across the Deschutes River bridge north of Sherar, Ore., on the afternoon of Aug. 12, 1977, with mixed BN/WP power. This canyon was the scene of the "Deschutes River wars" between 1908 and 1910, when crews of the OT and Des Chutes Railroad (controlled by E. H. Harriman and the UP) both were building on either side of the river, exchanging gunfire and sabotaging each others equipment. At one point the OT had to come across the river and use the same side as the Des Chutes and the situation became tense. Finally, in 1910, the two sides came to an agreement for joint use of the line following Harriman's death the year before. UP later abandoned most of its own line; a part of the roadbed is visible across the river above the rear of the train in this photo.—STEVE PATTERSON

In a magnificent scene reflecting the beauty of the Pacific Northwest, the Nelson Turn leaving South Nelson, B.C., on July 14, 1987, passes along Kootenay Lake. GP38-2 2080, built in 1972, pilots the Tuesday-only local on the 104-mile return trip to its base at Kettle Falls, Wash. The route from the Canadian border to Nelson was constructed in 1893. Unfortunately, scenes such as this may be thing of the past; in 1991 BN announced its intention to abandon the northern 35 miles of the branch from Salmo to Troup Junction, ending service to Nelson.— JAMES A. SPEAKER

LEFT: Could these locomotives have met before . . . say, in Ohio 15 years ago? Two leased former Penn Central/Conrail GP38-2's (BN rosters them as GP38E's) and GP38X 2181 (ex-PC/CR 7858) roll the southbound "Highball" local through the Palouse hills near Garfield, Wash., on the morning of July 19, 1991. The Spokane-based daylight run operated on an out-and-back schedule to the Palouse region three times a week, serving numerous pea, lentil, and grain elevators, as well as a thriving interchange with BN-owned Washington, Idaho & Montana (a lumber hauler built by Potlatch lumber and operated by Milwaukee Road until it left the West in 1980). The Highball pictured is strictly a timber train with 18 empty box cars and log bunks bound for direct interchange to the W&IM at Palouse. Within a month the grain will be ready to harvest, and the Highball will grow heavy with covered hoppers.—BLAIR KOOISTRA

CHAPTER 12

NEBRASKA DIVISION

BRANCH LINE TO MAIN LINE

Prior to the BN merger, things were pretty quiet in the Nebraska Division. Although the Burlington between Chicago and Denver was a busy, well-maintained main line, much of the rest of the state was served by secondary mains that headed north to Sioux City, Iowa, west to Alliance, Neb., and south to Kansas City. Many of these mains were in excellent condition thanks to the efforts of Ernest (Ernie) Potarf, who retired as Vice President-Operations of the "Q" prior to the merger. Potarf had been General Manager-Lines West of CB&Q, and earlier a rail-detector-car technician. While GM, he convinced Burlington management to lay 112-pound rail from Lincoln to Sheridan, and second-hand 112- and 115-pound welded rail west of Sheridan to the NP connection in Montana. The heavy rail would help BN cope with the initial flood of coal traffic immediately after the merger.

In the central and southern part of the state, branch lines took off seemingly in every direction, to serve the abundant wheat- and corn-producing areas. The big player in Nebraska was Union Pacific, whose Overland Route followed the Platte and South Platte rivers across the length of the state. At merger, no one could foresee the vast changes that would come to the state that proudly cheers on the University of Nebraska "Cornhuskers" each football season.

The changes were triggered, of course, by Powder River coal. Nebraska was the state that had to be crossed for coal trains to reach power plants well to the east of the coal fields, but the rail lines were in no condition to handle the tremendous traffic volumes coal would bring—so they were rebuilt, at a cost of millions. Two bridges over the Missouri River, at Rulo, Neb., and Sioux City had to be replaced to handle the coal traffic; the $8 million Rulo project also cut up to two days off the travel time for grain trains moving to Kansas City and Gulf ports. The Ravenna-Lincoln 2nd Subdivision line became a crucial link in the central coal corridor, with every other siding eventually extended to form double track. The 1st Subdivision route from Lincoln south to Kansas City became a coal gateway as well. The old Chicago-Denver main west of Lincoln was eclipsed by the coal lines, but remains an important intermodal and merchandise route, but with no regular coal business. After the bridge over the Missouri River at Sioux City was upgraded, the 10th Subdivision from Ashland north to Sioux City and the GN line beyond began handling Minnesota-bound coal and grain traffic, as well as through trains from old Frisco territory after BN acquired that road in 1980.

At merger, Nebraska was part of the Omaha Region, encompassing two divisions, the Lincoln and Alliance, reaching as far west as Gillette, Casper and Denver, south to St. Joseph, Mo., east along the Iowa and Missouri border, and north to South Sioux City. As of 1992, the Nebraska Division was based in Lincoln, with lines west to Ravenna (until 1991, it extended west to Alliance), Sterling and Brush,

Colo.; north to Aberdeen, S.D., and Willmar, Minn.; east to Bayard and Creston, Iowa, and south to Kansas City, encompassing approximately 3,238 miles of track.

Although the Nebraska Division includes the ex-GN Sioux City-Willmar line, a former Chicago & North Western (ex-Minneapolis & St. Louis) branch in Minnesota, and several old Milwaukee Road lines in South Dakota and Iowa, the preponderance of the division is made up of former CB&Q lines. Vestiges of the "Q" can be found all across the division, from Burlington heralds on bridges (and on employees caps) to refurbished 4-6-0 No. 710 on display at Lincoln's 1927-built depot. The division's dispatchers are based in the same depot, as well as Galesburg, Lincoln, McCook and Minneapolis (Northtown).

CB&Q predecessor Burlington & Missouri River Rail Road first reached Lincoln in July 1870, and the city has been an operational and maintenance hub of railroading ever since. Nebraska's state capital boasts the large—three miles long and a half mile wide—Hobson classification yard, opened in 1906 (extensively upgraded by Q in 1944 and modified by BN to handle coal trains), and a diesel service center, with over 300 units assigned for maintenance. BN's principal car repair and automated wheel shop, located in the Havelock neighborhood of Lincoln, once rebuilt Burlington steam locomotives. Havelock was originally platted as a separate town around the B&MR shops, but has been a part of Lincoln since

ABOVE: Southern Nebraska is one of the few locations on the BN that can still boast of an extensive network of branch lines. These lines serve grain elevators in Nebraska's most-productive agricultural areas, helping to contribute to the railroad's substantial grain business. Some of these lines have even been upgraded, such as the 9.5-mile branch from York to Benedict, rebuilt in 1989 with some funding coming from shippers. To celebrate the upgrading of the line, BN conducted a "Gold Spike" ceremony in Benedict on Oct. 17, 1989, bringing in business cars *Missouri River* and *Meramec River* pulled by GP39M 2823 (ex-CB&Q GP30 940). The last spike was driven by Nebraska State Senator Scott Moore. With the permission from the elevator operator, photographer Foley climbed to the top of Benedict's "prairie skyscraper" to capture this panoramic view of the special and the surrounding countryside that endorses Nebraska's sometimes undeserved flatland image.—M. B. FOLEY FACING PAGE, TOP: Central City depot.—STEVE GLISCHINSKI

the 1930's. Shops celebrated its centennial in 1991.

Rail traffic out of Lincoln is continuous, thanks to the fact that four lines (to Ravenna, Hastings, Omaha and Kansas City) all tie together there. But another location competes with Lincoln for the title of busiest point on the division: the at-grade crossing with Union Pacific's Omaha-Cheyenne Overland Route at Grand Island, Neb. The crossing here has become an operating headache, thanks to the ever-increasing number of both UP and BN coal trains. UP's main also sees the passage of its fleet of inter-modal trains bound to and from the C&NW at Fre-mont, Neb., making "GI" the busiest rail location in the state. BN has proposed building a 2.5-mile grade separation that would take its tracks over the UP.

The other busy terminals are in the two largest cities served by the division, Omaha (and neighboring Council Bluffs, Iowa) and Kansas City. Both are important points for interchanging coal and merchandise traffic to other railroads. The Kansas City suburb of Overland Park, Kan., became home to BN's operating department after it moved from St. Paul in 1983. When the operating department moved, so did BN's fleet of office cars, which are based at the ex-CB&Q Murray Yard in North Kansas City, Mo., BN's main facility in the area.

It's easy to think of the Nebraska Division as nothing but prairie flatland, but thanks to the Missouri, Platte and Republican rivers, such is not the case. The river valleys near McCook, Ashland, Plattsmouth, Omaha, and Kansas City all belie the area's reputation for lack of scenery. The rolling hills of western Iowa are a delight to the eye, whether along the busy main west of Creston or on the ex-Milwaukee main-turned-branch to Bayard, Iowa. The Nebraska Division offers more than just high-speed main lines and coal trains: The network of southern Nebraska branch lines, though diminished, is still impressive. Some have been upgraded, such as the 9th Subdivision branch between Lincoln and the Omaha Public Power District plant at Arbor,

ABOVE: A pair of EMD "GP5's—former GN GP9's built with components from traded-in FT's in 1959—on the Sioux Falls-Yankton Turn pass a fallen comrade, ex-Milwaukee Road FP7 103C, on display at a farm near Tea, S.D. RIGHT: Later the same day, June 18, 1980, a cycle rider waits for the local to clear his shaded stopping point. This ex-GN branch in southeastern South Dakota was abandoned in 1981. Most of the main and secondary lines in eastern South Dakota were moved into the Nebraska Division when the Lakes Division was eliminated in 1991.—BOTH PHOTOS, RON LUNDSTROM

south of Nebraska City. It was rebuilt to handle coal traffic, with the first coal train arriving at the plant in August 1978. Hubs for branchline activity are McCook and Hastings, from which locals run in all directions. Two secondary main/branch lines even probe south into Kansas: the 88-mile 19th Subdivision from Orleans Junction to Oberlin (the subdivision actually originates at Oxford Junction), and the 131-mile 20th Sub from Flynn to St. Francis.

In Colorado, the 7th Subdivision line from Sterling east to Wallace, Neb., was rehabilitated in the mid-1970's as a result of the coal boom. A new 17.6-mile spur was built from Wallace north to the Nebraska Public Power District's Gerald Gentleman Station south of Sutherland to bring coal to the power plant.

Amtrak also plays a role in the Nebraska Division. Each night, its *California Zephyr* rolls from one end of the division to the other, en route to and from Chicago, Denver and the West Coast. According to dispatchers, the *CZ* is still the hottest train on the Nebraska Division, and "will not be delayed without severe consequences." Although not equipped with domes or an observation car, it carries on the streamlined tradition begun by the *Denver Zephyr* on Nov. 8, 1936*, stopping at towns like Hastings, Holdrege and McCook under cover of darkness.

*On May 31, 1936, CB&Q shifted the Pioneer and Mark Twain Zephyrs to the Chicago-Denver route. Operating as the Advance Denver Zephyrs, they were a preview of the new, larger trains to come.

LEFT: One of the hottest trains on the Nebraska Division— and one of the few non-coal trains on the Ravenna line— was Seattle-Birmingham intermodal train 22. On the second day of 1989, the eastbound hotshot behind tiger-striped GP50 3140 and a B30-7A has just departed the crew change point of Ravenna, Neb., as it passes a windmill in country little changed since rails were first laid through this area in the 1880's. Train 22 has since been consolidated with train 20 on the same route.—STEVE GLISCHINSKI ABOVE: With the Omaha skyline in the background, a westbound empty coal train churns up South Omaha hill heading out of the Missouri River Valley en route back to the coal fields on Aug. 3, 1986. Four GE diesels, led by C30-7 5043 provide the power on this summer day.—PAUL F. DELUCA, COLLECTION OF ALLEN RIDER

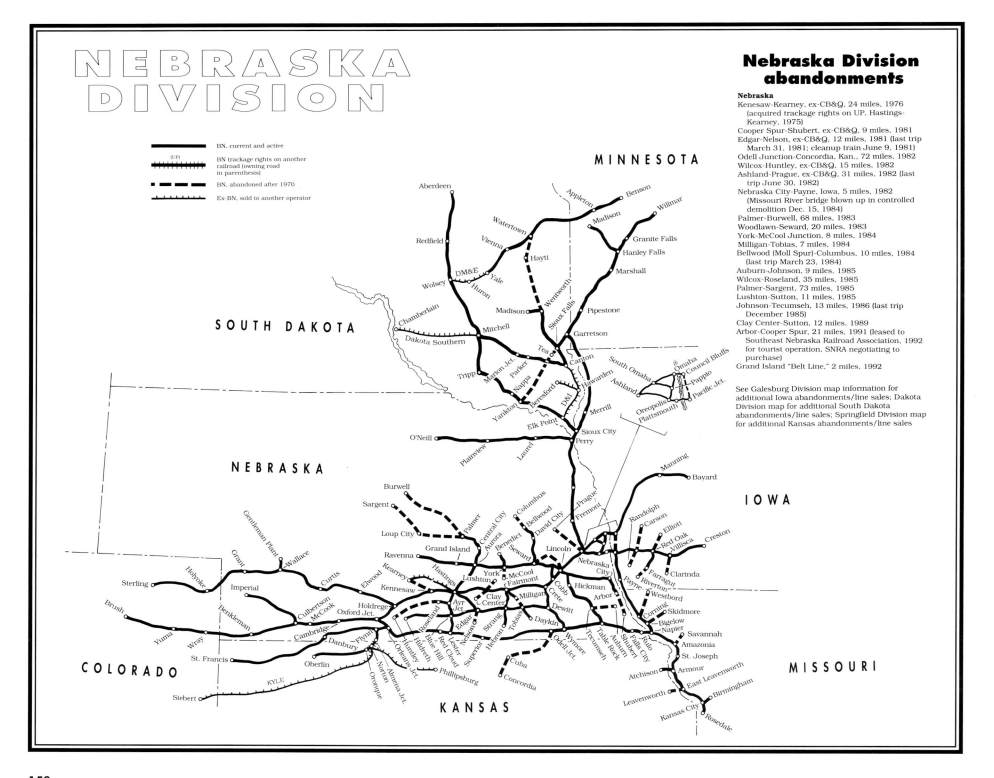

NEBRASKA DIVISION

Nebraska Division abandonments

Nebraska

Kenesaw-Kearney, ex-CB&Q, 24 miles, 1976 (acquired trackage rights on UP, Hastings-Kearney, 1975)
Cooper Spur-Shubert, ex-CB&Q, 9 miles, 1981
Edgar-Nelson, ex-CB&Q, 12 miles, 1981 (last trip March 31, 1981; cleanup train June 9, 1981)
Odell Junction-Concordia, Kan., 72 miles, 1982
Wilcox-Huntley, ex-CB&Q, 15 miles, 1982
Ashland-Prague, ex-CB&Q, 31 miles, 1982 (last trip June 30, 1982)
Nebraska City-Payne, Iowa, 5 miles, 1982 (Missouri River bridge blown up in controlled demolition Dec. 15, 1984)
Palmer-Burwell, 68 miles, 1983
Woodlawn-Seward, 20 miles, 1983
York-McCool Junction, 8 miles, 1984
Milligan-Tobias, 7 miles, 1984
Bellwood (Moll Spur)-Columbus, 10 miles, 1984 (last trip March 23, 1984)
Auburn-Johnson, 9 miles, 1985
Wilcox-Roseland, 35 miles, 1985
Palmer-Sargent, 73 miles, 1985
Lushton-Sutton, 11 miles, 1985
Johnson-Tecumseh, 13 miles, 1986 (last trip December 1985)
Clay Center-Sutton, 12 miles, 1989
Arbor-Cooper Spur, 21 miles, 1991 (leased to Southeast Nebraska Railroad Association, 1992 for tourist operation, SNRA negotiating to purchase)
Grand Island "Belt Line," 2 miles, 1992

See Galesburg Division map information for additional Iowa abandonments/line sales; Dakota Division map for additional South Dakota abandonments/line sales; Springfield Division map for additional Kansas abandonments/line sales

Legend

BN, current and active

BN trackage rights on another railroad (owning road in parenthesis)

BN, abandoned after 1970

Ex-BN, sold to another operator

RIGHT: Hub for Nebraska Division operations both in CB&Q days and for BN is Hobson Yard, Lincoln. Until 1983, Hobson was a hump facility that, at its peak, switched 2,000,000 cars yearly. Today the hump is gone and Hobson is "flat-switched." At the northeast corner of the yard is the diesel shop, maintenance home to the fleet of LMX B39-8's. A pair SW10's (BN's designation for SW1000's) pull a cut of cars through Hobson following a spring thundershower in 1989.—STEVE GLISCHINSKI ABOVE: Photographed from Nebraska route S55A, a westbound manifest pulled by rare GP20 2054 (ex-Q 918) and GP38-2 2304 cants into the big curve west of Cobb on the Hastings Line. Cobb is the junction of the passenger line that goes directly to downtown Lincoln and the three-mile freight line to Cushman, at the west end of Hobson Yard. The 2054 was one of a handful of GP20's on BN's roster that survived unrebuilt into the 1990's.—GREG SHOEMAKER BELOW: One of the last depots still to be manned by an agent in Nebraska was the large ex-CB&Q brick structure at Grand Island. The Nebraska Public Service Commission approved its closing on Oct. 29, 1991. "G.I." is one of the busiest rail locations in the state, thanks to the at-grade crossing of BN's coal-heavy Ravenna Line and UP's Overland Route. SW10 574 rests between switching assignments at the Grand Island depot in April 1991.—DAN MUNSON

Burlington Northern's presence in Kansas City nearly doubled with the 1980 acquisition of Frisco. The subsequent rerouting of much BN traffic through "K.C." has helped that city rival Chicago as a hub for Burlington Northern. En route to Cotton Belt's ex-Rock Island Armourdale Yard for interchange to SSW, double-stack train 53 negotiates the West Bottoms area of Kansas City on Jan. 5, 1990. At Armourdale, a St. Louis-Southwestern crew will climb aboard to take the train west over UP trackage rights to Herington, Kan., where it will swing onto the former Rock Island/SP "Golden State Route" to New Mexico and California.—DAN MUNSON

BELOW: On Aug. 4, 1989, BN's Palmer Turn, working the 17th Subdivision branch north of Aurora, Neb., was going about its business as usual when its SD9 suffered a failure. The train was pulled back to Aurora, and the trainmaster ordered power to be taken from a passing freight, which happened to include GE B32-8 demonstrater 5497, one of three leased to BN by GE beginning in 1984. The technologically advanced unit had to push the branch line train 20 miles to Central City, where it is seen running around the train to be properly positioned. The grade crossing visible behind the locomotive is U.S. 30, which parallels the Union Pacific main line across Nebraska; the BN crosses the UP at grade immediately behind the photographer. This view is graphic evidence of how quickly the railroad scene can change: The depot was torn down early in 1991, and the GE has been returned to its builder.—M. B. FOLEY RIGHT: CB&Q had several crossings of the Missouri River in Nebraska: at Omaha, where trains used Union Pacific's bridge, at Plattsmouth, Nebraska City and Rulo. The Nebraska City crossing has been abandoned, and a new bridge has been placed at Rulo, but the other two bridges are still in use. Plattsmouth, 21 miles south of Omaha on the 3rd Subdivision (and home to a CB&Q car repair shop until 1931) is the location of a bridge over the Missouri that was first opened on Sept. 12, 1880. Used heavily by coal trains, the river crossing presented a problem for the new BN in the 1970's: At its west end a sharp 12-degree curve restricted train speeds to 10 mph. The solution was a line change, completed Nov. 30, 1976, that eliminated the 10-mph curve replacing it with a five-degree curve through a deep cut good for 40 mph operation. To create the cut, an estimated 1.2 million cubic yards of earth had to be moved, 4,000 feet of new rail laid and U.S. Highway 34 relocated. On Sept. 26, 1983, a westbound manifest comes across the Missouri River bridge and through the 180-foot-deep cut. Next to BN's structure are toll bridges carrying automobile traffic across the river to Pacific Junction, Iowa, itself once an important junction point for CB&Q, whose Council Bluffs-Kansas City line crossed the Chicago-Denver main there.—JOHN BJORKLUND

CHAPTER 13

DENVER DIVISION

MOUNTAINS, PLAINS AND COAL COUNTRY

Some of the heaviest trains on Burlington Northern roll across the Denver Division. Countless unit trains of coal roll out of the mines of the Powder River Basin, mines that are responsible for the incredible growth in BN coal traffic over the last two decades.

In contrast to other divisions, the Denver runs more in a compass north-south direction, rather than east-west. As of 1992, it included all or parts of seven states: Montana, Wyoming, South Dakota, Nebraska, Colorado, Texas, plus BN's only foray into New Mexico. The northern border is at Laurel, Mont.; the southern end, at Texline, Texas, is more than 1,000 miles away. The eastern outpost is Ravenna, Neb., a small-town crew-change point in central Nebraska's sand hill country.

Almost all of the "Denver's" lines are heavy-duty welded-rail mains, as befits a division with coal as its primary commodity (grain and agricultural products are also important traffic sources). Division headquarters are at Denver while dispatchers' functions are handled by a state-of-the-art facility at Alliance, Neb., and an older facility at McCook.

Much of the Denver Division is comprised of old Colorado & Southern lines, controlled by CB&Q since December 1908 and remaining a "Q" subsidiary until merger. C&S was then a BN subsidiary until merged into the system on Dec. 31, 1981. The C&S main line extended from a connection with CB&Q at Orin Junction, west of Wendover, Wyo., southward through Cheyenne, Wyo., Denver and

Trinidad, Colo., to Texline, where it connected with C&S subsidiary Fort Worth & Denver.

In 1992, the former C&S Texline-Denver main line is the 340-mile 1st Subdivision of the Denver Division. The C&S, and BN's Denver Division, actually exists in two separate pieces—that expanse north of Denver, and that south of Southern Junction, 5.7 miles south of old Union Station in Pueblo, Colo. (119 miles from Denver). Between South Denver and Southern Junction, BN owns no property, controls no movements and has no input on daily operations. This trackage is owned by Santa Fe and Rio Grande, which operate it jointly between Denver and Bragdon, north of Pueblo (BN uses only AT&SF between Bragdon and Southern Junction.).

C&S obtained trackage rights over Santa Fe in 1899 and abandoned its own route. In October 1918, the parallel Santa Fe and Rio Grande lines were interlinked to form a joint double track, with C&S—as a Santa Fe tenant—also receiving access to the Rio Grande line. Operations on this "Joint Line" are under the control of the two owning railroads, with crews for BN trains supplied by Santa Fe. Southbound loaded coal trains require helpers to get over the grades between South Denver and Palmer Lake, 52 miles.

South of Southern Junction, operations are just as interesting. Santa Fe goes its own way, but BN and D&RGW operate joint double track to Walsenburg. This line is "dark" (non-signaled) territory, with the eastward (southbound) track owned and dis-

patched by D&RGW, while the westward (northbound) is owned and controlled by BN. Rio Grande has trackage rights from Walsenburg to Trinidad, 37 miles, but in recent years has rarely used them. At Trinidad, BN trackage turns east, cutting across the far northeast corner of New Mexico for 80 miles to the Texas state line where the C&S ended.

Stretching from Denver to Wendover, Wyo., is the 237-mile 11th Subdivision, which hosts a variety of merchandise trains and locals. North of the "Mile High City," the railroad meanders along the Front Range of the Rockies. North of Fort Collins to Cheyenne, steep grades have precluded the line from becoming a primary coal route. Branches (some of the very few on the Denver Division) head from Prospect Junction in Denver to Golden, to serve the Coors Brewery; Fort Collins to La Porte and Greeley; Broomfield to Lafayette; and Longmont to Barnett.

The remainder of the Denver Division is made up of ex-CB&Q lines, plus the new Donkey Creek-Bridger Junction "Orin Line" completed in 1979. The 6th Subdivision, part of the "central corridor" coal route, begins at connections with Montana Rail Link at Jones Junction and Huntley, Mont., and cuts through northeast Wyoming to Sheridan, a crew-change point and helper station. Loaded coal and grain trains headed west require a push from Sheridan to Parkman or all the way to Anita or Jones Junction. East of Sheridan, pushers are also used on the Nerco Branch, pushing from branch coal mines east to Ulm or Clearmont or west to Parkman

162

ABOVE: Heavy snows muffle the sounds of idling diesel units as two SD40-2's wait for their next assignments at Denver's 23rd Street diesel shop. It's 2:30 a.m., three days after Christmas 1987, and there is little activity around the BN terminal this snowy night.—STEVE PATTERSON FACING PAGE, TOP: The sign atop an employee walkway over the tracks at Gillette, Wyo., says it all. The Denver Division encompasses the coal country that has made the transportation of "black diamonds" one of BN's most-important commodities.—DAVID SCHAUER

DENVER DIVISION

MONTANA

Huntley
Jones Jct.
Moran Jct.
Anita
Laurel
Silesia
Lodge Grass
Fromberg
Red Lodge
Bridger
West Decker Mine
Spring Creek Mine
East Decker Mine
Frannie
Big Horn Mine
Parkman
Cody
Greybull
Kleenburn
Dutch
Sheridan
Ulm
Clearmont
Buckskin Mine
Rawhide Mine
Kendrick
Fort Union Mine
Clovis Point Mine
Eagle Butte Mine
Donkey Creek
Gillette
Moorcraft
Campbell
Caballo Mine
Belle Ayr Mine
Coal Creek Mine
Caballo Rojo Mine
Cordero Mine
Jacobs Ranch Mine
Thermopolis
Reno
Wind River Canyon
Black Thunder Mine
Boysen
Rochelle Mine
Antelope Mine
North Antelope Mine
Bonneville
Bill
Lead
Deadwood
Kirk
Rochford
Newcastle
Hill City
Keystone
Custer
Edgemont

SOUTH DAKOTA

Powder River
Casper
Shawnee Jct.
Crawford
Bridger Jct.
Rutland
Orin
Belmont
Wendover
Guernsey
Torrington
Alliance
Lakeside
Hyannis
Mullen

WYOMING

Chugwater
Dunning
Broken Bow
Northport
Bridgeport
Ravenna

NEBRASKA

Cheyenne
Sidney

Rex
La Porte
New Raymer
Fort Collins
Sterling
Barnett
Longmont
Greeley
Boulder
La Fayette
Union
Broomfield
Brush
Golden
Denver
South Denver
Climax
Castle Rock
Leadville
Palmer Lake
Colorado Springs
COLORADO
Bragdon
Pueblo
Southern Jct.
Walsenburg
Trinidad
Des Moines
OKLAHOMA
Mount Dora
Clayton
Texline
NEW MEXICO
TEXAS

——— BN, current and active
BN trackage rights on another railroad (owning road in parenthesis)
- - - BN, abandoned after 1970
——— Ex-BN, sold to another operator

Denver Division abandonments and additions

Colorado
Wyoming state line-New Raymer, ex-CB&Q, 38 miles, 1974
New Raymer-Sterling, ex-CB&Q, 36 miles, 1977
Erie-Longmont, ex-CB&Q, 12 miles, 1984
La Porte-Rex, ex-C&S, 13 miles, 1984

Line sales:
Leadville-Climax, ex-C&S, 14 miles, to Leadville, Colorado & Southern, 1987 (tourist passenger service began May 28, 1988)

Wyoming
Hereford, Colo-Carpenter, ex-CB&Q, 6 miles, 1974 (part of the Sterling-Cheyenne branch, abandoned from Carpenter-Cheyenne in 1969)

New construction:
Donkey Creek-Belle Ayr, 18.2 miles, 1972
Dutch-Decker, Mont., 16 miles, 1972
Campbell-Eagle Butte, 14 miles, 1976
Belle Ayr-Cordero Mine, 5.7 miles, 1976
Cordero Mine-Reno, 23.1 miles, 1977
Reno-Black Thunder-Jacobs Ranch, 6 miles, 1977
Reno-Bridger Junction (Orin), 83.3 miles, 1979

Several additional spurs have been constructed from these lines to reach individual mines.

SCALE
0   50   100 Miles

ABOVE: At 2 a.m. on the cool night of Sept. 16, 1988, an SD9 and SD40-2 6370 idle at Denver's 23rd Street diesel shop. The 6370 is right at home in Denver: It was built as C&S 922 in 1974. Santa Fe and C&S trains used to work out of the C&S Rice Yard, but eventually, C&S trains were transferred to the ex-CB&Q 38th Avenue Yard, with motive power serviced at the diesel shop at 23rd Street. C&S handled all terminal services for Santa Fe in Denver using a fleet of BN switchers with dual C&S/AT&SF lettering.—TOM KLINE RIGHT: Fur trading posts and an occasional ranch were the only settlements in the Denver area until 1857, when gold was discovered at Cherry Creek. With "Pike's Peak or Bust" painted on their wagons, 100,000 emigrants reached Denver by 1860, and the city became of one of richest mining regions in the world. LMX B39-8's and a fuel tender leave the modern Denver skyline behind as they head up the former C&S to Cheyenne.—STEVE PATTERSON

on the main. Westbound coal and grain trains originating east of Sheridan receive helpers at Clearmont.

Sheridan is the beginning of coal country: To the west is Kleenburn (named for the "clean burning" characteristics of the coal found there), location of the Big Horn mine. To the east, at Dutch, the 22.6-mile Nerco branch heads north into Montana to serve three mines. East of Dutch the 6th Subdivision continues for 90 miles to a crew change at Gillette, Wyo.

Gillette marks the start of the 5th Subdivision, extending 121 miles east to a crew change at Edgemont, S.D. Ten miles east of Gillette are the Campbell and Donkey Creek junctions, where coal lines head north and south. From Campbell, the 13th Subdivision juts 14 miles north, with six mine spurs branching off the main like a pine tree.

Donkey Creek is the beginning of the north-south Orin Line, the 10th Subdivision. BN has this line all to itself for the first 15 miles to Caballo, where the first coal mine is located. South of that point the line is joint with C&NW, with BN's Alliance dispatchers in control (the entire line is CTC-equipped). The Orin Line is home to 11 coal mines served by the two railroads, with the first 65 miles a maze of wye tracks and spurs used to reach the various coal facilities. Grades of up to one percent are common.

The largest operation on the 127-mile line is the Black Thunder Mine near Reno, 25 miles south of Belle Ayr. The three-mile 15th Subdivision coal spur heads east from Reno to serve both the Black Thunder and Jacobs Ranch mines. Black Thunder opened in 1977 and is now the largest coal mine in the world, with annual shipments of 24,000,000 tons.

Bill, Wyo. (milepost 85.4) is the center of C&NW coal operations. BN and C&NW trains part company 32 miles south of Bill at Shawnee Junction, after descending 7.5-mile Walker Hill (westbounds face grades up to one percent on Walker). Ten miles later, the Orin Line enters the ex-CB&Q 7th and 8th subdivisions at Bridger Junction.

To the west of Bridger is the lonely 383-mile 8th Subdivision. This secondary main carries no coal and has not been extensively rebuilt. Though it may lack the traffic density of the coal lines, the 8th Sub does possess great scenic beauty, particularly through short, scenic Wind River Canyon near Thermopolis, Wyo. This farthest west of ex-CB&Q lines ties into the ex-NP (now MRL) main at Laurel. One of its primary functions is to divert through freight traffic away from the busy coal routes.

South Dakota doesn't have very many main lines,

Continued on page 168

LEFT: The year 1980 is but four days old as a quartet of units led by SD40-2 6829 reflect the last rays of the setting sun at Castle Rock, Colo. Judging by the exhaust, the train of mixed merchandise just might be outpacing the traffic on parallel Interstate 25. With three carriers—BN, AT&SF and D&RGW—rail traffic on the Joint Line is among the most intense in Colorado, and route congestion has periodically thwarted proposals for Amtrak passenger service between Denver and La Junta or Albuquerque.—STEVE PATTERSON

BN's only service in New Mexico is provided by the former C&S line which cuts across the far northeast corner of the state, passing through several small communities, such as Des Moines (one of two cities of that name on BN, the other is in Iowa) and Clayton. En route from the Powder River Basin to a utility in Texas, three GE's and a pair of Santa Fe run-through units pass the motel and lounge in tiny Mt. Dora, N.M. in May 1986.—JOHN BJORKLUND

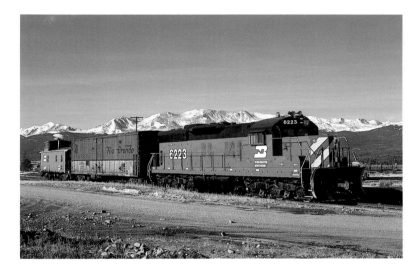

C&S had an extensive narrow-gauge network west of Denver right into the 1930's. Declining traffic and the Great Depression led to abandonments, with the last of the lines dropped in 1941, with one exception: the 14-mile branch line from Leadville to Climax. The branch was not connected to the rest of the C&S following the abandonment of the South Platte-Climax line in 1937, but did have a rail connection with Rio Grande at Leadville. C&S narrow-gauge operations came to a complete end on Aug. 25, 1943, when 2-8-0 No. 76 pulled the last slim-gauge train between Leadville and Climax, after which the line was converted to standard gauge. Following conversion, the branch became the highest standard-gauge rail operation in the U.S.; the elevation at Climax is 11,400 feet. This line was also home to the last operating standard-gauge Class I steam locomotive in regular service, C&S 2-8-0 641, which ran until Oct. 11, 1962. The chief source of traffic for the railroad was a molybdenum mine at Climax, which has closed. The branch was sold in November 1987 to the tourist-carrying Leadville, Colorado & Southern, which began operations May 28, 1988. Motive power for the new railroad includes a pair of ex-BN GP9's. For years a six-wheel trucked SD9 was standard power for the Leadville line, as evidenced by this view of chop-nosed 6223, former C&S 828, toting one car at Leadville in 1981.—PHOTOGRAPHER UNKNOWN Passing Colorado Springs old passenger station (now Giuseppe's Depot Restaurant) and a pair of Rio Grande units (including GP30 3006), Oakway SD60's lead both loaded and empty coal trains on D&RGW trackage in May 1987. Santa Fe had its own main through Colorado Springs, but it was rife with grade crossings and was removed in 1974 in favor of using the Rio Grande. This move resulted in single-track operation, with improved passing sidings, for 33 miles between Palmer Lake through Colorado Springs to Crews, just south of the "Springs."—MIKE DEL VECCHIO

Utilizing the southern entry into the Powder River Basin via Guernsey and Bridger Junction, a KK057 train, led by a mix of C30-7's and SD60M's, heads down the Alliance-Sterling main through the sandstone cuts north of Northport, Neb., April 28, 1991. At Northport, the train will turn west on the Denver Division's 7th Subdivision 133 miles to Bridger Junction, where it will head north on the Orin Line to the Jacobs Ranch mine. The 056/057 trains operate between the mine and American Electric Power's (reporting marks AEPX) Ohio River transload facility at Metropolis, Ill. In 1991 AEPX trains were among the most numerous coal movements, with nearly three trainsets in transit each way daily between Wyoming and Illinois. Only Houston Power & Light (UFIX) trains ran more frequently.— MIKE ABALOS

but BN's coal route across the far southwestern corner of the state helps make up for it. Edgemont, S.D., serves as a crew-change point and junction between the 5th Subdivision from Gillette and the 111-mile 4th Subdivision from Alliance. CB&Q and subsequently BN maintained a branch north from Edgemont into the Black Hills region, reaching 107 miles to Deadwood and Lead. This branch was cut back to Custer in 1983, and Edgemont in 1986.

Fifty-three miles east of Edgemont, the railroad climbs Crawford Hill, with loaded coal trains picking up helpers at Crawford for the run up to Belmont. From Belmont it's a 44-mile trip into Alliance. Here, BN's 110-acre facilities include a major locomotive shop, yard and the dispatching offices. From Alliance east the 12th Subdivision winds 238 miles to Raven-

na, where Nebraska Division jurisdiction begins.

Two other lines complete the picture of the Denver Division. From Alliance, 3rd Subdivision rails reach south to Northport, junction with the 7th Sub from Bridger Junction and intersection with Union Pacific's busy coal route to Wyoming. At Sidney, BN bridges UP's Overland Route before heading into Colorado and a connection with another UP line at Sterling. BN utilizes trackage rights over 23 miles of UP between Sterling and Union, Colo., but BN dispatchers control the route. UP downgraded this line in 1987, but, at BN's insistence, retained the ABS signaling, since this is a busy coal artery for BN.

From Union into Denver the rails are those of the 2nd Subdivision, with the Nebraska Division main from McCook joining at Brush, where a wye allows

trains to head east or west. This through Alliance-Denver route, opened in 1900, can be very congested, with coal trains and time freights moving from siding to siding as Denver can make room. Also opened in 1900 was the route west through the North Platte River Valley from Northport to the C&S and mining areas at Guernsey, Wyo. This route was originally projected to reach Salt Lake City. Today it's part of BN's 133-mile 7th Subdivision to Wendover and Bridger Junction, connecting with the C&S to Denver and the new Orin Line.

Main lines running through Wind River Canyon, over Crawford Hill, along the Front Range of the Rockies and over the plains of western Nebraska help make the Denver Division one of contrast—and of rugged beauty.

RIGHT: BN train 195 (a daily priority freight between Fort Worth and Seattle) treads down Mason Street in Fort Collins, Colo., on May 20, 1990. This is the former C&S main line between Denver and Cheyenne, whose route down the middle of Mason Street has long been a headache for both the railroad and the city. The problem has been escalated by Fort Collins growth—in the 1950's it numbered around 15,000 citizens, but in the early 1990's the city boasts a population of nearly 90,000. The street trackage, combined with the rolling nature of the geography north of Denver, forced the railroad to route Powder River coal trains to the more round-about ex-CB&Q route into Denver via Sterling, Colo., then down the joint line to reach southern points. In 1992, the Fort Collins trackage hosted approximately 6-10 trains per day.—DAVE SCHAUER

BELOW: The new fills and cuts created during the massive rebuilding of the grade over Nebraska's Crawford Hill are clearly visible in this photograph of westbound train 369 descending near Rutland. Completed in 1982, the realignment reduced maximum curvature and included double-tracking and CTC. Although this improved the trackage, it didn't eliminate the need for helpers, which still must be attached to eastbound coal trains to assist them in negotiating the 1.55 percent grade up the hill. On this December 1981 day, 369's consist includes three SD40-2's, an ex-Q GP20 and an SD9.—COLLECTION OF ALLEN RIDER

ABOVE: Burlington's 107-mile branch from Edgemont to Deadwood, S.D., was CB&Q's own "mountain railroad." Running through the heart of the Black Hills, the rugged terrain included six steep grades (up to 3 percent), 16-degree curves and four tunnels carved out of solid rock. The Burlington & Missouri River (a Q subsidiary) built north from Edgemont in 1890 under the name Grand Island & Wyoming Central, reaching Deadwood on Jan. 24, 1891. The last eight miles from Englewood into Deadwood were finished by three-railing the narrow-gauge Deadwood Central Railroad line. Eventually Q gained full control of the DC, along with the three-foot-gauge Black Hills & Fort Pierre from Lead to Piedmont. In addition to smaller narrow-gauge power, CB&Q's Black Hills line also saw the use of Burlington 2-6-6-2 Mallet engines. In diesel-era Burlington days, SD9's ruled the lines, with the exception of the spur to Lead, worked by an SW1. BN continued to operate all the Black Hills trackage, but as light-density trackage came under the increased scrutiny of management, BN began its exodus from the Black Hills. First to go was the Hot Springs branch in 1977, followed by the lines north of Custer in 1983. The last portion of the line from Edgemont to Custer was abandoned in 1986. The line east out of Hill City to Keystone remains, operated by the steam-powered Black Hills Central tourist line, which has been in operation for more than 35 years. Heading from Deadwood back to Edgemont, ex-Q chop-nosed SD9 6158 leads three other SD9's south through Rochford, S.D., in July 1980. Visible back in the consist is the SW1 assigned to the Lead spur, no doubt en route to Alliance for inspection or maintenance.—JOHN BJORKLUND

ABOVE: BN meets the competition: Despite BN's vigorous objections, Chicago & North Western was able to enter the Powder River Basin in 1984 with Union Pacific's help. The C&NW/UP team has been successful in winning several coal contracts away from BN, but in the 1990's, coal business continued to boom for all three railroads. On Sept. 9, 1991, at West Reno, Wyo., the competitors meet as North Western Dash 8-40C 8552 passes new SD60M 9280 in charge of a BN unit coal train. In late 1991, C&NW began returning to its original dark yellow and green colors, rather than the light yellow used during the 1980's, which tended to fade badly in the harsh Western sun. New C&NW 8552 was thus delivered in the old colors.—STEVE PATTERSON

On the north end of the Orin Line, helpers are the rule for BN coal trains. From Donkey Creek south it's uphill on double track to milepost 8 on a 1.4 percent grade; from there, it's downhill to milepost 16.4 on a 1.25 percent slope. Although that 1.25 percent grade is no problem for east- (south) bound trains, north- (west) bound loaded trains require assistance to surmount it. Based at Belle Ayr, helpers assist loaded coal trains westbound to Donkey Creek or eastbound to Reno Junction. BN's helpers also will occasionally help C&NW trains having problems. On the double track south of Donkey Creek near milepost 4, SD40-2 7224 assists a southbound lead by the 7267 on Sept. 8, 1991. Standard helper power in the late 1980's and early 1990's were pairs of SD40-2's spliced by a fuel tender.—STEVE PATTERSON

*D*espite its location away from most U.S. population centers, Wyoming is one of the most-visited states along the BN system. Photographers head to the state to capture the drama of BN and C&NW coal trains pulling seemingly endless strings of coal hoppers out of the Powder River Basin. However, there is another, quieter, and often overlooked side to the Burlington Northern in Wyoming, west of the coal country.

The 8th Subdivision of the Denver Division strikes west from a connection with the coal line at Bridger Junction, east of Orin, Wyo., and traverses 383 miles of Wyoming and Montana before linking with Montana Rail Link at Laurel, Mont. Along the way, the lonely line passes through scenic Wind River Canyon, between Thermopolis and Bonneville, Wyo. The Wind River cut a deep gorge through the earth between these two communities that isn't particularly long (about 10 miles) but is narrow, with rock walls that shoot straight up as high as 2,500 feet above the river. The Wind River flows north from Shoshoni (Bonneville) through the Canyon. At the north mouth of the chasm, several tributaries come together at what is called "the wedding of the waters." Here the Wind River becomes the Big Horn River, flowing north into Montana.

Wind River Canyon is representative of over a billion years of geology, with rock units from the earth's Paleozoic, Precambrian and Cambrian eras overlying each other. Although a scenic wonder, it was way off Burlington's main passenger routes, and never saw Zephyr or Vista-Dome service. Still, if you look at an old CB&Q system map or passenger timetable, you'll always see Wind River Canyon designated. For many years, Denver-Billings trains 29 and 30 provided passenger service along the line. In the 1950's both trains carried a sleeper, with 29 having a dining car for breakfast and lunch, and 30 a diner for dinner. Northbound 29 passed through the Canyon in mid-morning, while southbound 30 passed through in early evening. In the

1960's the train became coaches only and was comprised of an E-unit pulling heavyweight equipment, mostly mail and express cars; it resembled a typical local "milk run." Economics and the loss of its postal service contract caught up with the trains in 1967, and the service was discontinued.

Although never a priority passenger route, the line through the canyon once rated exemplary freight power. Back in the mid-1960's, when the Q first received its U25C and U28C models from General Electric, it assigned some of the new locomotives to Lincoln-Laurel trains 75/78 which operated via Casper and the Wind River Canyon. The big new six-axle power was needed to keep the trains on their assigned schedules through the "up and down" territory of western Nebraska and central Wyoming. After the merger, the emergence of Powder River coal, and the building of the Orin Line, the route began to serve as a way to divert freight traffic away from the busy coal lines. As of 1992, seven scheduled freight or intermodal trains ran through the canyon daily.

Thermopolis (Greek for "hot city") is the site of the world's largest mineral hot springs and the starting point for canyon visitors. Heading south on U.S. 20, you'll see the canyon walls begin to rise up about five miles south of town. From a distance, the canyon almost resembles a lump of clay, with a large gap carved through it. Train speeds through this rocky area are 25-30 mph. The line passes through four tunnels as it progresses south along the river. When in the heart of the gorge, the canyon resembles Rio Grande's main line through Colorado's Glenwood Canyon before interstate highway construction ruined it.

At the south end of the canyon is Boysen Dam, built by the Bureau of Reclamation. Completed in 1951, the earth filled dam is 1,100 feet long and 230 feet high. Its construction required 12 miles of railroad to be relocated at government expense. Just north of the dam the railroad enters the line change,

crossing the river on a tall bridge and heading into a 7,100-foot tunnel which takes the railroad past the dam and under part of the reservoir. This tunnel became the longest on CB&Q when this new line opened for traffic Sept. 15, 1950. Under the river bridge, the abandoned original tunnel used by the Q is still visible. The line emerges from the Canyon at this point, and heads across the high plains toward Bonneville.

Between Bonneville and Orin, the C&NW once had its own line, which paralleled the Q before turning west at Bonneville (actually, a half mile east) to Riverton and the end of C&NW track at Lander, Wyo. The U.S. Government dictated a trackage rights arrangement on the parallel Burlington during World War II, with 86 miles of North Western trackage pulled up from Illco to Shobon in 1944. Eventually C&NW resorted to trackage rights over BN between Orin and Casper as well. In 1972, the Riverton-Lander line was abandoned, and on October 1, 1988, the Riverton-Shobon line was sold to Bonneville Transloaders (which named it the Bad Water Line); C&NW then cut service back to Casper. BN interchanges with the Bad Water (which has abandoned its line from Riverton to Shoshoni, leaving only 3.2 miles in service) at Bonneville.

Seventy-five miles north of Wind River Canyon, just west of Greybull, the 8th Subdivision passes through scenic Sheep Creek Canyon, with rock formations and rushing river waters similar to Wind River. Further north, at Frannie, Wyo. the 42-mile 9th Subdivision branch line to Cody connects with the main line; this was Q's entrance to Yellowstone National Park and the Big Horn Basin, completed in 1901. It is one of the few true "branch" lines on the Denver Division.

Remote canyons and light rail traffic contribute to the mystique of these lines through central Wyoming. Although well off the beaten path of BN routes, their beauty and isolation make them all the more worth a visit.

CB&Q builders found a way out of Wyoming's Big Horn Basin by charting a route along the Wind River and the Wind River Canyon, located between Thermopolis and Shoshoni. The Canyon is about 10 miles long, ending four miles south of Thermopolis at the "Wedding of the Waters." There, the fast-flowing Wind River becomes the meandering Big Horn River, which winds its way north into Montana. Winding north along the river and through the scenic canyon, a westbound freight, headed by two SD45's and a pair of SD40-2's makes a picturesque sight near Boysen, Wyo., on Oct. 2, 1984.—JOHN BJORKLUND

CHAPTER 14

SPRINGFIELD DIVISION

HEART OF THE FRISCO

Springfield, Mo., was the crossroads of the Frisco. A busy division point and location of SLSF's principal locomotive shop, the southwest Missouri town continues to be important to BN, serving as home of the Springfield Division, which includes lines in eight states. BN acquired Frisco to enter the growing markets in the Sunbelt states served by SLSF. The Springfield Division serves as the gateway to these states, linking ex-CB&Q lines at Kansas City and St. Louis to the old Frisco Lines. From Springfield, the "Queen City of the Ozarks" and home of the division's dispatchers, lines reach out in all directions: to St. Louis, Kansas City, Tulsa, Memphis and the Southeast. Principal yards on the division include Lindenwood in St. Louis, Tennessee Yard near Memphis and Springfield Yard at its namesake city. Springfield serves as an important locomotive facility; in 1992 over 250 units were assigned there for maintenance.

The Springfield Division was also the first BN territory served by intermodal *Expediter* trains. In 1985, with the cooperation of the Brotherhood of Locomotive Engineers and the United Transportation Union, the railroad begin operation of these short, fast, cabooseless, TOFC-trains. Initial service was on the Birmingham-Kansas City, Kansas City-Dallas, St. Louis-Dallas, and St. Louis-Birmingham ex-Frisco routes.

From Springfield, the 3rd Subdivision reaches from Nichols Junction, at the west end of the city, nearly to Murray Yard in North Kansas City, 202

miles. This route is one of the more important of the former Frisco lines, offering BN access to the important rail crossroads of Kansas City from the south. The line heads northwest out of Springfield into far eastern Kansas, then north through Fort Scott and Olathe, approaching Kansas City from the southwest. The division actually ends four miles south of Murray Yard on the Kansas/Missouri state line. From that point, BN trains utilize trackage rights on Kansas City Terminal to the south foot of the double-track swing span—Hannibal Bridge—over the Missouri River, where Nebraska Division jurisdiction begins; Murray Yard lies just north of the span. Hannibal Bridge opened in 1917 (the original bridge at this site opened in 1869). Frisco's Rosedale Yard in southwestern Kansas City, Kan., was used for a few years after the merger, then was dismantled, with all work handled at Murray Yard.

Just south of Fort Scott, at Edward, the 7th Subdivision main line cuts off from the Kansas City line, heading south 84 miles to a connection with the Springfield-Tulsa route at Afton, Okla. Trains from Kansas City to points in Oklahoma and Texas can use this route to bypass Springfield. This line crosses the 8th Subdivision at Columbus, Kan. To the east, the 8th Sub runs 56 miles east to Pierce City, Mo., while to the west the line pierces deep into Kansas, reaching Wichita and Medora, 203 miles west of Columbus. West of Medora, SLSF once reached to Ellsworth, Kan., 56.4 miles. This was abandoned in 1986, but the 17-mile segment

between Lyons and Lorraine, now isolated from the system, was retained because Santa Fe has trackage rights over the route (negotiated before BN acquired SLSF) to reach branchline trackage. Branches in the Columbus area include lines to Joplin and Webb City, Mo., and Pittsburg, Kan.

To the southwest of Springfield, the 2nd Subdivision reaches 184 miles from Nichols Junction to the Fort Worth Division connection at Claremore, Okla., 26 miles from Tulsa's Cherokee Yard. The entire route is governed by CTC, serving as a funnel for BN between the Midwest and Texas. Forty-two miles from Springfield, the former Frisco route to Fort Smith, Ark., and Paris, Tex., left the main line at Monett, Mo. This line was SLSF's original route to Texas and included two tunnels and its steepest mainline grade. The Monett-Fort Smith portion was transferred to Arkansas & Missouri in 1986, while the line to Paris was broken up between KCS and the Kiamichi Railroad, with 89 miles of the route through Oklahoma abandoned.

The 1st Subdivision main line heads northeast out of Springfield to St. Louis. Using the Terminal Railroad Association of St. Louis (TRRA), BN is able to connect the former Frisco with the old Burlington line to Hannibal and West Quincy, Mo. (BN also has trackage rights from Granite City to Toland, Ill., via Union Pacific). The St. Louis route doesn't enjoy the traffic most of the others out of Springfield do, but includes a scenic highlight: Dixon Hill, between Arlington and Dixon, Mo. The original Dixon Hill

ABOVE: Mississippi Rambler: Northtown-Memphis train 144 is 35 miles south of Linden-wood Yard in St. Louis as it makes its way across a short trestle at Crystal City, Mo., on the 276-mile 6th Subdivision "River Line"—the River Division in Frisco days. The train began its trip along the Mississippi River, and when it completes its run, it will still be alongside the Father of Waters. Only on the Savanna-Galesburg-Quincy, Ill., portion of the trip has 144 been away from water's edge for any substantial distance. On this October 1990 day, GP39E 2903 (ex-GN GP35 3031) leads a pair of SD40-2's on the final leg of 144's journey to Memphis.—COL. D. A. WOODWORTH JR. FACING PAGE, TOP: Tennessee Yard, east of Memphis at Capleville, Tenn., is BN's gateway to the Southeast. The yard opened in June 1957 and was the first "hump yard" on the Frisco. Memphis was an important mid-system hub for SLSF, and has remained important for BN, with cars sorted at Tennessee for Birmingham, Mobile and Pensacola as well as other points.—CHARLES STREETMAN

consisted of nine miles of 2.2 percent grade westbound from Arlington to Dixon. A 1945 line change reduced the grade to 1.6 percent as the line cuts through rock outcroppings and forests high above the Gasconade River. At Cuba, the 43-mile branch to Buick heads south. This line includes part of the new 32.7-mile Missouri Mineral Belt line (also called the "lead spur") opened by SLSF in 1967 to furnish rail service to new lead mines then opening in the area. This line extension was built with concrete ties.

The St. Louis area is a hub for BN train activity, with transfer runs connecting the ex-Frisco Lindenwood Yard and the TRRA at Madison, Ill. One of BN's most important customers is the Chrysler Fenton plant on the 1st Subdivision, the only automotive plant served directly by the railroad on the entire system. South of St. Louis, former Frisco rails follow close to the Mississippi for 276 miles to River Junction near Memphis, offering quick access for BN customers from the St. Louis area to the Southeast. The 6th Subdivision, Frisco's old River Division, includes an 17.8-mile branch from Hayti to Kennett, Mo., and a 6.4-mile spur from Blytheville to Amorel, Ark. One principal customer on the division is Nucor Steel at Blytheville, for whom BN bought several new gondolas from Trinity Industries in 1989.

Back at the east end of Springfield is Teed, the junction between the St. Louis line and the 293-mile 4th Subdivision to Memphis and Tennessee Yard. Another route which benefited from Frisco's aggressive use of CTC, the 4th Sub cuts across the hills of south central Missouri, encountering some one percent grades between Springfield and Thayer, then passes through northeast Arkansas to the Mississippi River at Memphis, linking with the 6th Subdivision main from St. Louis at River Junction at Turrell, Ark. To cross the Mississippi, BN uses a massive single-track bridge opened in 1892, the first to span the river at Memphis. There is a great deal of industrial traffic generated in this city, notably at the President's Island Industrial Park, served by a daily transfer run from Tennessee Yard. The hump at Tennessee was the original home for two of the four SD38-2's received by the Frisco in 1979 exclusively for hump yard service. The yard itself is located southeast of the city at Capleville.

East of Memphis, the 5th Subdivision quickly leaves the state of Tennessee, cutting across northern Mississippi to Amory, junction with the 10th Subdivision south to Boligee. The 5th Subdivision continues east to Birmingham, encountering several grades in the hilly country between Amory and Birmingham. At that city BN interchanges with Birmingham Southern, CSX and Norfolk Southern, and maintains an intermodal hub center. From Boligee, the 10th sub continues south to Pensacola, Fla., BN's only penetration of the Sunshine State, while the 11th Subdivision reaches to Mobile on former Alabama, Tennessee & Northern trackage. To travel the 25 miles between Boligee and York, trains used trackage rights over NS's Birmingham-New Orleans main line, also used by Amtrak's *Crescent*.

The AT&N originally had its own line from Reform to York, which crossed SLSF at Aliceville (on the Amory-Pensacola main). In the early 1970's, the AT&N Tombigbee River bridge between Aliceville and York collapsed, and Mobile-bound trains began using the Southern between Boligee and York. In 1992, BN realigned its Pensacola and Mobile lines, employing trackage rights over CSX which will result in the abandonment of some ex-Frisco trackage.

At the important Gulf port of Mobile, BN maintains a terminal on Blakely Island in Mobile Bay, using a car float to reach island trackage. Because of weight limits on the island, only small units can be used, including BN's lone remaining SW1.

The Frisco may be gone, but its tradition of fast freight service lives on in the well-maintained, high-speed main lines it bequeathed to BN, now an intregal part of the Springfield Division.

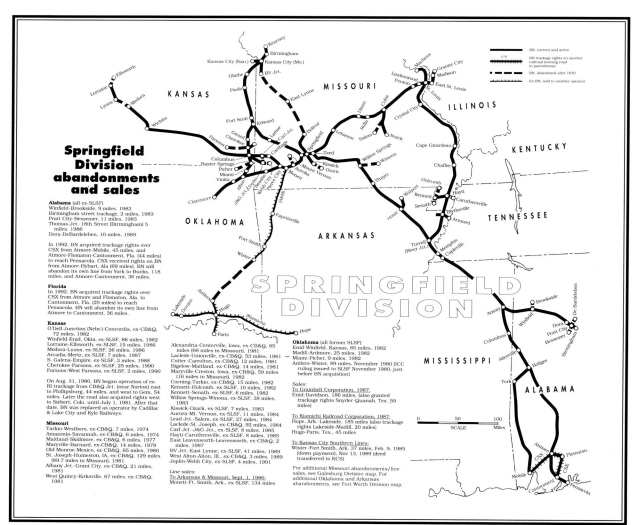

Springfield Division abandonments and sales

Alabama (all ex-SLSF)
Winfield-Brookside, 9 miles, 1983
Birmingham street trackage, 2 miles, 1983
Pratt City-Bessemer, 11 miles, 1983
Thomas Jct.-18th Street (Birmingham) 5 miles, 1986
Dora-DeBardeleben, 10 miles, 1989

In 1992, BN acquired trackage rights over CSX from Atmore-Mobile, 45 miles, and Atmore-Flomaton-Cantonment, Fla. (44 miles) to reach Pensacola. CSX received rights on BN from Atmore-Hybart, Ala (69 miles). BN will abandon its own line from York to Bucks, 118 miles, and Atmore-Cantonment, 36 miles.

Florida
In 1992, BN acquired trackage rights over CSX from Atmore and Flomaton, Ala. to Cantonment, Fla. (29 miles) to reach Pensacola. BN will abandon its own line from Atmore to Cantonment, 36 miles.

Kansas
O'Dell Junction (Nebr.)-Concordia, ex-CB&Q, 72 miles, 1982
Winfield-Enid, Okla, ex-SLSF, 86 miles, 1982
Lorraine-Ellsworth, ex-SLSF, 15 miles, 1986
Medora-Lyons, ex-SLSF, 26 miles, 1986
Arcadia-Mertz, ex-SLSF, 7 miles, 1987
S. Galena-Empire, ex-SLSF, 3 miles, 1988
Cherokee-Parsons, ex-SLSF, 25 miles, 1990
Parsons-West Parsons, ex-SLSF, 2 miles, 1990

On Aug. 31, 1980, BN began operation of ex-RI trackage from CB&Q Jct. (near Norton) east to Phillipsburg, 44 miles, and west to Gem, 54 miles. Later the road also acquired rights west to Siebert, Colo. until July 1, 1981. After that date, BN was replaced as operator by Cadillac & Lake City and Kyle Railways.

Missouri
Tarkio-Westboro, ex-CB&Q, 7 miles, 1974
Amazonia-Savannah, ex-CB&Q, 6 miles, 1974
Maitland-Skidmore, ex-CB&Q, 6 miles, 1977
Maryville-Barnard, ex-CB&Q, 14 miles, 1978
Old Monroe-Mexico, ex-SLSF, 65 miles, 1980
St. Joseph-Humeston, IA, ex-CB&Q, 129 miles (89.7 miles in Missouri), 1981
Albany Jct.-Grant City, ex-CB&Q, 21 miles, 1981
West Quincy-Kirksville, 67 miles, ex-CB&Q, 1981

Alexandria-Centerville, Iowa, ex-CB&Q, 85 miles (68 miles in Missouri), 1981
Laclede-Unionville, ex-CB&Q, 53 miles, 1981
Cotter-Carrolton, ex-CB&Q, 12 miles, 1981
Bigelow-Maitland, ex-CB&Q, 14 miles, 1981
Maryville-Creston, Iowa, ex-CB&Q, 59 miles (16 miles in Missouri), 1982
Corning-Tarkio, ex-CB&Q, 15 miles, 1982
Kennett-Holcomb, ex-SLSF, 10 miles, 1982
Kennett-Senath, ex-SLSF, 6 miles, 1982
Willow Springs-Winona, ex-SLSF, 38 miles, 1983
Kissick-Ozark, ex-SLSF, 7 miles, 1983
Aurora-Mt. Vernon, ex-SLSF, 11 miles, 1984
Lead Jct.-Salem, ex-SLSF, 27 miles, 1984
Laclede-St. Joseph, ex-CB&Q, 92 miles, 1984
Carl Jct.-J&G Jct., ex-SLSF, 8 miles, 1985
Hayti-Caruthersville, ex-SLSF, 8 miles, 1985
East Leavenworth-Leavenworth, ex-CB&Q, 2 miles, 1987
BV Jct.-East Lynne, ex-SLSF, 41 miles, 1989
West Alton-Alton, Ill., ex-CB&Q, 3 miles, 1989
Joplin-Webb City, ex-SLSF, 4 miles, 1991

Line sales:
To Arkansas & Missouri, Sept. 1, 1986:
Monett-Ft. Smith, Ark., ex-SLSF, 134 miles

Oklahoma (all former SLSF)
Enid-Winfield, Kansas, 85 miles, 1982
Madill-Ardmore, 25 miles, 1982
Miami-Picher, 9 miles, 1982
Antlers-Wister, 89 miles, November 1980 (ICC ruling issued to SLSF November 1980, just before BN acquisition)

Sales:
To Grainbelt Corporation, 1987:
Enid-Davidson, 186 miles (also granted trackage rights Snyder-Quanah, Tex. 59 miles)

To Kiamichi Railroad Corporation, 1987:
Hope, Ark.-Lakeside, 185 miles (also trackage rights Lakeside-Madill, 20 miles)
Hugo-Paris, Tex., 45 miles

To Kansas City Southern Lines:
Wister-Fort Smith, Ark. 37 miles, Feb. 9, 1985 (down payment); Nov 13, 1989 (deed transferred to KCS)

For additional Missouri abandonments/line sales, see Galesburg Division map. For additional Oklahoma and Arkansas abandonments, see Fort Worth Division map.

Legend:
BN, current and active
BN trackage rights on another railroad (owning road in parentheses)
BN, abandoned after 1970
Ex-BN, sold to another operator

SCALE — 0 50 100 Miles

RIGHT: Moving "as the crow flies" on straight trackage near Grandview, Mo., south of Kansas City, a unit coal train heads south on Kansas City Southern rails. The train was turned over to KCS at Knoche Yard, a facility of the Joint Agency (with Soo Line, ex-Milwaukee Road) in Kansas City. KCS serves four power plants (in Arkansas, Louisiana, Missouri and Texas) with coal trains originating on BN; power from both railroads runs through on the other. The billboard on the bridge advertises the Kansas City-New Orleans *Southern Belle* passenger train, discontinued by KCS on Nov. 2, 1969, 20 years before this 1989 view.—MIKE SCHAFER

LEFT: BN uses, as did Frisco, three-unit lash-ups of SW1500's (BN classifies them "SW15's") to pull its daily cross-town transfer runs between Tennessee Yard and the President's Island Industrial Park in Memphis, Tenn. In this view the train is on Memphis Port Authority trackage heading toward the causeway to President's Island. This large industrial park is served by BN, Illinois Central and Union Pacific (ex-Missouri Pacific) over track owned by the Port Authority. On a snowy day in January 1982, two of the three switchers are still wearing their Frisco colors as they make their way to President's Island.—DAVID M. JOHNSTON

RIGHT: At Boligee, Ala., southbound BN trains have two route choices—straight through to Pensacola, Fla., or turning southwest to reach Mobile. On Dec. 29, 1985, Extra 3060 South is opting for the latter and is waiting on the south leg of the interchange track as Amtrak 19, the New York-New Orleans *Crescent,* passes on Norfolk Southern trackage. SLSF and, later, BN used the NS (formerly Southern, ex-Alabama Great Southern Railway) between Boligee and York, Ala., to connect its Amory-Pensacola route to the York-Mobile line. After the Amtrak train passes, the 3060 will head southwest the 25 miles to York, where a crew change will be made and the train will traverse the 142-mile 11th Subdivision into Mobile. A 40-mph speed limit and several restricted bridges on the 11th Sub resulted in BN negotiating for trackage rights over CSX from Atmore, Ala., to reach Mobile, which should make scenes such as this a thing of the past.—MEL FIVEASH BELOW: The small yard at Pensacola could arguably be considered the east end of the huge BN system, although Birmingham, Ala., would be another contender. On July 5, 1990, GP39M 2803 (an ex-Cotton Belt unit) switches the Pensacola yard. The 2803 is one of the few rebuilt units repainted in BN's original colors; most of the remanufactured units received the new "whiteface" scheme.—F. L. BECHT

ABOVE: One of the most unique diesel stories on the BN involves the unit assigned to switch the boat slip on Blakely Island in Mobile, where small switchers are necessary because of weight limits on various railroad structures. For 31 years until 1979, 45-ton GE switcher No. 11—"The Crab"—worked the car float. In a strange twist of fate, the 45-tonner was replaced in 1979 by a secondhand SW1—which formerly belonged to BN. BN got the unit back when it acquired the Frisco in 1980, renumbering it 70 (and stenciling "MOBILE ALA. SW1" on its sideframe), and it became the sole remaining SW1 on the BN roster in the 1990's. The unit rests between assignments adjacent to the Blakely Island boat slip in the spring of 1992.—JOHN A. CRAFT

ABOVE: Memphis-bound 144 makes its way over Gravois Road in St. Louis on Oct. 20, 1991. The bas-relief FRISCO LINES on the concrete highway overpass harkens to an era when structures were built for railroads expecting to be around forever.—SCOTT MUSKOPF RIGHT: Framed by one of the arches of the Eads Bridge across the Mississippi River, a pair of SD40-2's negotiate their train along the Merchants Elevated on St. Louis' waterfront in September 1986. Opened on July 4, 1874, Eads was the first bridge across the Mississippi in the St. Louis area; it carried both road and rail traffic and by the mid-1990's will carry St. Louis' new light-rail line into Illinois. BN trains off the River Line on the Galesburg Division enter Terminal Railroad Association of St. Louis trackage near Branch Street just north of this scene, proceed along TRRA's Merchants Elevated to Gratiot tower, then swing west to Grand Avenue to enter the ex-Frisco main to Lindenwood Yard.—COL. D. A. WOODWORTH, JR.

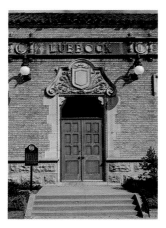

CHAPTER 15

FORT WORTH DIVISION

ACROSS THE PRAIRIES

The Fort Worth Division only covers two states, Texas and Oklahoma, but it still covers a large geographic area, including crossing the State of Texas from New Mexico all the way to the Gulf Coast. The division is an example of the lean, slimmed-down divisions now operated by the company, nearly all comprised of main lines. It represents the post-Frisco BN in a big way, melding together the lines of former subsidiary Fort Worth & Denver with the southern part of the old Frisco. The former lines of the two railroads join at Quanah, Texas, and in Dallas/Fort Worth. Division dispatching functions in 1992 were handled in Springfield, Mo., and McCook, Neb. In downtown Fort Worth, Burlington Northern Railroad maintains it general offices, which moved from St. Paul in 1984. Plans call for a new headquarters "campus" to be built outside downtown Fort Worth.

From Texline, on the New Mexico border far northwest in the Texas panhandle, the former FW&D main line stretches for 778 miles southeast to the Gulf of Mexico at Galveston. This trackage makes up three subdivisions: the 117-mile Texline-Amarillo 3rd Sub, the 320-mile Amarillo-Fort Worth 2nd Subdivision, and the 341-mile 1st Subdivision from Fort Worth to Galveston. The latter includes 67 miles of trackage rights over Union Pacific in the Fort Worth/Dallas area. Between Houston and Galveston, BN variously runs over the rails of the

Houston Belt & Terminal and Santa Fe. Secondary lines are few, extending from Amarillo to Bushland, Wichita Falls to Abilene, Estelline (once the world's largest cattle-shipping point) southwest to Sterley and Dimmitt, and a 53-mile line heading from Sterley to Lubbock. Another 32-mile branch heads north from Childress to Wellington. This line and the 9th Subdivision Childress-Sterley-Lubbock route are abandonment candidates. The Estelline-Sterley line included a 790-foot tunnel at milepost 288.7 between Quitaque and Sterley, the last railroad tunnel in Texas (there were once six). This line could be abandoned because BN gained trackage rights over Santa Fe between Amarillo and Lubbock. BN continues to serve Lubbock via this route and can also still reach Dimmitt from Plainview, where AT&SF crosses the BN's Estelline-Dimmitt line.

Most of these lines were once part of the Fort Worth & Denver, incorporated under the laws of Texas on May 26, 1873, as the Fort Worth & Denver City Railway Company. The first track was laid in November 1881 north of Fort Worth, with the object to connect with a railroad from Denver, which eventually turned out to be the Colorado & Southern. FW&DC reached Wichita Falls in 1882; the New Mexico boundary was reached on Jan. 26, 1888. On Dec. 19, 1898, C&S bought the FW&DC. C&S wished to gain access to southern Texas and was able to achieve this goal with control of the Trinity &

Brazos Valley Railway in 1905; in 1906 a half-interest in the line was sold to the Rock Island.

The T&BV had lines between Fort Worth and Galveston which included trackage rights over several other lines. Business was poor on the T&BV, and the road fell into receivership in 1914. It emerged in 1930, when the name was changed to Burlington-Rock Island Railroad Company, reflecting its ownership. In 1931 alternate operation of the B-RI between Dallas and Teague was begun, whereby every five years either the Rock Island or FW&DC would run the line. Alternating operation was extended to Galveston in 1950, the same year B-RI was dissolved, becoming the Joint Texas Division (JTD) of the FW&DC and the Chicago, Rock Island & Gulf—the Texas lines of the Rock Island.

Trains of both roads ran through from Dallas to Galveston, with both lines using Missouri-Kansas-Texas trackage from Dallas to Waxahachie (FW&D trains used the Rock between Fort Worth's North Yard and Dallas). Both railroads' power and cabooses were intermixed on trains, and it was common to see one railroads "motors" (a Burlington term for locomotives) and cabooses on the other railroad's train. JTD had a joint seniority agreement, with the crews working for JTD and running whatever train needed them; they were mixed without rivalry and were decided by who was available, not by the operating road. Crews were changed at the halfway point

ABOVE: On Sept. 27, 1991, two SD40-2's and a B30-7A tug 5,400 tons of Houston-Seattle intermodal No. 91 up the 1.2 percent westbound grade east of Bellevue, Texas, on the rolling profile of the 2nd Subdivision. The rail was laid down on this part of the Fort Worth & Denver City in 1882, under the supervision of former UP Chief Engineer Grenville M. Dodge. It's easy to see why FW&D's builders were able to reach Wichita Falls from Fort Worth (114 miles) in short order—they just followed the contours of the land!—RICK KNUTSON FACING PAGE, TOP: Spanish Renaissance Revival is clearly the mark of the handsomely restored Lubbock depot of the Fort Worth & Denver South Plains Railway, which reached that city in 1928 when the railway was leased to FW&DC. The building became a restaurant in 1976 and Lubbock's first historic landmark in 1979.—MIKE BLASZAK

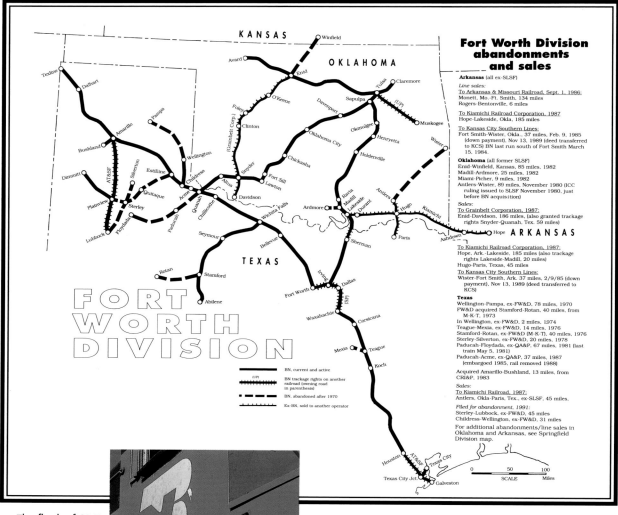

Fort Worth Division abandonments and sales

Arkansas (all ex-SLSF)
Line sales:
To Arkansas & Missouri Railroad, Sept. 1, 1986:
Monett, Mo.-Ft. Smith, 134 miles
Rogers-Bentonville, 6 miles

To Kiamichi Railroad Corporation, 1987:
Hope-Lakeside, Okla, 185 miles

To Kansas City Southern Lines:
Fort Smith-Wister, Okla., 37 miles, Feb. 9, 1985 (down payment), Nov 13, 1989 (deed transferred to KCS) BN last run south of Fort Smith March 15, 1984.

Oklahoma (all former SLSF)
Enid-Winfield, Kansas, 85 miles, 1982
Madill-Ardmore, 25 miles, 1982
Miami-Picher, 9 miles, 1982
Antlers-Wister, 89 miles, November 1980 (ICC ruling issued to SLSF November 1980, just before BN acquisition)
Sales:
To Grainbelt Corporation, 1987:
Enid-Davidson, 186 miles, (also granted trackage rights Snyder-Quanah, Tex. 59 miles)

To Kiamichi Railroad Corporation, 1987:
Hope, Ark.-Lakeside, 185 miles (also trackage rights Lakeside-Madill, 20 miles)
Hugo-Paris, Texas, 45 miles
To Kansas City Southern Lines:
Wister-Fort Smith, Ark. 37 miles, 2/9/85 (down payment), Nov 13, 1989 (deed transferred to KCS)

Texas
Wellington-Pampa, ex-FW&D, 78 miles, 1970
FW&D acquired Stamford-Rotan, 40 miles, from M-K-T, 1973
In Wellington, ex-FW&D, 2 miles, 1974
Teague-Mexia, ex-FW&D, 14 miles, 1976
Stamford-Rotan, ex-FW&D (M-K-T), 40 miles, 1976
Sterley-Silverton, ex-FW&D, 20 miles, 1978
Paducah-Floydada, ex-QA&P, 67 miles, 1981 (last train May 5, 1981)
Paducah-Acme, ex-QA&P, 37 miles, 1987 (embargoed 1985, rail removed 1988)

Acquired Amarillo-Bushland, 13 miles, from CRI&P, 1983
Sales:
To Kiamichi Railroad, 1987:
Antlers, Okla-Paris, Tex., ex-SLSF, 45 miles.

Filed for abandonment, 1991:
Sterley-Lubbock, ex-FW&D, 45 miles
Childress-Wellington, ex-FW&D, 31 miles

For additional abandonments/line sales in Oklahoma and Arkansas, see Springfield Division map.

Map legend:
BN, current and active
BN trackage rights on another railroad (owning road in parenthesis)
BN, abandoned after 1970
Ex-BN, sold to another operator

SCALE — 0 50 100 Miles

The flank of SD7 856 shows the ownership and maintenance base of the 30-year old unit while at Houston, February 1983.—TOM KLINE SD40-2 7021, a 14-year veteran, idles near the ex-FW&D 9th Street Yard, as seen from the Santa Fe station used by Amtrak.—BRUCE GUSTAFSON

---

of Teague. This operation ended when the Rock Island was liquidated in 1980, with FW&D/BN purchasing Rock's half ownership. Main shop facility for FW&D was at Childress, Texas, which remained open until 1982. The FW&DC name was shortened to Fort Worth & Denver on Aug. 7, 1951. C&S and FW&D became BN subsidiaries in 1970, with FW&D fully absorbed by BN on Dec. 31, 1982.

One of the main functions of the old FW&D main line is to serve as a conduit for coal headed from the Powder River Basin to Texas power plants. One of BN's largest customers is the Houston Lighting & Power plant at Smithers Lake, on the Santa Fe. These trains are turned over to AT&SF at Tower 55 in Fort Worth for final delivery to Smithers Lake, south of Houston. BN also hauls coal for the Central Power & Light Company Coleto Creek plant outside of Victoria, Texas. These moves begin on Rio Grande's Craig Branch in Colorado and are turned over to BN in Denver; BN hands them off to SP in Fort Worth, who hands them to Cotton Belt in Corsicanna for final delivery.

The old lines of the "Denver" aren't the only ones on the division. North of Irving, Texas (between Dallas and Fort Worth), is the former Frisco main line (Frisco used CRI&P from Irving to Fort Worth and Dallas). Now the 4th Subdivision of the Fort Worth Division, this 282-mile line reaches north through Sherman, Texas, to Cherokee Yard in Tulsa, Okla. It carries merchandise and important intermodal trains from and to northern and western points to the important Dallas/Fort Worth gateway, as well as a coal trains destined for points on the Kiamichi Railroad. BN also has trackage rights out of Tulsa over Union Pacific (former Missouri Pacific) to Muskogee. Cherokee's hump yard in Tulsa is the northern gateway to the division. In 1979, Frisco purchased four SD38-2's to work the humps in Memphis and at Cherokee. The two units that worked Tulsa included special slow-speed controls and extra ballasting. Because of the unusual downhill approach configuration of Cherokee's hump, the two SD's assigned there carry extended low-range dynamic brakes to assist in controlling train speed during downhill humping operations. The SD38-2's continued to work Cherokee right into the 1990's.

Ten miles south of Cherokee Yard, at Sapulpa, the 102-mile 5th Subdivision main heads for Oklahoma City. This was once the route of the Frisco's crack *Meteor* passenger train and has more than 100 curves—not what you'd expect in this part of the country. At Oklahoma City, the 6th Subdivision heads into Texas to connect with the old FW&D line at Quanah; this city was once also home to Frisco subsidiary Quanah, Acme & Pacific and its connection to the Santa Fe. The old through-train service to the Santa Fe was moved in the 1970's from the QA&P to the connection at Avard, Okla. Today, the Tulsa-Enid-Avard route is the 7th Subdivision, continuing its role as a connection to AT&SF, now for BN rather than Frisco. BN has trackage rights over Santa Fe 11 miles from Avard to reach the AT&SF yard at Waynoka, while Santa Fe has rights over BN from Perry 37 miles east to Camp to serve an isolated branch line. This branch is the vestigial remains of what once was Santa Fe's freight-only half of a dual main line that ran through the state.

LEFT: At Amarillo, Texas, the former FW&D Fort Worth-Texline main crosses Santa Fe's busy transcontinental freight main. Four SD40-2's are banging across the AT&SF "diamond" guarded by East Tower en route east on July 24, 1983; the tower was removed in May 1990.—JOE MCMILLAN ABOVE: With the skyline of Tulsa barely visible through the haze of a September 1986 day, an *Expediter* intermodal train behind a single SD40-2 picks its way through the ex-Frisco Cherokee Yard. Rebuilt and expanded by SLSF in 1959 at a cost of over $5 million, Cherokee serves as an important northern gateway to BN's Fort Worth Division, with traffic to and from the Midwest funneled through for points in Texas.—RICK KNUTSON

BN's presence in Oklahoma used to be larger, but two 1987 line sales altered the picture. Grainbelt Corporation purchased the 186-mile line south of Enid to Davidson, Okla. This route crosses the 6th Subdivision at Snyder, and BN granted the company 59 miles of trackage rights to reach Quanah, Texas. The Kiamichi Railroad picked up the route into Arkansas, which heads east from the 4th Subdivision at Lakeside to Hope, Ark. Kiamichi also was granted 20 miles of trackage rights from Lakeside to Madill to interchange traffic to BN. This regional carrier, which has won several awards for quality customer service, also picked up the 45-mile Antlers-Hugo-Paris (Texas) line. Both carriers serve as important interchange partners for Burlington Northern, delivering staple rail traffic such as paper, lumber and chemicals.

The Fort Worth Division really has two faces. One is that of fast, mainline trains crossing vast prairie territory, often punctuated only by grain elevators. These "prairie skyscrapers" contrast sharply with the other face of the Fort Worth Division, the modern steel-and-glass skyscrapers found near BN's facilities in cities like Fort Worth, Houston and Tulsa. In both cases, this trackage is BN's critical link to markets in the growing Southwest.

ABOVE: Houston Lighting & Power is one of BN's better coal customers, receiving the bulk of the coal trains on the old FW&D into Fort Worth. At that city they are handed off to the Santa Fe for final delivery to the power plant at Smithers Lake, near Houston. Seen at the plant on Santa Fe rails, C30-7 5568 leads the train through the rotary dumping shed. The first two of 104 coal hoppers have already been unloaded; this operation normally takes about four hours as the train moves through at four mph.— TOM KLINE RIGHT: SD40-2's 6362 and 6372 were less than two months old when they pulled an inspection trip from Denver south over the C&S and FW&D lines in May 1973. The train had run south to Houston and was on its way back north when it paused in downtown Dallas on May 30, 1973. —GERALD A. HOOK

"Covered wagons" in the form of Electro-Motive E- and F-units and Alco FA's survived well into the Burlington Northern era and made a fascinating sub-chapter of BN history. Although the FA's vanished early on, F's and E's survived in one form or another well into the 1990's. This sparkling-clean pair of F9's (in tandem with a Duluth, Missabe & Iron Range unit) perhaps epitomize the 1970's as being the height of BN's covered-wagon era, when F-units could be found piloting intercity passenger trains, merchandise freights and business and excursion specials. F9A 774 and F9B 775 pose for photographers at Fort Frances, Ont., on the evening of Aug. 7, 1976, after having piloted the *Bicentennial Friendship Train* from Duluth, Minn., to Fort Frances over the Duluth, Winnipeg & Pacific and Duluth, Missabe & Iron Range. The public excursion, sponsored by the Lake Superior Museum of Transportation of Duluth in conjunction with BN, DW&P and DM&IR, commemorated the nation's Bicentennial and the United States' long-standing friendship with Canada.—STEVE GLISCHINSKI

Despite being one of the more modern railroads in the country, Burlington Northern right into the 1980's continued to operate the largest fleet of streamlined EMD "cab units"—locomotives whose design and technology were rooted in the 1930's and 1940's. These locomotives included rebuilt E8 and E9 units in Chicago commuter service, as well as over 100 F3, F7 and F9 freight units. Since both BN and its predecessors were such major users of these classic locomotives, its only proper they be saluted in these pages. This is appropriate, because it can be argued that BN's "cab unit" era did not end until 1992, when the last of the E-units (owned by the West Suburban Mass Transit District and leased to BN but still wearing Cascade green) were retired from the commuter pool. And in a sense, a bit of the cab-unit era continues with BN's "Executive" locomotive fleet.

Following the "Cab Unit Chronicle," readers will find an explanation of BN's train symbols. BN is one of the last users of numeric symbols, rather than "alpha" codes used by most Class I rail carriers. While it is a relatively simple system, an explanation is in order, since it has undergone several changes in recent years. Like BN itself, the trains symbols continue changing, in order to make operations more efficient for America's largest railroad.

CHAPTER 16

A CAB-UNIT CHRONICLE

BN AND THE COVERED WAGON TRAIL

When Burlington Northern was formed, the new company inherited a massive fleet of "covered wagons" or cab units—bulldog nosed F-units and streamlined E7's, 8's and 9's from EMD and square-jowled FA's from Alco. Although the E-unit count had been declining along with the number of passenger trains, GN and particularly NP both still had substantial numbers of freight and passenger F3's, F7's and F9's on their rosters. While all the predecessor roads had purchased new second-generation diesels by merger time, only CB&Q and SP&S had been able to make substantial retirements of their cab-unit fleets. Frisco's later entry into BN (1980) rendered the subject moot, for its last "covered wagons" were sold to Precision National Corporation in 1974.

Thanks to CB&Q's steady replacement of first-generation units, at merger BN received but one F from the Q: F7A 168A. This last survivor of Burlington's F fleet was retired in September 1970 without receiving its intended number, 796. Other oddities were NP's last two FT's, FTA 5409D and FTB 5404C. The pair were retired in May 1970. Incredibly, an ex-NP A&B FT set survives in service in 1992 on the Sonora-Baja California Railroad in Mexico.

At merger, E-units came from CB&Q (19 E7's, 37 E8's and 16 E9's), GN (10 E7's) and SP&S (lone E7 No. 750). GN had 116 F-units of all types, but by far the biggest fleet of F's came from NP: over 150 units, including two FP7's, the only models of their kind on BN. SP&S contributed some of the more-interesting

units in addition to the lone E7: two F3A's, four F7A's, 11 Alco FA1's and a single FA2. The net result: BN at merger owned close to 400 cab units.

Early on, the E-units were the most vulnerable to retirement because of the decline in passenger train-miles. Six GN E7's continued to hold down secondary passenger trains on their old lines: St. Paul-Superior, Grand Forks-Winnipeg, and Seattle-Vancouver, B.C. By the advent of Amtrak, only four ex-GN E7's—which once pulled the first streamlined *Empire Builder*—remained in passenger service.

Some Burlington E7's remained in long-distance service, with unit 9920 actually painted in BN colors (see page 90). The remaining GN and CB&Q units had no more passenger trains to pull and briefly entered the freight pool, but all had left the roster by the end of 1972.

Concurrent with the retirement of the E7's was the purging of SP&S FA's. These were real dinosaurs, the last of their breed to see regular freight service on a U.S. carrier. None ever were painted in BN colors, but they did receive 4100-series BN numbers. By early 1972, only five FA's were left in revenue service: 4100, 4108, 4114, 4116 and 4120. The last trip for the Alco cab units was on May 16, 1972, when the 4116 tied up at North Vancouver. Six of the old Alcos were traded in on new GE units, and GE in turn rebuilt the six into cab-control and power cars for "push-pull" commuter operation on the Long Island Rail Road.

Burlington's E8's and E9's turned out to be true

survivors. With the Amtrak takeover, BN sold 21 E8's to the new passenger carrier in 1972. Also in 1972, five other E8's and all 16 E9's were sold to the newly formed West Suburban Mass Transit District, which took over ownership of BN's Chicago-Aurora commuter service. The units were rebuilt for WSMTD by Morrison-Knudsen in 1973-74 and leased back to BN for service. BN retained title to five other units, and in 1977 four of them went to WSMTD, were rebuilt and went back to work pulling commuter trains (the remaining seven E8's were sold for scrap or parts 1972-75). This fleet of 25 E's remained intact right into January 1992—the last fleet of E's still in regular service in the U.S. Metra, the Chicago commuter authority, began replacing the venerable units with new EMD F40PHM-2's, with the E's running their last miles in late 1992 ending a nearly 53-year tradition of Burlington E-units, which can be traced back to the stainless-steel E5's of 1940.

Immediately after the merger, F-units roamed freely around the BN system—even returning to ex-Burlington lines. They remained in command on passenger trains on the former NP and SP&S lines, and supplemented newer SDP40/45 units on the transcontinental *Empire Builder* and *Western Star*. When Amtrak was created, F's actually regained the *Empire Builder* assignment, as BN transferred the newer SDP's to the freight pool. Ultimately, Amtrak bought 15 units. Many units that became excess passenger power and weren't leased to Amtrak were transferred into the freight pool.

ABOVE: You can almost feel the biting North Dakota cold in this frigid scene from February 1979. Bucking through snowdrifts caused by an eastern North Dakota storm the night before, the F-units powering train 132 show why the streamlined carbody of the F's were good snow fighters as they blast through Gardner, N.D. The five units on this day were more than a match for the snow delivered by Mother Nature. In the late 1970's, trains 131/132, operating between Grand Forks, N.D., and Willmar, Minn., were a regular haunt for cab units as were other secondary trains of the Twin Cities Region. The trains utilized former Great Northern trackage between the two cities, pausing to do local work where needed and traversing the busy Fargo-Moorhead terminal. The primarily flat geography of the region allowed the F's to sprint at speeds up to 50 mph.—STEVE GLISCHINSKI

FACING PAGE, TOP: Generally well-maintained mechanically, after 27 years of exposure to moisture and salt air, the sheet metal panels of F9A 804 could withstand the forces of nature no more, erupting in a display of rust no amount of Cascade green paint could hide. Posing in the warm winter sunlight at Seattle's Interbay engine terminal in January 1980, 804 had two months of life left in its worn carbody before a blown piston forced its retirement to the deadline at Livingston, Mont.—BLAIR KOOISTRA

In the early 1970's, the aging F's were replaced as the railroad received more new units which could bump other power to secondary assignments held by cab units. In the early post-merger years, the F's had also been good fodder for trade-in on these new units. By 1975, only 22 of the 116 F's GN had contributed to BN were still on the roster. But as the decade progressed, the coal boom BN was experiencing began taking more and more new units, leaving little extra power elsewhere. There was such a shortage of motive power that in 1974 six ex-SP&S F's that had been converted to power units for rotary snowplows and painted maintenance-of-way red were brought back into freight service, for a time retaining their red paint.

In late 1974, a reversal of policy took place: BN began overhauling the F's rather than retiring them. The intention was to keep the units rolling another five years. The first unit completed was F7A 744 (ex-NP second 6017A), which rolled out of the former GN Dale Street Shops in St. Paul on April 9, 1975.

With this new lease on life, retirements were suspended and the units became the primary power on secondary trains in three areas: the Twin Cities, Seattle and Portland regions. The fleet stabilized at 116 units: five F3A's and one B, 22 F7A's and 14 B's, 37 F9A's and 36 B's, plus one ex-NP FP7. This fleet was reduced by one when F7A 730 was wrecked. Overhauled F's even enjoyed the distinction of powering several director's and inspection trains.

The 50-plus F's based at the east of the system worked primarily out of two ex-GN facilities: Belknap Street roundhouse in Superior, Wis, and the 1907-era roundhouse in Grand Forks, N.D. Both had nearly 20 units assigned. Minneapolis (Northtown) had fewer than 10 units, including three F7B's that worked as a "sandwich" between pairs of SD9's on Northtown's hump. Another two F's were based at Dilworth, Minn. The Seattle and Portland regions had 62 F-units assigned in 1979, all based in Washington state: 22 at the ex-NP facility in Auburn, 14 each at Seattle (Interbay) and Spokane (Parkwater), and 12 at the former SP&S facility in Vancouver, Wash. By the end of the decade, BN's fleet of F's comprised the largest roster of streamlined carbody units on any U.S. railroad.

LEFT: Among the most-photographed cab-unit survivors of BN were the 25 E-units used in Chicago-Aurora commuter service. In the afterglow of an evening rush hour, one of the troopers hustles a three-car dinky through Naperville Curve toward Chicago in August 1988.—MIKE SCHAFER

BN's western F's roamed freely across the state of Washington on secondary trains, and even made it down the "Inside Gateway" to the Western Pacific. F's also were regulars on Seattle-Vancouver (B.C.) time freights as well as the "Sumas Time Freight" which went north from Auburn to Sumas, Wash.—on the Canadian border—where it picked up interchange from CP Rail and British Columbia Hydro. Ironically, this was also one of the last stands of NP's FT's in the 1960's. Another job, the Cle Elum Turn, occasionally got up to seven F's because of the 2.2 per cent eastbound grade of Stampede Pass.

Spokane-assigned F's ventured quite far east. At least two sets of three or four units were regularly assigned to Essex, Mont., as helpers for eastbound trains over Marias Pass (they were maintained at Whitefish). The F's lost their helper assignment to F45's after making last pushes over Marias on July 20, 1980; they then worked branchlines throughout eastern Washington. F's were also assigned as helpers over Stevens Pass in Washington (as they had been on GN) until the late 1970's when they too were replaced by F45's.

In the Dakotas, Minnesota and Wisconsin, F's held down secondary train assignments. Until 1972, cab units were the exclusive power for BN's ex-GN ore and taconite unit trains, but they were gradually superseded by newer power. Some of the F's assigned to ore service even had "creep" controls installed to permit loading at extremely low speeds.

As the 1970's drew to a close, coal business continued to grow and there still was not enough power to replace the covered wagons. The units were in good shape, and the future still looked bright. However, beginning in late 1979 and lasting through 1981, an economic recession caused traffic levels to dip. Coal business remained in a growth mode, but other more-vulnerable commodities slacked off. Suddenly newer power was available for secondary runs, and minority and older power could finally be replaced. The first to go were BN's fleet of ex-NP and SP&S Alcos, which were all stored by April 1980 and removed from the roster by autumn.

The west-end F-units came next. By November 1980, 42 units were for sale. Still, thanks to their sheer numbers, many continued to roll into 1981, even as the recession worsened. The delivery of 40 new GP39-2's in spring 1981 hastened the units' demise. That summer was the end for F's on the Pacific Division, with the last run taking place on July 29 as F7A 732 led the Kalama Time Freight from Seattle to Auburn flying white flags to mark the

BELOW: With Mt. Hood looming in the background, FA1 4100 leads a former NP RS3, F9A and RS11 motoring east near North Dalles, Wash., in May 1972 in its last days of service. The last trip for BN's Alco cab units was May 16, 1972, when the 4116 tied up at Vancouver, Wash. BN's public relations office in Portland made arrangement for the FA's to lead wherever possible for journalists recording the the last days of operation.—MIKE SCHAFER RIGHT: In the late 1970's, the state of Washington became one of the last bastions for covered-wagon freight operations. Mount Rainier makes an impressive backdrop as F7A 602 and mates wheel through South Tacoma, Wash., with a southbound out of Seattle in 1978.—GREG STADTER

last covered-wagon trip on the division. On the Spokane and Portland divisions, the F's lasted longer, where four F9's stayed in service until winter.

In the Midwest, the F's ran strong right into September 1981 when more and more were stored; a few continued to roll in Minnesota and North Dakota as late as February 1982. In August and September 1982, many of the F9's were traded in to GE for new units, while two others ended up with preservation groups. Three F7's went to shortline Seattle & North Coast and two others ultimately landed on the *Minnesota Zephyr* dinner train. The shell of F7A 668 (ex-GN 454A) ended up being painted NP colors for display at Bandana Square, a shopping mall at the old NP Como Shops in St. Paul. Five F9A's and a like number of B's were converted to power units for rotary snowplows, and the F-unit era on BN was over. Or so it was thought.

The 10 units converted for snowplow duty turned out to be the basis of a partial F-unit revival. In 1987, one of the plow "A" units was donated to the Inland Empire Chapter-National Railway Historical Society, and its NP paint and number were restored. Then came the big surprise: Plow units 972567 (ex-NP 6700A) and 972574 (ex-NP 7002C) were sent to the BN shops at West Burlington, Iowa, for a complete rebuilding that essentially converted them into new units similar to a GP38-2. After release from West Burlington in October 1990, the units were sent to Mid-America Car in Kansas City for new paint. What emerged from the paint shop looked unlike any other BN F-unit—or any BN locomotive for that matter. The new scheme included the liberal use of cream and Brunswick green, with black trucks, white roof and red pinstripes, looking very "Continental"—and capped off with chrome heralds.

The new units, termed F9-2's and renumbered BN-1 and BN-2, first appeared in public Oct. 13-14, 1990 for the Dwight D. Eisenhower Centennial in Abilene, Kan. Since that time, the reconstituted F's—based in North Kansas City with the business car fleet— have traveled systemwide, and have even gone off-line on CSX and Rio Grande

The cab-unit fleet may also be expanded. BN still has other plow units that could be converted back to locomotives, and in mid-1992 the company reacquired two Chicago commuter E's. Some day they may join BN 1 and 2 in carrying on the long history of cab units on BN and its predecessors.

ABOVE: Engineer "Sonny" Wells has the white flags flying on former NP F7A 732 as he brings southbound train 53675-29 into Auburn, Wash., on the afternoon of July 29, 1981—the last trip of an F-unit in regular service on BN's then-Pacific Division. Management made a special point of placing the F on the point out of Seattle on that day's Kalama Time Freight for the final run to Auburn, where the 732 was removed, sent to the roundhouse and "retired," according to BN records, after 2,728,519 miles of service.—BLAIR KOOISTRA BELOW: Here is a scene to warm the heart of any cab-unit aficionado: A set of cab units in perfect A-B-A formation roll west with train 190 at 50 mph near Kandiyohi, Minn. Except for the Cascade green paint, this could easily be a scene from the 1950's, rather than January 1978.—STEVE GLISCHINSKI

ABOVE: Two F's clad in maintenance-of-way red pass their days at Havre in 1991 waiting for snowstorms and subsequent plow duty. Mild winters since 1980 have rendered "plow" F's virtually moribund, save for two units which in 1990 were rebuilt for special service.—PAUL D. SCHNEIDER FAR RIGHT: In a classic silk-purse-from-a-sow's-ear tale, BN transformed a pair of snowplow F-units into "Executive" locomotives. The units received new Electro-Motive 645-model prime movers, modern Dash-2 electrical systems, tightlock couplers and Blomberg trucks. BN's new F-unit era began in Kansas City at 5:08 a.m., Sunday, Oct.14, 1990, when rebuilt F9A&B-2's BN-1 and BN-2 departed the Amtrak station pulling ten passenger cars destined for Abilene, Kan. The occasion was the 100th anniversary of Gen. Dwight D. Eisenhower's birth, celebrated in his Abilene home town. AT&SF, BN and UP each provided special trains to move World War II veterans and others to the celebration. BN used the event to officially unveil its new executive train power. At sunrise on Oct. 14, the resurrected F's are blasting west at Ogden, Kan., on UP rails en route to Abilene.—DAN MUNSON ABOVE RIGHT: The rebuilt F9's also include small, detail touches, including EMD "F9" plates, old-design builder plates, a chrome BN nose herald and a special plate fabricated by the railroad listing the earlier road numbers the units carried. BN routinely ferries the units around the system on the point of freight or intermodal trains from their home base at North Kansas City.—STEVE SMEDLEY

BN TRAIN SYMBOLS

On M-day in 1970, BN elected to abolish Northern Pacific's old 600-series freight symbols, instead opting for the GN and Q's primarily double-digit train symbols, with some freight trains in the 100-series. The Frisco, acquired by BN in 1980, employed an alphabetical symbol system, and when it came into the fold, some of the trains originating or terminating on ex-Frisco lines received alpha symbols, such as Portland-Birmingham "PBF" and "BPX".

On Jan. 1, 1985, BN implemented a major renumbering of its trains. The new system continued to favor numerals, but a priority numbering system—which indicates generally how "hot" a train is—was adopted. Simply stated, the lower the number the higher a train's priority. Thus, Chicago-Seattle intermodal No. 1 is the "hottest" in 1992. An alpha-numeric combination is employed for unit trains with basic differences for coal, grain and mineral moves.

General Freight Trains

The freight symbols adopted in 1985 are prioritized into five catagories:

1-99	Intermodal and auto trains
100-299	Merchandise trains
300-900	Regional merchandise trains
1000-1800	Amtrak trains
11000-96000	Local trains

BN formerly used certain numbers within the 1-100 range as *Expediters*, but this moniker has largely been dropped with reference to high-priority trains as simply "intermodal." Almost all of these are dedicated intermodal services, Chicago-Laurel No. 19 being one of the few exceptions since it also carries merchandise. The 300-900 series freights for many years were referred to as "regional" primarily because they tended to travel in the 100- to 300-mile

range. Now, these are also referred to as merchandise trains, inferring they have no less priority than the 100-299-series operations. Amtrak trains received the 1000-series because several of their trains, notably the *Empire Builder*—Nos. 7 and 8 in Amtrak timetables—conflicted with BN priority trains (BN train 7/8 is a Chicago-Tacoma Sea-Land double stack running on much of the *Builder* route).

Local trains, which use the five-digit 11000-96000 series, are primarily mainline turns, industrial locals or "out-one-day, back-the-next" branch trains, typically requiring only one crew. A catch-all for the current system are symbols for trains run as "Extras." These consist of one alpha symbol followed by a two- or three-digit numeric code. The one alpha is represented by a "X" for Extra and the numeric code is geographically based, such as "X03." Examples of Extras are work trains or special passenger runs or excursions, and others not covered by the regular symbol system.

Other unusual numbers are generated when a train originates from a terminal other than its normal point of origin. In this case, BN assigns the normal symbol, but attaches a two-alpha code representing the originating station. For example, normally train 100 runs from Pasco to Chicago. However, a "100WF" originates in Whitefish (WF), Mont., and runs to Chicago.

Unit Trains

Unit coal trains have their own two-alpha, three-digit number symbols. The two alpha characters represent the origin mine (example: AA = Antelope Mine, BB = Big Sky, etc.). The three-digit numbers represent the route or destination. For instance, QQ050 originates at the Caballo Mine (QQ) while the KK050 originates at the Jacobs Ranch Mine (KK), but both trains travel the same route from Wyoming to Fort Worth, where they are interchanged to Santa Fe.

AT&SF takes them to Smithers Lake, Texas, which is what the "050" represents.

When BN began unit coal-train service, a one alpha/two-digit code for the trains was employed, but with the coal boom BN began to run out of these types of symbols. The present system created room for additional mine and route destination codes.

At merger, grain trains ran as Extras. BN later adopted a one-alpha ("G" for grain)/two-number symbol. The current unit grain-train symbols were adopted in the late 1980's, with numbers based on geographic corridors (including some three-digit numbers). A "G28" is a loaded unit grain move from Grand Forks, N.D., to Galveston, Texas; "G29" is the empty reverse move. A train using the same route but originating at an alternate point, such as Willmar, Minn. (WM), would be a "G28WM."

Potash trains use the symbol "UP" for "unit potash" followed by a three-digit number for the geographic corridor: "UP 202" runs from Northgate, Alta., to Chicago. Its reverse move would be "UP 203," but most empty grain and potash cars return in regular merchandise trains. For taconite moves, the system is similar to the coal trains, with the two alpha codes designating mine of origin or the interchange point where BN gets the train; the three-digit number represents route or destination. Thus, NT400 is a unit taconite train originating at National Taconite (Keewatin, Minn.) destined for Granite City, Ill. (400). Like coal, taconite trains return empty as unit trains, which in this case would be "NT401".

BN also operates other unit mineral trains on an infrequent basis. These include bentonite clay trains out of Greybull, Wyo., moving to Minnesota or Texas, and sulphur trains off the Duluth, Winnipeg & Pacific at Superior, Wis. These use a two-alpha/three-digit code, such as "UB 400" ("unit bentonite," 400 the route/destination). The sulphur trains are symboled "US500" for "unit sulphur" with 500 the route/destination.

BURLINGTON NORTHERN
1992